P9-DJU-882

CHELSEA HOUSE PUBLISHERS
Modern Critical Views

HENRY ADAMS
EDWARD ALBEE
A. R. AMMONS
MATTHEW ARNOLD
JOHN ASHBERY
W. H. AUDEN
JANE AUSTEN
JAMES BALDWIN
CHARLES BAUDELAIRE
SAMUEL BECKETT
SAUL BELLOW
THE BIBLE
ELIZABETH BISHOP
WILLIAM BLAKE
JORGE LUIS BORGES
ELIZABETH BOWEN
BERTOLT BRECHT
THE BRONTËS
ROBERT BROWNING
ANTHONY BURGESS
GEORGE GORDON, LORD BYRON
THOMAS CARLYLE
LEWIS CARROLL
WILLA CATHER
CERVANTES
GEOFFREY CHAUCER
KATE CHOPIN
SAMUEL TAYLOR COLERIDGE
JOSEPH CONRAD
CONTEMPORARY POETS
HART CRANE
STEPHEN CRANE
DANTE
CHARLES DICKENS
EMILY DICKINSON
JOHN DONNE & THE
    17th-CENTURY POETS
ELIZABETHAN DRAMATISTS
THEODORE DREISER
JOHN DRYDEN
GEORGE ELIOT
T. S. ELIOT
RALPH ELLISON
RALPH WALDO EMERSON
WILLIAM FAULKNER
HENRY FIELDING
F. SCOTT FITZGERALD
GUSTAVE FLAUBERT
E. M. FORSTER
SIGMUND FREUD
ROBERT FROST

ROBERT GRAVES
GRAHAM GREENE
THOMAS HARDY
NATHANIEL HAWTHORNE
WILLIAM HAZLITT
SEAMUS HEANEY
ERNEST HEMINGWAY
GEOFFREY HILL
FRIEDRICH HÖLDERLIN
HOMER
GERARD MANLEY HOPKINS
WILLIAM DEAN HOWELLS
ZORA NEALE HURSTON
HENRY JAMES
SAMUEL JOHNSON
BEN JONSON
JAMES JOYCE
FRANZ KAFKA
JOHN KEATS
RUDYARD KIPLING
D. H. LAWRENCE
JOHN LE CARRÉ
URSULA K. LE GUIN
DORIS LESSING
SINCLAIR LEWIS
ROBERT LOWELL
NORMAN MAILER
BERNARD MALAMUD
THOMAS MANN
CHRISTOPHER MARLOWE
CARSON MCCULLERS
HERMAN MELVILLE
JAMES MERRILL
ARTHUR MILLER
JOHN MILTON
EUGENIO MONTALE
MARIANNE MOORE
IRIS MURDOCH
VLADIMIR NABOKOV
JOYCE CAROL OATES
SEAN O'CASEY
FLANNERY O'CONNOR
EUGENE O'NEILL
GEORGE ORWELL
CYNTHIA OZICK
WALTER PATER
WALKER PERCY
HAROLD PINTER
PLATO
EDGAR ALLAN POE

POETS OF SENSIBILITY &
    THE SUBLIME
ALEXANDER POPE
KATHERINE ANNE PORTER
EZRA POUND
PRE-RAPHAELITE POETS
MARCEL PROUST
THOMAS PYNCHON
ARTHUR RIMBAUD
THEODORE ROETHKE
PHILIP ROTH
JOHN RUSKIN
J. D. SALINGER
GERSHOM SCHOLEM
WILLIAM SHAKESPEARE (3 vols.)
    HISTORIES & POEMS
    COMEDIES
    TRAGEDIES
GEORGE BERNARD SHAW
MARY WOLLSTONECRAFT SHELLEY
PERCY BYSSHE SHELLEY
EDMUND SPENSER
GERTRUDE STEIN
JOHN STEINBECK
LAURENCE STERNE
WALLACE STEVENS
TOM STOPPARD
JONATHAN SWIFT
ALFRED LORD TENNYSON
WILLIAM MAKEPEACE THACKERAY
HENRY DAVID THOREAU
LEO TOLSTOI
ANTHONY TROLLOPE
MARK TWAIN
JOHN UPDIKE
GORE VIDAL
VIRGIL
ROBERT PENN WARREN
EVELYN WAUGH
EUDORA WELTY
NATHANAEL WEST
EDITH WHARTON
WALT WHITMAN
OSCAR WILDE
TENNESSEE WILLIAMS
WILLIAM CARLOS WILLIAMS
THOMAS WOLFE
VIRGINIA WOOLF
WILLIAM WORDSWORTH
RICHARD WRIGHT
WILLIAM BUTLER YEATS

Further titles in preparation.

Modern Critical Views

PHILIP ROTH

Modern Critical Views

PHILIP ROTH

Edited with an introduction by

Harold Bloom

Sterling Professor of the Humanities
Yale University

1986
CHELSEA HOUSE PUBLISHERS
New York
New Haven   Philadelphia

813.54
Phi

PROJECT EDITORS: Emily Bestler, James Uebbing
ASSOCIATE EDITOR: Maria Behan
EDITORIAL COORDINATOR: Karyn Gullen Browne
EDITORIAL STAFF: Laura Ludwig, Linda Grossman, Perry King
DESIGN: Susan Lusk

Cover illustration by Kye Carbone

Copyright © 1986 by Chelsea House Publishers, a division of Chelsea House Educational Communications, Inc.

Introduction copyright © 1986 by Harold Bloom

All rights reserved. No part of this publication may be reproduced or transmitted, in any form or by any means, without the written permission of the publisher.

Printed and bound in the United States of America

Library of Congress Cataloging in Publication Data

Philip Roth.
    (Modern critical views)
    Bibliography: p.
    Includes index.
    1. Roth, Philip—Criticism and interpretation—Addresses, essays, lectures. I. Bloom, Harold.
II. Series.
PS3568.0855Z83   1986   813'.54   85–21325
ISBN 0–87754–661–4

Chelsea House Publishers
Harold Steinberg, Chairman and Publisher
Susan Lusk, Vice President
A Division of Chelsea House Educational Communications, Inc.
133 Christopher Street, New York, NY 10014

860248

Contents

Editor's Note

This volume gathers together what, in its editor's judgment, is a representative selection of the best criticism so far devoted to the fiction of Philip Roth, arranged in the order of critical publication. The editor's "Introduction" centers upon Roth's major achievement, the trilogy *Zuckerman Bound*, with its epilogue *The Prague Orgy*. By insisting upon the profound moral intensity of Roth's vision, the editor sets himself at some variance with much received opinion upon Roth's work.

The chronological sequence of criticism begins with Stanley Edgar Hyman's generous and accurate prophecy of Roth's future, founded upon the early evidence of *Goodbye, Columbus* and *Letting Go*. Hyman's judgment is complemented by two further exegeses of *Goodbye, Columbus*, Stanley Trachtenberg's meditation upon "the hero in stasis," and Jonathan Raban's analysis of "two meal scenes."

Portnoy's Complaint, Roth's most famous and scandalous work, provokes Bruno Bettelheim's impersonation of what might be called "Dr. Spielvogel's revenge" upon his patient, Alexander Portnoy. It is supplemented here by what Theodore Solotaroff calls his "personal view" of Roth and his achievement up through *Portnoy's Complaint*. The exuberant controversy continues with Allen Guttmann's judicious survey of Roth's early work, including *Portnoy's Complaint*, and Tony Tanner's sympathetic observations upon the deliberately "unfinished" quality of the book, since Portnoy himself is so clearly a transitional figure for Roth.

Irving Howe's notorious condemnation of Roth and *Portnoy's Complaint* is the inevitable centerpiece in this volume, since it inspired Roth to the enormous counterattack of *Zuckerman Bound*—in particular, of *The Anatomy Lesson*. I have juxtaposed it here with Roth's best and most revealing critical performance, in which he looks at Kafka, and, in that mirror, beholds much of himself.

The final group of essays begins with John N. McDaniel's overview of Roth through *My Life as a Man*, rightly emphasizing Roth's artistic courage. Sanford Pinsker's defense of *The Breast* as comic allegory is counterbalanced by Mary Allen's restrained and effective feminist analysis, which concludes that Roth is incapable of surmounting his personal obsession with masochistic men and destructive women. Hermione Lee's emphasis is interestingly different in her brilliant account of Roth's quest for literary self-identity. Finally, Sam B. Girgus acutely examines Roth's relation to the developing tradition of American Jewish writing, emphasizing Roth's profound sense of the limits of freedom. This book in a sense comes full circle here, back to the editor's "Introduction," which salutes Roth as the most authentic instance of moral heroism in that tradition.

Introduction

Philip Roth's *Zuckerman Bound* binds together *The Ghost Writer*, *Zuckerman Unbound* and *The Anatomy Lesson*, adding to them as epilogue a wild short novel, *The Prague Orgy*, which is at once the bleakest and the funniest writing Roth has done. The totality is certainly the novelist's finest achievement to date, eclipsing even his best single fictions, the exuberantly notorious *Portnoy's Complaint* and the undervalued and ferocious *My Life as a Man*. *Zuckerman Bound* is a classic apologia, an aggressive defense of Roth's moral stance as an author. Its cosmos derives candidly from the Freudian interpretation of ambivalence as being primal, and the Kafkan evasion of interpretation as being unbearable. Roth knows that Freud and Kafka mark the origins and limits of a still-emerging literary culture, American and Jewish, which has an uneasy relationship to normative Judaism and its waning culture. I suspect that Roth knows and accepts also what his surrogate, Zuckerman, is sometimes too outraged to recognize: breaking a new road both causes outrage in others, and demands payment in which the outrageous provoker punishes himself. Perhaps that is the Jewish version of Emerson's American Law of Compensation: nothing is got for nothing.

Zuckerman *Bound* merits something reasonably close to the highest level of aesthetic praise for tragicomedy, partly because as a formal totality it becomes much more than the sum of its parts. Those parts are surprisingly diverse: *The Ghost Writer* is a Jamesian parable of fictional influence, economical and shapely, beautifully modulated, while *Zuckerman Unbound* is more characteristically Rothian, being freer in form and more joyously expressionistic in its diction. *The Anatomy Lesson* is farce bordering on fantasy, closer in mode and spirit to Nathanael West than is anything else by Roth. With *The Prague Orgy*, Roth has transcended himself, or perhaps shown himself and others that, being just past fifty, he has scarcely begun to display his powers. I have read nothing else in recent American fiction that rivals Thomas Pynchon's *The Crying of Lot 49* and episodes like the story of Byron the light bulb in the same author's *Gravity's Rainbow*. The *Prague Orgy* is of that disturbing eminence: obscenely outrageous and yet brilliantly reflective of a paranoid reality that has become universal. But the Rothian difference from Nathanael West and Pynchon should also be emphasized. Roth paradoxically is still engaged in moral prophecy; he continues to be outraged by the outrageous—in societies, others and himself. There is in him nothing of West's Gnostic preference for the posture of the Satanic editor, Shrike, in *Miss Lonelyhearts,* or of Pynchon's Kabbalistic doctrine of sado-anarchism. Roth's negative exuberance is not in the service of a negative theology, but intimates instead a nostalgia for the morality once engendered by the Jewish normative tradition.

This is the harsh irony, obsessively exploited throughout *Zuckerman Bound,* of the attack made upon Zuckerman's *Carnovsky* (Roth's *Portnoy's Complaint*) by the literary critic Milton Appel (Irving Howe). Zuckerman has received a mortal wound from Appel, and Roth endeavors to commemorate the wound and the wounder, in the spirit of James Joyce permanently impaling the Irish poet, physician and general roustabout, Oliver St. John Gogarty, as the immortally egregious Malachi (Buck) Mulligan of *Ulysses.* There is plenty of literary precedent for settling scores in this way; it is as old as Hellenistic Alexandria, and as recent as Saul Bellow's portrait of Jack Ludwig as Valentine Gersbach in *Herzog.* Roth, characteristically scrupulous, presents Appel as dignified, serious and sincere, and Zuckerman as dangerously lunatic in this matter, but since the results are endlessly hilarious, the revenge is sharp nevertheless.

Zuckerman Unbound makes clear, at least to me, that Roth indeed is a Jewish writer in a sense that Saul Bellow and Bernard Malamud are not, and do not care to be. Bellow and Malamud, in their fiction, strive to be North American Jewish only as Tolstoi was Russian, or Faulkner was American Southern. Roth is centrally Jewish in his fiction, because his absolute concern never ceases to be the pain of the relations between children and parents, and between husband and wife, and in him this pain invariably results from the incommensurability between a rigorously moral normative tradition whose expectations rarely can be satisfied, and the reality of the way we live now. Zuckerman's insane resentment of the moralizing Milton Appel, and of even fiercer feminist critics, is a deliberate self-parody of Roth's more-than-ironic reaction to how badly he has been read. Against both Appel and the covens of maenads, Roth defends Zuckerman (and so himself) as a kind of Talmudic Orpheus, by defining any man as "clay with aspirations."

What wins over the reader is that both defense and definition are conveyed by the highest humor now being written. *The Anatomy Lesson* and *The Prague Orgy,* in particular, provoke a cleansing and continuous laughter, sometimes so intense that in itself it becomes astonishingly painful. One of the many aesthetic gains of binding together the entire Zuckerman ordeal (it cannot be called a saga) is to let the reader experience the gradual acceleration of wit from the gentle Chekhovian wistfulness of *The Ghost Writer*, on to the Gogolian sense of the ridiculous in *Zuckerman Unbound*, and then to the boisterous Westian farce of *The Anatomy Lesson*, only to end in the merciless Kafkan irrealism of *The Prague Orgy*.

I will center most of what follows upon *The Prague Orgy*, both because it is the only part of *Zuckerman Bound* that is new, and because it is the best of Roth, a kind of coda to all his fiction so far. Haunting it necessarily is the spirit of Kafka, a dangerous influence upon any writer, and particularly dangerous, until now, for Roth. Witness his short novel, *The Breast*, his major aesthetic disaster so far, surpassing such livelier failures as *Our Gang* and *The Great American Novel*. Against the error of *The Breast* can be set the funniest pages in *The Professor of Desire*, where the great dream concerning "Kafka's whore" is clearly the imaginative prelude to *The Prague Orgy*. David Kepesh, Roth's Professor of Desire, falls asleep in Prague and confronts "everything I ever hoped for," a guided visit with an official interpreter to an old woman, possibly once Kafka's whore. The heart of her revelation is Rothian rather than Kafkan, as she integrates the greatest of modern Jewish writers with all the other ghosts of her Jewish clientele:

> "They were clean and they were gentlemen. As God is my witness, they never beat on my backside. Even in bed they had manners."
> "But is there anything about Kafka in particular that she remembers? I didn't come here, to her, to Prague, to talk about nice Jewish boys."
> She gives some thought to the question; or, more likely, no thought. Just sits there trying out being dead.
> "You see, he wasn't so special," she finally says. "I don't mean he wasn't a gentleman. They were all gentlemen."

This could be the quintessential Roth passage: the Jewish joke turned, not against itself, nor against the Jews, and certainly not against Kafka, but against history, against the way things were, and are, and yet will be. Unlike the humor of Nathanael West (particularly in his *The Dream Life of Balso Snell*) and of Woody Allen, there is no trace of Jewish anti-Semitism in Roth's pained laughter. Roth's wit uncannily follows the psychic pattern set out by Freud in his late paper on "Humor" (1928), which speculates that the superego allows jesting so as to speak some "kindly words of comfort to the intimidated ego." The ego of poor Zuckerman is certainly intimidated enough, and the reader rejoices at being allowed to share some hilarious words of comfort with him.

When last we saw the afflicted Zuckerman, at the close of *The*

Anatomy Lesson, he had progressed (or regressed) from painfully lying back on his playmat, *Roget's Thesaurus* propped beneath his head and four women serving his many needs, to wandering the corridors of a university hospital, a patient playing at being an intern. A few years later, a physically recovered Zuckerman is in Prague, as visiting literary lion, encountering so paranoid a social reality that New York seems, by contrast, the forest of Arden. Zuckerman, "the American authority on Jewish demons," quests for the unpublished Yiddish stories of the elder Sinovsky, perhaps murdered by the Nazis. The exiled younger Sinovsky's abandoned wife, Olga, guards the manuscripts in Prague. In a deliberate parody of James's "The Aspern Papers," Zuckerman needs somehow to seduce the alcoholic and insatiable Olga into releasing stories supposedly worthy of Sholom Aleichem or Isaac Babel, written in "the Yiddish of Flaubert."

Being Zuckerman, he seduces no one and secures the Yiddish manuscripts anyway, only to have them confiscated by the Czech Minister of Culture and his thugs, who proceed to expel "Zuckerman the Zionist agent" back to "the little world around the corner" in New York City. In a final scene subtler, sadder, and funnier than all previous Roth, the frustrated Zuckerman endures the moralizing of the Minister of Culture, who attacks America for having forgotten that "masterpiece," Betty Mac-Donald's *The Egg and I*. Associating himself with K., the hero of Kafka's *The Castle*, Zuckerman is furious at his expulsion, and utters a lament for the more overt paranoia he must abandon:

> . . . here where there's no nonsense about purity and goodness, where the division is not that easy to discern between the heroic and the perverse, where every sort of repression foments a parody of freedom and the suffering of their historical misfortune engenders in its imaginative victims these clownish forms of human despair . . .

That farewell-to-Prague has as its undersong: here where Zuckerman is not an anomaly, but indeed a model of decorum and restraint compared to anyone else who is at all interesting. Perhaps there is another undertone: a farewell-to-Zuckerman on Roth's part. The author of *Zuckerman Bound* at last may have exorcised the afterglow of *Portnoy's Complaint*. There is an eloquent plea for release in *The Anatomy Lesson*, where Zuckerman tries to renounce his fate as a writer:

> It may look to outsiders like the life of freedom—not on a schedule, in command of yourself, singled out for glory, the choice apparently to write about anything. But once one's writing, it's *all* limits. Bound to a subject. Bound to make sense of it. Bound to make a book of it . . .

Zuckerman bound, indeed, but bound in particular to the most ancient of Covenants—that is Roth's particular election, or self-election. In his critical book, *Reading Myself and Others* (1975), the last and best essay, "Looking at Kafka," comments on the change that is manifested in Kafka's later fiction, observing that it is:

> . . . touched by a spirit of personal reconciliation and sardonic self-acceptance, by a tolerance of one's own brand of madness . . . the piercing masochistic irony . . . has given way here to a critique of the self and its preoccupations that, though bordering on mockery, no longer seeks to resolve itself in images of the uttermost humiliation and defeat . . . . Yet there is more here than a metaphor for the insanely defended ego, whose striving for invulnerability produces a defensive system that must in its turn become the object of perpetual concern—there is also a very unromantic and hardheaded fable about how and why art is made, a portrait of the artist in all his ingenuity, anxiety, isolation, dissatisfaction, relentlessness, obsessiveness, secretiveness, paranoia, and self-addiction, a portrait of the magical thinker at the end of his tether . . .

Roth intended this as commentary on Kafka's "The Burrow." Eloquent and poignant, it is far more accurate as a descriptive prophecy of *Zuckerman Bound*. Kafka resists nearly all interpretation, so that what most *needs* interpretation in him is his evasion of interpretation. That Roth reads himself into his precursor is a normal and healthy procedure in the literary struggle for self-identification. Unlike Kafka, Roth tries to evade, not interpretation, but guilt, partly because he lives the truth of Kafka's terrible motto of the penal colony: "Guilt is never to be doubted." Roth has earned a permanent place in American literature by a comic genius that need never be doubted again, wherever it chooses to take him next.

STANLEY EDGAR HYMAN

A Novelist of Great Promise

Television has destroyed boxing in our time, perhaps permanently by killing the neighborhood clubs at which young fighters learn their craft. As a result boys are brought up into the big time too soon, and acclaim and fortune are won by the semi-skilled who then naturally continue to be semi-skilled. Consequently, we will probably never again see fighters with the artistry of Archie Moore or Ray Robinson.

In the literary arenas the same thing is done by gushy reviewing. Philip Roth is a case in point. In 1959, at the age of 26, he published his first book, *Goodbye, Columbus*, consisting of the title novella and five short stories. It was greeted with a cascade of adulation, of which some remarks quoted on the back of the paperback reprint are a fair sample. "One catches lampoonings of our swollen and unreal American prosperity that are as observant and charming as Fitzgerald's," Alfred Kazin wrote in the *Reporter*. "At twenty-six he is skillful, witty, and energetic and performs like a virtuoso," Saul Bellow wrote in *Commentary*. "What many writers spend a lifetime searching for—a unique voice, a secure rhythm, a distinctive subject—seem to have come to Philip Roth totally and immediately," Irving Howe wrote in the *New Republic*.

The next year, *Goodbye, Columbus* won the National Book Award as "the most distinguished work of fiction published in 1959." Roth was promptly awarded a Guggenheim fellowship as well as a grant from the National Institute of Arts and Letters with a citation saying in part:

From *On Contemporary Literature: An Anthology of Critical Essays on the Major Movements and Writers of Contemporary Literature*, edited by Richard Kostelanetz. Copyright © 1964 by Avon Book Division, The Hearst Corporation.

"*Goodbye, Columbus* marks the coming of age of a brilliant, penetrating, and undiscourageable young man of letters." Undiscourageable? Who had tried?

The merits of *Goodbye, Columbus* and its author are immediately evident. The novella shows a sardonic wit, and the sharp eye of a born writer. The Patimkin way of life, with its white hair "the color of Lincoln convertibles" and its 23 bottles of Jack Daniels each with a little booklet tied around its neck, decorating the unused bar, has been rendered for all time. There are other sure touches: the cherry pits under Neil's bare feet in the TV room; the Ohio State sentimental record of the title. The long monologue by Patimkin's unsuccessful half-brother Leo at the wedding is a masterpiece: funny, moving, perfect.

But the faults of *Goodbye, Columbus* are as readily visible. The novella has no values to oppose to Patimkin values other than a small Negro boy who admires Gauguin's Tahiti, which seems a considerable overmatch. Some images are bad, like Brenda treading water "so easily she seemed to have turned the chlorine to marble beneath her"; the language is sometimes as inadequate as: "I failed to deflate the pout from my mouth." Most important, the novella shows Roth's architectonic weakness. Many of the incidents do not advance the action; the end is merely a running-down.

The stories show the same balance of strength and weakness. "Defender of the Faith" is the only one of them that seems wholly successful to me. "Eli, the Fanatic" reaches one high point of power and beauty, when Tzuref replies to all the smooth talk about the 20th century with: "For me the Fifty-eighth," but the rest of the story is rambling and diffuse. "The Conversion of the Jews," with its pat moral, "You should never hit anybody about God," is ultimately hokum, as "You Can't Tell a Man by the Song He Sings" is immediately hokum. "Epstein" is an inflated joke.

The minor result of the shower of praise and coin that Roth received was to make him arrogant. In a speech, "Writing American Fiction," at a 1960 symposium, he knocked off his elders and betters: Malamud displays "a spurning of our world," Salinger tells us "to be charming on the way to the loony bin," and so on. The major, and really unfortunate result has been to convince Roth that he has nothing further to learn. Three years later, *Letting Go* appears with the same merits and the same faults as *Goodbye, Columbus*.

Let us get the faults out of the way first. Since the novel is six times as long as the novella, it shows Roth's architectural weakness six times as strongly. It never in fact becomes a novel, with a unified dramatic action, but falls apart into two narratives which have only a pat complementarity: the failure of Gabe Wallach in the world of personal relations, specifically with the divorcée Martha Reganhart, despite every advantage; and the limited success of Paul and Libby Herz in the same world, despite every handicap. For the rest, it is a series of comic set pieces and vignettes: dirty diapers and high thought among the instructors at Midwest universities; Swedish modern and espresso in Jewish apartments in Brooklyn; the Kodachrome European trips of Central Park West dentists.

The prose is still quite lame in spots. Characters experience "relief—though by no means total relief" and children eat "manipulating their food like Muzak's violinists their instruments." There are letters that no one would ever have written, and long pedestrian explanations of past events by the author. In the style of college humor magazines, Roth will interrupt a scene to remark: "It's the little questions from women about tappets that finally push men over the edge." At the same time, there is a balancing pomposity; the book has no fewer than *three epigraphs*—by Simone Weil, Wallace Stevens, and Thomas Mann—any one of which would do for a dissertation on Covenant Theology.

A two-page history of the marital sex life of the Herzes has a clinical leadenness that would sink the most buoyant novel. Beyond that there is cocktail-party Freud. A pathetic event finally ends the liaison between Gabe and Martha. Martha's older child, Cynthia, pushes her younger brother, Mark, off the top of a double-decker bunk, which results in Mark's death. Roth spends laborious pages showing us why—it was penis-envy! Finally, Gabe's weakness is Hegelian essence: "He is better, he believes, than anything he has done in life has shown him to be." Not being the sum of his actions, Gabe is not really anything in the book.

The virtues of *Letting Go*—of Roth, really—are equally impressive. He has the finest eye for the details of American life since Sinclair Lewis. When Margie Howells of Kenosha moves in with Gabe as an experiment in Bold Free Union, she comes with Breck shampoo, an Olivetti, an electric frying pan, a steam iron, and a copy of the *Oxford Book of Seventeenth-Century Verse*. The Spiglianos (he is the chairman of Gabe's department) have 11 budgetary tins in their kitchen, one labelled: "John: Tobacco, scholarly journals, foot powder."

Roth's ear is just as remarkable as his eye. When Blair Stott, a Negro on pot, talks hip, it is the best hip, and a delight. When Gabe and Martha quarrel over money, every word rings true, and the reader can feel a sick headache coming on. No manner of speech seems to be beyond Roth's powers. An elderly Midwest woman says to Gabe: "You talk to the top professors and you see if they're not Masons." Paul recalls necking with a girl in high school, sitting in her living room while her father called out from the bedroom: "Doris, is that you, dolly? Is somebody with you? Tell him thank you, dolly, and tell him it's the next day already, your father has to get up and go to work soon, tell him thank you and good night, dolly."

If Gabe is a thin Hegelian essence, Martha is a gorgeous rich *Existenz*. She *is* the total of what she does. "A woman at least realizes there are certain rotten things she's got to do in life and does them," Martha explains to Gabe. "Men want to be heroes." She is bawdy and vulgar, honest and decent, funny and heartbreaking. Gabe's effort, as he finally recognizes when he loses her, had been to turn her into a sniveling Libby. Martha's vitality dominates the book, and if Gabe's final "letting go" of the world is at all poignant, it is poignant chiefly in that he had a chance to keep Martha and failed it.

The best of *Letting Go* comes from the marvelous quality of Roth's imagination. A fellow-dentist with whom Gabe's father goes ice-skating is characterized in a phrase; he only makes "little figure eights, and all the time, smiling." The failure of Paul's father in the frozen foods business is one magnificent sentence: "One day, creditors calling at every door, he got into the cab of a truckful of his frozen rhubarb and took a ride out to Long Island to think; the refrigeration failed just beyond Mineola, and by the time he got home his life was a zero, a ruined man." At her low point, Libby, who has converted from Roman Catholicism to Judaism on marrying Paul, tries to commit suicide; when that fails she decides to make potato pancakes, "to bring a little religion into her house."

Two episodes of almost indescribable complexity, at once awful and uproarious, are the clearest sign of Roth's great promise. One is Libby's abortion, which becomes entangled with the effort of an elderly neighbor, Levy, to steal a job-lot of jockey briefs from another elderly neighbor, Korngold; it culminates in a horrifying and splendid scene when they both invade the Herz bedroom just after Libby comes home from the operation. The other is Gabe's mad effort to persuade a scoundrel named Harry Bigoness to sign a legal document that will enable the Herzes to keep their adopted baby. Eventually Gabe steals the baby in the night and drives it to Gary, Indiana, to confront Bigoness.

Roth may be the Lewis of Suburbia, but he is potentially much more. His "Writing American Fiction" speech rejects all the easy affirmations of America, and concludes on Ralph Ellison's sombre final image of the Invisible Man waiting underground. Roth really does know how hard life is. *Letting Go* concludes with Gabe, who has tried to do good without attachment, as Lord Krishna recommends in the *Gita,* left with little good achieved and no attachments either. I think that after he has seasoned longer, after another book or two, if he is prepared to learn from his mistakes, Philip Roth will be a fine novelist. Providing, that is, that all the matchmakers and promoters leave him alone.

STANLEY TRACHTENBERG

The Hero in Stasis

Always a difficult business at best,
coming of age has, in recent fiction, become even more tentative. Mediating between the compulsive affirmation of Saul Bellow, Bernard Malamud, and Herbert Gold and the surrealistic agony of Joseph Heller, John Hawkes, and Thomas Pynchon, a novel of compromise has developed in which the heroic mode is static, lacking either motion or confirmation of inactivity, surrendering the options of experience by default. This novel of immobility received early if hesitant outline in *The Catcher in the Rye* with Holden Caulfield's inability to make sense of his experience; but no sooner had Salinger suggested the pattern than he abandoned it for a mystical affirmation. The full flowering of the form had to wait for the obsessively introspective, generally unread, first novels of Eugene Mirabelli, Peter Cohen, Alfred Grossman, Herbert Lobsenz, and of best selling Philip Roth, which characteristically fix their adolescent heroes in a ceremony of perpetual innocence.

Unlike the traditional initiation, which requires either surrender to or victory over the community, the contemporary one insists only that the initiate define his situation—or in contemporary terminology that he search for identity. Yet the current hesitant hero rejects even that limited quest. Unhappy with tradition he nonetheless feels disinherited by the decline of man's image from its fixed position in a Hellenic Chain of Being to its present existential uncertainty. The sense of possibility is diminished, the need for discovery neutralized. As a result, the Neil Klugmans (Roth's *Goodbye, Columbus*), the Georges (Mirabelli's *The Burn-*

From *Critique* 2, vol. 7 (Winter 1964–65). Copyright © 1965 by the Bolingbroke Society, Inc.

ing Air), and the Roberts (Cohen's *Diary of a Simple Man*) have become increasingly reluctant either to confirm their own values or to accept those of society. They are willing to take only a limited risk in their encounters with the destructive element of experience, and less willing to resolve its contradictions they are characterized either by a complete lack of involvement or by a parasitic one.

Since neither posture is the result of motion, the uncommitted hero must begin with rather than arrive at his estimate of experience, substituting irony for examination. This inaction contrasts sharply with the modern tradition of sensitive adolescents in American fiction, which reaches back at least as far as Sherwood Anderson, Fitzgerald, and Thomas Wolfe. Primarily romantics they left the hero's enthusiasm for life modified but essentially unchanged by his confrontation with reality. In the current initiation, disengagement is exposed not as choice but as evasion. It does not lead toward the insight of, say, Carson McCullers, for whom growing up is the realization that isolation is the natural state and that love is not reciprocal. Neither do these inactive adolescents arrive at the counter statement of Saul Bellow's passionate if contingent belief in the communal nature of life and love, which, for such questors as Tommy Wilhelm (*Seize the Day*) subsumes the personal one. While the static hero does attempt a redemptive personal relation, it is anchored in an image rather than a reality of self and thus collapses into a sentimental confession of inadequacy. Rather than confirming his maturity, he uncertainly marks time, projecting a counterfeit identity either solely determined by or entirely independent of that of others. Either way it is an identity in which even he no longer believes and which isolates him at the same time as it renders that isolation precarious.

Of the two stances the dependent is perhaps the more immediately destructive, transposing the roles through which each sex determines its identity. Submitting himself for judgment, the boy looks to the girl not merely to corroborate his authority, self won, but to provide it, and no longer reticent she does not submit to him but accepts him on an equal basis, fulfilling her own emotional demands, ultimately defeating his. She may sleep with him in the process, but this has become more a test of her own adequacy than of his. Missing is the American girl's maternal fondness for the shiftless ne'er-do-well. No longer content with making a man of him, she is concerned only that he make a woman of her, and though she encourages the game of sex she is aware that playing house is not a home. Seduction, then, has little to do with surrender, and a non-virginal norm is accepted as part of any meaningful experience. Even chastity no longer suggests the exclusive sufficiency of a single male, but has become rather fidelity to one at a time. Though she resents this male dependence, the girl nonetheless encourages it, under the disguise, even to herself, of fulfillment, and released, or at least relieved, pursues the pattern of life that seems most promising to her.

This sexual generosity predictably discomforts the male ego rather than satisfies it. The questor on the same old quest finds that he is awarded the prize at the outset and is thus prevented from discovering his fitness for it. He finds also that he is no longer the only prizewinner, and with this means of establishing his identity withdrawn in spirit though it remains in body, he becomes uncertain of his worth and unsure of how to determine it. The girl is thus not man-destroying in the classically frigid way. Far from it. But the result is the same as if she were. It is in her very measuring herself against the hero and the consequent shift in relations that his vulnerability to her challenge lies. In the vacuum of values, breathing is difficult, and unable to recognize the inadequacy of his assumptions and so to substitute more realistic ones, he thrashes helplessly in a burning air.

It is this pattern of experience which informs Philip Roth's novella, *Goodbye, Columbus*. The tone is set at Neil Klugman's introduction to Brenda Patimkin by her insistence on his holding her glasses, a gesture which suggests not so much that he will be more clearsighted as that he will be more introspective and certainly more servile. Neil begins by resenting Brenda for the very pretensions that keep him in awe of her, and that are, in addition to her good looks, the reason for her appeal. To the opulent vulgarity of Short Hills, where the Patimkins live, Neil opposes the honesty and unpretentiousness of Newark, where his aunt and uncle relax in an alley, "each cool breeze sweet to them as the promise of afterlife." Much of this proves to be hot air, however, for despite his resentment of Brenda's patronizing references, he never suggests that she visit his aunt, who has recognized the snobbishness in his characterization of the wealthy Patimkins as not having to live over the store.

Invited to Short Hills, Neil is conscious of his inadequacy in the competitive environment in which Brenda lives, even in such remote terms as that of his appetite. But in response to her almost wistful observation that she feels pursued, Neil objects, " '*You* invited *me*, Brenda.' " He has recognized neither her need nor his own, and while he thus implicitly admits that it is Brenda who controls the situation, he does not realize that it is a control she inherits by default. Neil suffers a meaningful blow to his self-esteem when Brenda extorts the admission that he loves her by a literal and symbolic game of hide-and-seek. Later she will challenge him again with an invitation to run track. Although it almost exhausts him, he does outdistance her, and sensing the one area in which he can legitimately triumph, he continues to run each morning thereafter. So much pleasure does Brenda take in her own defeat that she admits for the first time that she loves him, although they had made love long before.

Paralleling Neil's adventures with the Patimkins are his encounters with a Negro boy, who comes to the library where he works to look at a book of Gauguin paintings. When another borrower threatens to charge out the book, Neil, who has been able to maneuver to protect it, pleads with the boy to take it out himself. The boy, however, rejecting his own environment as Neil has rejected his, prefers to visit the glass-brick magnificence of the library rather than take the book home where "somebody dee-*stroy* it." Eventually Neil abandons him for a week-long visit with the Patimkins, subconsciously recognizing the similarity of their positions by coupling himself with the boy in a nightmare in which they are both forced to leave Paradise. It is during this visit that Brenda takes complete charge, on one occasion summoning him to make love to her, after an argument with her mother and the loss of a cache of $300 from her father have cut off the two main sources of her own strength.

Despite their physical intimacy, Neil, who felt "a hollowness when Brenda was away," worries about her ending the affair when she returns to school in the fall. Made to feel insecure by her failure to suggest marriage, which would legitimatize *him*, he proposes more as a test of authority than as a physical convenience, that she buy a diaphragm. However during an argument which follows her refusal, he admits his uncertainty as the real reason for his insistence. Brenda too suggests they are talking about something other than the diaphragm when she objects to buying it because it would be so conscious a thing to do. Having recognized Neil's insecurity and her own power over him, she does not want to acknowledge either the fact of their sexual relations or the permanence of their union. Only after Neil has accepted the situation and the force has gone out of the gesture does she agree to it. It proves to be the excuse for their final separation, when on her return to school, her mother discovers it among her possessions. But the issue had long since been decided. " 'Neil, you don't understand,' " she defends herself when he proposes that she nonetheless spend her holiday with him rather than at home. " 'They're still my parents. They did send me to the best schools, didn't they? They have given me everything I've wanted, haven't they?' " Neil does not, in fact, understand. What she has wanted and what she received from them was the force of authority, not the material benefits she confuses it with, and with the meaning of the terms thus hidden, he can only assert his own frustration and inadequacy. When he rejects both the demands of his job and the urging of his family to follow her to school, the collapse of his integrity leaves nothing to sustain her and she returns to the field of force exerted by her parents in the very middle class substantiality that Neil both envies and condemns.

Left to find some meaning in his experience, Neil can only dream of a pursuit he would not earlier acknowledge. "What was it inside me," he thinks, "that had turned pursuit and clutching into love and then turned it inside out again? What was it that had turned winning into losing, and losing—who knows—into winning?" Neil's admission that he can no longer love Brenda is true, but in a different sense than he is aware of. It is true because he has been exposed and not because he has done the exposing. He had known Brenda's values from the first tennis game he witnessed her play, had seen and remarked on her crudeness, her obtuseness, her childishness, and had accepted it all. Unable to see why his assertion of self-sufficiency failed under her challenge, he can only regard that failure as hers rather than his. His consequent retreat from the search for his own manhood ends, symbolically, with the desire to break the windows of her school library. The possibilities of experience held in those glasses at the first meeting have in fact been shattered. Separated from and faintly contemptuous of his own background, resentful of Brenda's, Neil never confronts either of his opposing drives. Instead he implies that somehow things have worked out for the best, and in so doing substitutes a pretended understanding of Brenda's social aspirations for an insight into his own complicity in their failure of love. . . .

If, then, as Ihab Hassan has said of the contemporary novel (*Radical Innocence,* Princeton, 1961), the initiate is the rebel-victim, the existential self in recoil, the static hero has become his own executioner, allowing a destructive drift to determine his fate. Reluctant to insist on his integrity, he is humble as a result of weakness rather than conviction, and both insures and welcomes the contempt he consequently gets. In his desire for a romantic innocence in the face of his intimation of guilt, he manifests an incapacity for action coupled with a refusal to acknowledge his complicity in its cause. His attachment to people remains as unreciprocal and as uncomprehending as that to things and his difficulties thus constitute an attitude which agonizes over human inconvenience rather than its condition. As such they seem suspiciously as though they could be resolved if only he were to get the girl or the job, or if he were five inches taller.

Unable to reconcile a limited sense of possibility with the even more limited achievement that has resulted from it, unwilling to assess both himself and his experience, the static hero remains restless for lack of definition. Though he suggests perspective by adopting an ironic view-point, the irony fails to relieve the pressure, for rather than a way of sustaining contradictions it attempts to understand experience by taking an attitude toward it. It is thus adopted more as the result of indecision than of encounter, and though the static hero perceives its incongruities, he does not regard life as fundamentally incongruous. Lacking awareness his experience remains accretion rather than development. Above all he lacks the resources to cope with the confusion caused by the disappearance of the standard symbols of maturity, a confusion which is itself absorbed into the mystery of the initiation rite. Effect becomes cause. Unable to accept the truth his experiences have revealed, he is unable to discover his own identity. Finally he is left to search for new pledges, new insignias of sufficiency, whose definition prohibits his ever finding them.

JONATHAN RABAN

Two Meal Scenes
from "Goodbye, Columbus"

Neil Klugman the narrator is a young librarian from a poor Jewish family. He lives with his aunt in the backstreets of the New York suburb of Newark, but has fallen in love with Brenda Patimkin, a college girl from an affluent middle-class Jewish family. In the first scene Neil eats in his aunt's house; in the second he goes out to dinner with the Patimkins. In the novel the two occasions are separated by eleven pages.

DINNER WITH AUNT GLADYS

My aunt called me and I steeled myself for dinner.

She pushed the black whirring fan up to *High* and that way it managed to stir the cord that hung from the kitchen light.

'What kind of soda you want? I got ginger ale, plain seltzer, black raspberry, and a bottle cream soda I could open up.'

'None, thank you.'

'You want water?'

'I don't drink with my meals. Aunt Gladys, I've told you that every day for a year already—'

'Max could drink a whole case with his chopped liver only. He works hard all day. If you worked hard you'd drink more.'

At the stove she heaped up a plate with pot roast, gravy, boiled potatoes, and peas and carrots. She put it in front of me and I could feel

From *The Technique of Modern Fiction*. Copyright © 1968 by Jonathan Raban. Edward Arnold Publishers, Ltd.

the heat of the food in my face. Then she cut two pieces of rye bread and put that next to me, on the table.

I forked a potato in half and ate it, while Aunt Gladys, who had seated herself across from me, watched. 'You don't want bread,' she said, 'I wouldn't cut it it should go stale.'

'I *want* bread,' I said.

'You don't like with seeds, do you?'

I tore a piece of bread in half and ate it.

'How's the meat?' she said.

'Okay. Good.'

'You'll fill yourself with potatoes and bread, the meat you'll leave over I'll have to throw it out.'

Suddenly she leaped up from the chair. 'Salt!' When she returned to the table she plunked a salt shaker down in front of me—pepper wasn't served in her home: she'd heard on Galen Drake that it was not absorbed by the body, and it was disturbing to Aunt Gladys to think that anything she served might pass through a gullet, stomach, and bowel just for the pleasure of the trip.

'You're going to pick the peas out is all? You tell me that, I wouldn't buy with the carrots.'

'I love carrots,' I said, 'I love them.' And to prove it, I dumped half of them down my throat and the other half on to my trousers.

'Pig,' she said.

DINNER WITH THE PATIMKINS

There was not much dinner conversation; eating was heavy and methodical and serious, and it would be just as well to record all that was said in one swoop, rather than indicate the sentences lost in the passing of food, the words gurgled into mouthfuls, the syntax chopped and forgotten in heapings, spillings, and gorgings.

To Ron: When's Harriet calling?

Ron: Five o'clock.

Julie: It *was* five o'clock.

Ron: Their time.

Julie: Why is it that it's earlier in Milwaukee? Suppose you took a plane back and forth all day. You'd never get older.

Brenda: That's right, sweetheart.

Mrs. P.: What do you give the child misinformation for? Is that why she goes to school?

Brenda: I don't know why she goes to school.

Mr. P. (*lovingly*): College girl.

Ron: Where's Carlota? Carlota!

Mrs. P.: Carlota, give Ronald more.

Carlota (*calling*): More what?

Ron: Everything.

Mr. P.: Me too.

Mrs. P.: They'll have to *roll* you on the links.

Mr. P. (*pulling his shirt up and slapping his black, curved belly*): What are you talking about? Look at that?

Ron (*yanking his T-shirt up*): Look at *this*.

Brenda (*to me*): Would you care to bare your middle?

Me (*the choir boy again*): No.

Mrs. P.: That's right, Neil.

Me: Yes. Thank you.

Carlota (*over my shoulder, like an unsummoned spirit*): Would *you* like more?

Me: No.

Mr. P.: He eats like a bird.

Julie: Certain birds eat a lot.

Brenda: Which ones?

Mrs. P.: Let's not talk about animals at the dinner table. Brenda, why do you encourage her?

Ron: Where's Carlota, I gotta play tonight.

Mr. P.: Tape your wrist, don't forget.

Mrs. P.: Where do you live, Bill?

Brenda: Neil.

Mrs. P.: Didn't I say Neil?

Julie: You said 'Where do you live, *Bill?*'

Mrs. P.: I must have been thinking of something else.

Ron: I hate tape. How the hell can I play in tape?

Julie: Don't curse.

Mrs. P.: That's right.

Mr. P.: What is Mantle batting now?

Julie: Three twenty-eight.

Ron: Three twenty-five.

Julie: Eight!

Ron: Five, jerk! He got three for four in the second game.

Julie: *Four* for four.

Ron: That was an error, Minoso should have had it.

Julie: *I* didn't think so.

Brenda (*to me*): See?

Mrs. P.: See what?

Brenda: I was talking to Bill.

Julie: Neil.

Mr. P.: Shut up and eat.

Mrs. P.: A little less talking, young lady.

Julie: *I* didn't say anything.

Brenda: She was talking to me, sweetie.

Mr. P.: What's this *she* business? Is that how you call your mother? What's dessert?

The phone rings, and though we are awaiting dessert, the meal seems at a formal end, for Ron breaks for his room, Julie shouts 'Harriet!'

and Mr. Patimkin is not wholly successful in stifling a belch, though the failure even more than the effort ingratiates him to me. Mrs. Patimkin is directing Carlota not to mix the milk silverware and the meat silverware again, and Carlota is eating a peach while she listens; under the table I feel Brenda's fingers tease my calf. I am full.

ANALYSIS

There are three main voices at work here: that of the narrator, Neil Klugman, that of Aunt Gladys and that of the chorus of Patimkins. We are given distinctive speech patterns for an educated New Yorker, a poor Jewish immigrant and a family of affluent suburbanites. On a merely technical level, Roth proves an exact recorder. Neil's quizzical mixture of formal and colloquial phrasing, Aunt Gladys's twisted Yiddish-English ('You'll fill yourself with potatoes and bread, the meat you'll leave over I'll have to throw it out') and the bright facetiousness of the Patimkins, are sharply rendered. But it is in the balancing of the dialogues that the real work of the novelist has been done.

Consider the rôle of Neil Klugman in both conversations. He does not say much, and when he speaks as the narrator he is alert but non-committal. Roth concentrates on Aunt Gladys and the Patimkins, allowing Neil to drift almost without comment between the two settings. Each grouping bears close resemblance to the other; people sitting down to a meal can be expected to talk and behave in a similar fashion, and Roth draws upon the established conventions of table manners. So that when the scenes do differ, we can infer that an important statement is being made about the two ways of life exemplified by Aunt Gladys and the Patimkin family.

At the first meal, Aunt Gladys talks about nothing but food and household economies. At the second, food is hardly mentioned at all, and the conversation consists of family wise cracks, sports talk and an occasional flippant intimacy between Neil and Brenda. We can immediately locate the two groups socially: one household where money is short and good food important, the other where both are taken for granted. By education and inclination, Neil hovers somewhere between the two classes: he is embarrassed both by Aunt Gladys's perpetual fussing and by the Patimkins' brashness.

But does Roth lead us towards an evaluative judgement of the groups or do we, as in the Hemingway dialogue, have to infer everything? Look at the structure of the dialogues, at the detailed narrative of the first and the bare script of the second. When Neil eats with Aunt Gladys, there is a warmth of description and documentation. His aunt is a strongly felt physical presence, complete with familiar prejudices and mannerisms. We feel that Neil *knows* her in a way that he cannot possibly know the Patimkins. When she exclaims '*Salt!*', Neil is able to explain 'pepper wasn't served in her home: she'd heard on Galen Drake that it was not absorbed by the body . . .' Even when Neil appears to resent Aunt Gladys, his complaints are tempered by irony, as when he announces 'I *steeled* myself for dinner'. We feel throughout the scene that both people have arrived at an intimate acceptance of one another.

In the second episode, the script form prevents Neil from making any interpretative comments. The banality of the conversation has to stand on its own, and we are immersed among a family of strangers making jokes that we don't altogether understand. No one bothers to make Neil feel at home: all the Patimkins sound complacently wrapped up in themselves. Roth further emphasizes the alien quality of their world by refusing to supply us with explanatory detail. Finally the choice between Aunt Gladys and the Patimkin family is ours, but Roth has subtly forced our hand.

BRUNO BETTELHEIM

Portnoy Psychoanalyzed

THERAPY NOTES FOUND IN THE FILES OF
DR. O. SPIELVOGEL, A NEW YORK PSYCHOANALYST

Monday, *The first hour:* A trouble-
some—aren't they all?—new patient, 33 years old, raised in Newark.
Typical petty bourgeois Jewish Orthodox background. He is highly intelligent, a compulsive talker, extremely narcissistic and exhibitionistic. His
intellectual arrogance he hides behind ironic self-deprecation. He cannot
stop the diarrhea of talk, since it is his way of denying his essential
constipation, his total inability to give of himself or of anything else. His
working for the underdog (some kind of public human relations work for
the poorest) is not only a denial of his own exploitativeness, but reflects
the feeling he has that only the most miserable could possibly accept him.

He gave me no chance to explain what psychoanalysis is all about,
claims to be well familiar with it, and proceeds to show that he lacks even
the slightest understanding. He seems to think it is a self-serving rattling
off of complaints, of accusations leveled at others and himself, instead of
serious introspection and the contemplation that it evokes. He is capable
of neither, because he feels himself so worthless that he cannot be serious
about anything that touches him—neither his own self, nor his parents,
nor those he cohabitates with. He wants to do everything himself without
any relation to, or contribution by, another person, in a typical masturbatory phallic fixation. He permits no one, including me, to make any

From *Midstream: A Monthly Jewish Review* 6, vol. 15 (June–July 1969). Copyright
© 1969 by the Theodor Herzl Foundation.

contribution to his life. Obviously he has spent years at his self-justifying ruminations, where even his self-criticism is meant only to show how shrewd and honest he is about himself. Mainly the self-criticism serves to let him go on exactly as before without the need to internalize his guilt to the degree that he would do something about it; it serves him to avoid any need to change. He is convinced that to rattle off in this way becomes psychoanalysis when he does it aloud with me listening.

Despite his long account of all that went wrong in his life begin-ning with infancy, there is absolutely no realization of his sickness: that he simply cannot relate to other persons. And how can he, since all he sees of the world are his own projections which he is certain are true pictures of reality?

He sees psychoanalysis as one vast catharsis, without the need for any deeper insight or internalization. Everything is just one huge ejacula-tion. So much so, that I doubt if he can establish even the minimal transference that would enable him to analyze. Probably his selecting me for an analyst typifies his unwillingness to give up his bondage to his Jewish past. I wonder if I should have insisted that he go to a gentile, American-born analyst. I may still have to transfer him to one.

In a brief talk before treatment began, I asked him why, given his feeling that his troubles originate with his Orthodox Jewish background, he selected me, who is not only Jewish, but European-born. He could not understand my point, saying that no gentile analyst could ever understand him. As if the issue were to find an analyst whose sympathy and under-standing were endless, as it was with his parents, and not his own coming to understand himself. His selecting me for an analyst suggests that deep down he does not want to transcend his own background, but chose an analyst who, because of his background, would not alienate him from what he pretends to hate, but without which he feels there would be nothing left of him or his life. It remains to be seen whether we can overcome this handicap.

Since he thinks his need is to spill out, uninterruptedly, I shall let him, for a full week. Then we shall see if he can stop the spilling enough for analysis to be possible.

He carries on as if to convince me that all the clichés of a spoiled Jewish boyhood are indeed valid: the overpowering, overindulging, over-protective mother and the ineffectual father. Essentially the hour was one long alibi. I am to understand that if he cannot meet life, cannot relate to another human being, it's not because of how he construes things, but because of his parents and their ritual background, along with two specific traumata. He is a master of the alibi, and like the clever lawyer he is, plays both sides of the road. He blames his misery on both kinds of trauma: the physical (an undescended testicle) and the psychological (his mother's threat of desertion, and with a knife). He must be certain I will see him as the suffering victim, no matter what kind of theories I hold about physical or emotional trauma as causing behavior like his. It is neither one, but only his self-hatred that forces him to defeat all those who love him (his parents, his sexual partners, etc.).

The tirade against his parents, especially his mother, is uninterruptable. A few times I indicated the wish to say something, but he only talked on the more furiously. It was like a satire on the complaints of most of my patients, and on the tenets of psychoanalysis: that of the dominating and castrating father, and of a mother too involved in herself and her own life, to pay much attention to her son. This extremely intelligent young Jew does not recognize that what he is trying to do, by reversing the Oedipal situation, is to make fun of me, as he does of everyone, thus asserting his superiority over me and psychoanalysis itself. His overpowering love for his mother is turned into a negative projection, so that what becomes overpowering is the mother's love for him. Overtly he complains that she could never let him alone, was all intrusive—behind which lies an incredibly deep disappointment that she was not even more exclusively preoccupied with him. While consciously he experienced everything she did as destructive, behind it is an incredible wish for more, more, more; an insatiable orality which is denied and turned into the opposite by his continuous scream of its being much too much.

Even the most ordinary, everyday request, such as her reminding him to send a card on his father's 66th birthday, is experienced by him as the most unreasonable demand, forcing on him a life of guilt, of indebtedness to his parents. Whatever the mother did for him was always too little; the smallest thing she requested was always asking too much.

Having to listen all day to the endless complaints of my patients about mothers who were never interested in whether they ate or did not eat, whether or not they defecated, whether or not they succeeded in school, it should have been refreshing to listen to an hour of complaints about a mother who did exactly that—but it was not. Because it was so obvious that he, too, felt cheated at not being given enough. No doubt, he is tortured by memories of his past, and by his present inability to be a man, to enjoy normal sex. But nowhere do I see any effort to free himself of this bondage to the past. He certainly makes the most of it. Obviously he expects my magic and that of psychoanalysis to do it for him.

An important clue, later to be followed up: He is fascinated by his father's constipation, which is so stark a contrast with his excessive masturbation and incessant, diarrhea-like talk. It seems like an interesting fixation at the phallic level, where the father's constipation made him so anxious about the ability to produce that to compensate, he produces without interruption—whether by masturbating, talking, or intellectual achievement. If he does not learn to hold in, to store, but continues the indiscriminate discharge, analysis will certainly fail.

If I should give a name to this first hour, I would call it *The most unforgettable character I've met.* Not because the patient thinks this is true of his mother, as he sees her (as it is of everyone and his mother) but because, while he wishes to believe this, his major effort is to impress me with himself as "The most unforgettable character I've ever met." Poor soul. Instead of trying to get from me the help he so desperately needs, he tries to impress me with his uniqueness. Everything he accuses his mother of, he is himself, in the extreme. She exploited him because she loved him so much. He exploits everyone because he loves no one.

Tuesday, *The second hour*

Despite the same incessant stream of talk, little new material. Speculations arrived at by the end of the last hour seem borne out today. As a child, he masturbated, preferably on the toilet, in line with the father's constipation which emerges ever more as a central experience leading to a negative identification. The father cannot let go. The son cannot hold anything in, or hold onto anyone. The father, out of incessant fear for the future, chose and stuck to his job of life insurance salesman. This is internalized by the son as fear for his masculinity. And for this he finds only one defense: the excessive masturbation that seems to prove his body is working, but at the price of self-disgust. Because what he wants is not a penis that gives pleasure, but an instrument that expels its content, a seeking of self-assurance, which his kind of masturbation cannot give him. Otherwise, it was a repetition of the first hour's contents. In the deliberately vulgar language of the patient, I would title this session *Whacking off.* He uses obscenity to impress others and fools himself into thinking himself liberated, while actually he expresses his loathing for himself.

Wednesday, *The third hour*

It becomes more and more clear that he has read too much about psychoanalysis, and understood nothing—for example about castration anxiety and the effect of seeing menstrual blood. What he does not see is how desperately he wishes he *had* a castrating father, how deeply disappointed he is because what he encounters instead is only what he experiences as a castrating mother. But even as he complains of how castrating she is, he cannot help admiring her inner strength, which alone seems to sustain the entire family. One gets the feeling that he has to see her as castrating, because he needs to see her as being strong enough to protect him. It becomes more and more clear that his true sickness is the refusal to recognize his parents' deep love for him, because that would mean the obligation to love them back, and later, other human beings. Instead he clings to his vision of all human relations as exploitative power plays.

A characteristic memory: The athletic cousin, Heshie, gets into a physical fight with his father. Although considerably the stronger, he lets the father pin him down and then defeat him in physical combat. My patient wonders and wonders about it. He cannot understand why his cousin lets this happen. He cannot see what, in his unconscious, he obviously senses: that while the father kept his son from marrying the gentile girl he loved, which led to the fight, the father's motive was deep love for his son. This cousin could realize, consciously or unconsciously, that to be overpowered by the deep love of another for oneself is the greatest victory possible in human relations, even if outwardly it seems like defeat. This my patient, unfortunately, is unable to consciously accept, and I fear never will. If he could, it would mean his problems were over and his analysis done.

That he could never have the closeness there was between Heshie and his father, that he can neither let go of nor enjoy the specific Jewishness of his background, that he denies what he craves—all this gives him the particular "*Jewish Blues*" that formed the leitmotif of this session.

Thursday, The fourth hour

He connects his exhibitionary masturbation on the bus to his having eaten un-Kosher food (lobster) for the first time. In his unconscious he thus recognizes the connection between oral and phallic anxiety, and how much of his sexual acting out is based on oral anxiety, how like the baby who shows off his phallus. From here, his associations move to what an anxious person his mother really is, with her endless stories of how she tries everything once only to find that any venturing out in the world leads to immediate punishment, if not destruction. Even an explicit memory—her first attempt to drive, which led to an accident and to so much anxiety that she never drove again—brings no realization of how anxiety-ridden she is. Because such an insight would destroy his image of her as the all-powerful, castrating woman. He has no realization that what he identifies with in his mother is not her strength, but her abysmal fear of life.

From talking of his resentment at the feeling that he owes his parents something—to get married and provide them with grandchildren, or to be a success in life they can brag about, as their friends and relatives do—he associates to his sexual desire for gentile girls. That is, he can only have sex if it is sex that his parents disapprove of. He is so tied to them that he cannot feel he has a separate existence unless he does something to hurt them. Of course this does not work, and even in the midst of having intercourse he is already dissatisfied, is already longing anxiously for the next girl to have sex with.

Clearly his promiscuity is one big effort to keep from his parents what they so much want, while making certain he is punished for it by getting nothing that is meaningful to him. For all his reading of psycho-analysis, he does not see that his promiscuity, particularly with gentiles, is one big reassurance that he is not having incestuous relations with his mother. By keeping his women ever-changing and meaningless to him, he remains faithful to his mother—not because she won't let him go but because he won't let go of her. Having enslaved himself to her, he projects the relation to see it as if she, or both parents, had enslaved him to them.

Another crucial memory: A fifteen year old boy is pushed too hard by his ambitious mother to perform, and hangs himself. Pinned to his shirt is a message he took for his mother: that she is to take the mah-jongg rules along when she goes out that night. My patient can see in it only the boy's obedience, and not the lethal venom at his mother who dares to enjoy a game with her friends instead of doing nothing all day except cater to her son.

As is typical for patients totally unable to form any human rela-tions, they complain endlessly of the deficiency of human relations in their childhood and try to provide for others what is, in fact, totally absent in their own lives. So this patient, it turns out, is Assistant Commissioner of the New York Committee on Human Opportunity, concerned in his work with improving the lives of others. In his profes-sional life he tries to prevent the poor from being exploited, while all he chases in his personal life is the chance to sexually exploit others.

The worst part of it is that he, who is so lacking in ego and the capacity to give, who is so driven to act out his uncontrolled instinctual tendencies, thinks he is suffering from a deficiency of the id. At one point he makes clear what he wants from me: to put the id back into this particular Yid. That is, he does not really want to analyze himself; does not want to get ego control over superego and id. All he wants of me is to rid him of all the pangs of conscience he still feels about his selfish and asocial behavior. This is how he conceives of the purpose of psychoanalysis. Indeed he offers to pay me an even higher fee if only I could do that for him.

He recalls masturbating once into a piece of liver which was then eaten at the family dinner. He has no inkling that this shows an extreme sexualization of the oral stage. But most of his seemingly phallic sexuality is really nothing but a screen for his fixation at the oral stage as it shows in his incessant demand to be given to. All the giving by both parents was not enough to fill him up. At least the girl he calls "monkey" understood him well. According to him she screams out against this great humanitarian whose job it is to protect the poor from their landlords, while his own sexual enjoyment comes of sexually degrading this girl who seems really to have fallen in love with him, who hoped their relationship might help her out of her own sexual, moral, human morass.

How wise Freud was to impose the sexual abstinence rule, and the rule against patients' reading in psychoanalysis. This patient uses his reading of Freud to masturbate with. Having no intention of analyzing himself, he wants me to do everything for him, as he expected of his mother, without his having to do anything for himself.

The only enjoyment he seems to get out of sex is cunnilingus. Like his incessant talking and his pleasure in four letter words, so it is with his preference for this perversion. All indicate that he was so intensely satisfied by the oral pleasure his mother provided, that he cannot conceive of its coming from anything else. He is, I am tempted to say, crazy in his efforts to wring oral satisfaction out of sex. In the language of the patient, this session exemplifies his "*cunt craziness.*"

Friday, The fifth hour

He begins the session by referring to Freud's paper on the misuse of sex to degrade the partner. Which leads to memories of his sexual relations with some upper-class gentiles. He recognizes that his feelings of Jewish inferiority, his resentment of anti-Semitism, are why he cannot find sexual satisfaction except through seducing his gentile partners into practices which to him are degrading. (The "monkey," who did not mind fellatio or even enjoyed it, he induces to have lesbian sex with a prostitute—at which point he is through with her. His excuse is that she had hinted at it; which she had. Since she really loves him, she wishes to please him in every way. She feels unworthy of him, feels that though she gives all she has, tries everything she knows, it seems never enough. So she tried to suggest her readiness to do whatever else might satisfy him. Her offer to do anything he might want of her is then used by him to exculpate himself that it is really her fault that he so degraded her that she wants to kill herself. All his life it is always the same desperate story: unable to love anybody, including himself, he cannot believe that anybody—his parents, the "monkey"—can do anything out of love for him.)

Since he has never known true empathy for anyone, he cannot see that these gentile girls had sex with him precisely because he lived up to their stereotyped notions of the dirty, sex-crazy Jew. Forcing them into what they view as perverted sex, proves to them they were right about Jews in the first place. They have selected this highly intelligent, thus seemingly very worthwhile Jew, because being specially admirable he threatened their image of Jews as inferior beings. But if even this very bright, this nice, concerned Jew wants nothing so much as to degrade them in sex, then their initial image of the "dirty" Jew is again confirmed. And my patient does his best to oblige. Still thinking he degrades only them, he degrades himself even more. This mutual exploitation extends also to what the pair use each other for: to defeat their parents. For my patient the worst he can do to his parents is to live with a gentile girl. While to sleep with a Jew is probably the worst these girls can do to their parents. How these neurotics always find each other! How they help each other act out their neurosis so there is no need to face it! His sex experiences certainly seem like an illustration to Freud's: *The most prevalent form of degradation in erotic life.*

Saturday, The sixth hour

Were I to see my patients only five hours a week, like most of my American colleagues, and not also on Saturdays, this patient's story might have developed very differently. Last night, going over my notes up to now, I came close to deciding that his narcissistic self-involvement, his deep oral fixation, his inability to relate, etc., would make analysis impossible and had pretty much decided to tell him so at the end of today's hour. I hoped that the shock might, later on, permit him to seek out another analyst; I planned to suggest a gentile one. With him he might begin to analyze, instead of misusing him as a prop to get rid of his guilt, while continuing to destroy all who have positive feelings for him.

If he had had to wait till Monday, probably nothing would have changed. Maybe that this was a Saturday, *the Sabbath,* had something to do with it. This I shall find out later. Anyway, today was an entirely different hour. Instead of regaling me with his sexual successes—in masturbation, cunnilingus, fellatio—he finally became a bit more human in recounting his sexual defeats, all by Jewish girls. It began with his recalling how he admired Jewish men like his father, their Sunday morning ball game, how he wished to identify with them but could not, because he wanted even more to possess his mother. From his girlfriend, the "monkey," he had to run because as soon as he had gotten a girl to the point where no further degradation was likely to occur, all attraction was gone. Unable as always to come through when the love of others for him was so obvious he could no longer deny it, his only solution was to run away. Blaming them for trying to put him in bondage—though all he wishes is to see them in bondage to him, and with him having no return obligation—he flees to Israel, the mother country.

There unconsciously (but so close to consciousness that I feel analysis may begin after all) he realizes that if he is no longer a Jew in a gentile world, if he can no longer blame on it (and with it justify) his whole pattern of demanding and receiving without ever giving, if he must manage without these excuses, he is nothing—cannot even manage an erection.

In desperation he tries to seduce a kibbutz girl by reversing the methods he used with his gentile girls. Them he had degraded and their debasement had made them extremely attractive to him, but also useless. Here instead, it is he who submits to debasement, particularly when the girl tells him what should long have been obvious: that his self-degradation is the more despicable because he is a man of such high intelligence. To her telling him how little she thinks of him, he reacts by inviting her to have intercourse with him. Blaming others as always, he tries to pin his impotence on his mother, claiming the kibbutz girl reminds him of her. He believes it to be the Oedipal (but genital) attachment that makes him impotent, while it is really his oral attachment, his wish to remain the suckling infant forever.

The long-suffering Jewish mother who suffers herself to be blamed for everything, is willing to thus serve her son. Never will he have to feel guilty about anything he does because he can always blame it on her. And in a way he can; but not as he thinks. He can blame her for what she has led him to believe: That whatever he wants he must immediately be given. This, the central theme of his life, he screams out at the kibbutz girl: "I HAVE TO HAVE." It is she who finally tells him that this belief of his—that he has to have what he wants, whatever it may cost the other—is not valid.

In a fantasy of being judged for his crimes, he realizes, at least for a moment, that blaming his mother will not get him off, cannot justify his behavior to others. This raises the hope that analysis might just succeed. So, instead of dismissing him, as I had planned, I said, "Now we may perhaps begin." Only the future will tell if I was not much too optimistic.

One more thought: He is very clever at presenting himself, and right after the first session I had the uneasy feeling that he wants to impress me as the most unforgettable patient I ever had. What if all he said so far was carefully prepared and selected? His determination not to permit me to interrupt with questions or interpretations suggests the possibility that he was afraid that any interference might throw him off his only seemingly stream of consciousness-like talk, while it was actually a carefully prepared story, designed to impress me. What if all he presented as the outpourings of his unconscious and preconscious, of his id and superego (the self-criticism, the fantasy about his being judged) would have been conscious ego productions? Was he trying to test me in order to find out whether I am smart enough not to mistake what was essentially a literary production for an effort at analysis?

If so, did I do the right thing not to insist on interrupting him, or on directing his associations, and tell him at the end of the last session that it is time to stop being a man of letters so that, through analyzing himself, he might finally become a man? Again, we shall see.

But even though what has happened so far was not more than an effort to tell a good story, it is significant that it is the "monkey" who emerges as having the greatest dignity. Though born desperately poor, social success means nothing to her. Having been married to one of the richest men of France meant nothing to her. When she felt used by him, she left him without another thought. Though aspiring to culture, she is not at all impressed by its trappings, nor by being invited to the mayor's mansion, because what is important to her is to be with him, not to attend a formal dinner. This she makes clear by having sex with him within view of the mayor's house, not caring what others may think of her or what she does there, while he is deathly afraid of how all this may look to others. He, as always, being involved only in himself, does not recognize that she is not motivated by any hedonist impulsiveness, but by the anxious question: "Are you taking me to the mayor's reception because you love me and want me near you, or because I am ornamental and therefore useful in your social climbing?"

If it was a literary production, what view must he have of himself as a person and as a Jew if social and sexual honesty, that is if true humanity—in his eyes—resides only in the poor "monkey"? Is it just another case then of the self-hating Jew living *in exile*?

THEODORE SOLOTAROFF

Philip Roth: A Personal View

One day in the fall of 1957, I was sitting in a course on Henry James at the University of Chicago. The semester had just begun, and there were a few new faces: one that I had been noticing belonged to a handsome, well-groomed young man who stood out in the lean and bedraggled midst of us veteran graduate students as though he had strayed into class from the business school. The text for the day was *Daisy Miller*, and toward the end of the hour, one of the other students began to run away with the discussion, expounding one of those symbolic religious interpretations of the story that were in fashion at the time everywhere but at Chicago. Eventually the instructor asked me what I thought of this reading, and in the rhetoric I had learned from my mentors among the Chicago critics, I said that it was idiotic. I was immediately seconded by the debonair young man, who, in a very precise and concrete way, began to point out how such a reading turned the purpose and technique of the story inside out. Like two strangers in a pickup basketball game who discover they can work together, we passed the argument back and forth for a minute or two, running up the score of common sense. It was one of those fine moments of communication that don't occur every day in graduate English courses, and after class we met, shook hands, and exchanged names. His was Philip Roth.

So began a relationship. Since we were leading complicated, busy, and quite different private lives, our paths didn't cross that much. But almost each time they did, a connection was made and the current flowed. Though I was five years older than Roth, we were rather alike in temperament—aggressive, aloof, moody, and, as graduate students go, worldly.

From *The Red-Hot Vacuum*. Copyright © 1969 by Theodore Solotaroff. Atheneum.

We also had a number of things in common that turned us on to each other. We were from roughly the same background—the practical, coarse, emotionally extravagant life of the Jewish middle class—as well as from neighboring cities in northern New Jersey. So there was an easy, immediate intimacy of a more or less common upbringing—Hebrew schools and YMHA's, the boardinghouses and boardwalks of Belmar and Bradley Beach, the Empire Burlesque House in Newark; the days and ways of possessive Jewish mothers and harassed Jewish fathers; the pantheons of our adolescence where Hank Greenberg, John Garfield, Norman Corwin, and Longy Zwillman, the outstanding racketeer in Essex County, were enshrined; and so many other "Jewish" artifacts, experiences, nuances of feeling and attitude, about which we found ourselves to be about equally nostalgic and contemptuous, hilarious and burdened. At the same time, we were both involved in the similar journey from the halfway house of semi-acculturation, whose household deity was neither Sholom Aleichem nor Lionel Trilling but someone like Jack Benny, into the realm of literature and culture. In our revolt against the exotic but intransigent materialism of our first-generation bourgeois parents, we were not in school to learn how to earn a living but to become civilized. Hence our shared interest in James. And, finally, we both thought of ourselves as writers who were biding their time in the graduate seminars we took and the freshman composition courses we gave. Hence our quick hostility toward any fancy, academic uses of James.

All of which meant that we were also somewhat wary of each other. Since each of us served as an objectification of the other's sense of position and purpose, we spent a lot of time secretly taking each other's measure, comparing and contrasting. Also I had more or less stopped writing, except for term papers, while Roth was writing all the time and was getting published. One of his stories had even been anthologized in a Martha Foley collection; two others had just been bought by *Esquire*; and he was also doing movie reviews for the *New Republic*. After a quarter or so Roth dropped out of graduate school in order to concentrate on his fiction; meanwhile I slowly forged on through the second year of the Ph.D. program. To our other roles came to be added those of the creative writer and the critic, respectively.

During this year I read several of the stories in manuscript that were to appear two years later in *Goodbye, Columbus*. Raised as I had been, so to speak, on the short-story-as-a-work-of-art, the cool, terse epiphanies of the Joyce of *Dubliners*, the Flaubert of *Un Coeur simple*, of Katherine Mansfield and Hemingway, I didn't at first know how to respond to a story in which the narrator says:

Though I am very fond of desserts, especially fruit, I chose not to have any. I wanted, this hot night, to avoid the conversation that revolved around my choosing fresh fruit over canned fruit, or canned fruit over fresh fruit; whichever I preferred. Aunt Gladys always had an abundance of the other jamming her refrigerator like stolen diamonds. "He wants canned peaches. I have a refrigerator full of grapes I have to get rid of. . . ." Life was a throwing off for poor Aunt Gladys, her greatest joys were taking out the garbage, emptying her pantry, and making thread-bare bundles for what she still referred to as the Poor Jews in Palestine. I only hope she dies with an empty refrigerator, otherwise she'll ruin eternity for everyone else, what with her Velveeta turning green, and her navel oranges growing fuzzy jackets down below.

But my resistance quickly toppled like tenpins. It was like sitting down in a movie house and suddenly seeing there on the screen a film about the block on which I had grown up: the details of place, character, incident all intimately familiar and yet new, or at least never appreciated before for their color and interest. This story of Neil Klugman and Brenda Patimkin was so simple, direct, and evident that it couldn't be "art," and yet I knew that art did advance in just this way: a sudden sweeping aside of outmoded complexities for the sake of a fresh view of experience, often so natural a view and so common an experience that one wondered why writers hadn't been seeing and doing this all along. The informal tone of the prose, as relaxed as conversation, yet terse and fleet and right on the button; the homely images of "stolen diamonds," of the Velveeta, and the oranges, that make the passage glow. Such writing rang bells that not even the Jewish writers had touched; it wasn't Malamud, it wasn't even Saul Bellow: the "literary" fuzz of, say, *Augie March* had been blown away, and the actualities of the life behind it came forth in their natural grain and color, heightened by the sense of discovery.

Such writing is much more familiar today than it was ten years ago: indeed, it has become one of the staples of contemporary fiction. But at the time the only other writer who seemed to be so effortlessly and accurately in touch with his material was Salinger. For a year or so after reading *Catcher in the Rye,* I hadn't been able to walk through Central Park without looking around for Holden and Phoebe Caulfield, and now here was this young semblable of mine who dragged me off for a good corned-beef sandwich or who gave me a push when my car wouldn't start, and who, somehow, was doing for the much less promising poetry of Newark, New Jersey, what the famous Salinger was doing for that of Central Park West. Moreover, if Roth's fiction had something of Salinger's wit and charm, the winning mixture of youthful idealism and cynicism, the air of immediate reality, it was also made of tougher stuff, both in the kind of life it described and in the intentions it embodied. Salinger's taste for experience, like that of his characters, was a very delicate one; Roth's appetite was much heartier, his tone more aggressive, his moral sense both broader and more decisive.

What fascinated me most about stories like "Goodbye, Columbus," "The Conversion of the Jews," and "Defender of the Faith" was the firm, clear way they articulated the inner situation we sensed in each other but either took for granted or indicated covertly—by a reference to Isabelle Archer as a *shiksa,* or by a takeoff on the bulldozing glottals of our father's speech, as we walked away from our literature or linguistics course. In such ways we signaled our self-ironic implication in things Jewish, but Roth's stories dealt directly with the much touchier material of one's efforts to extricate himself, to achieve a mobility that would do justice to his individuality. Social mobility was the least of it. This was the burden of "Goodbye, Columbus," where Neil Klugman's efforts early in the story to latch and hold on to the little wings of Brenda Patimkin's shoulderblades and let them carry him up "those lousy hundred and eight feet that make summer nights so much cooler in Short Hills than they are in Newark" soon take on the much more interesting, and representative, struggle to have her on his own terms, terms that lie well beyond money, comfort, security, status, and have to do with his sexual rights and ultimately his uncertain emotional and moral identity. At the end of the story, Neil stands in front of the Lamont Library and at first wants to hurl a rock through the glass front; but his rage at Brenda, at the things she had been given and has sacrificed him for, soon turns into his curiosity about the young man who stares back at him in the mirrored reflection and who "had turned pursuit and clutching into love, and then turned it inside out again . . . had turned winning into losing and losing—who knows—into winning. . . ."

Neil's prickly and problematic sense of himself, his resistance to the idea of being a bright Jewish boy with an eye for the main chance, for making sure, an idea that was no stranger to other desires—well, this was not simply fiction to me. Nor was the Patimkin package, where horse shows and Big Ten basketball and classy backhands still came wrapped in Jewish conformity and ethnocentricity. In story after story there was an individual trying to work free of the ties and claims of the community. There was Ozzie in "The Conversion of the Jews," who would not have God hedged in by the hostility of Judaism to Christianity; there was Sergeant Marx in "Defender of the Faith," who finally refused to hand over any more of his sense of fairness and responsibility to the seductive appeals of Jewish solidarity; or, on the other hand, there was Eli Peck, who refused to close the book of Jewish history to be more at ease with his landsmen in Suburbia. Or there was even poor Epstein, who managed to pry apart the iron repressions of Jewish family life to claim some final gratifications for himself. Or there was my special favorite, a very early story called "You Can't Tell a Man by the Song He Sings," in which a nice Jewish boy learns from two Italians—a juvenile delinquent and an ex-radical guidance teacher—that some dignities have to be won against the rules and regulations of upward mobility.

Such themes were as evocative to me as a visit from my mother, but I knew that I couldn't write the stories that embodied them in the way that Roth had. It was not just a matter of talent but of the intricate kind of acceptance that joins one's talent to his experience so that he can communicate directly. Though Roth clearly was no less critical of his background than I was, he had not tried to abandon it, and hence had not allowed it to become simply a deadness inside him: the residual feelings, mostly those of anxiety, still intact but without their living context. That is to say, he wrote fiction as he was, while I had come to write as a kind of fantasist of literature who regarded almost all of my actual experience in the world as unworthy of art. A common mistake, particularly in the overliterary age of the late Forties and Fifties, but a decisive one. So if I envied Roth his gifts, I envied even more his honesty, his lack of fastidiousness, his refusal to write stories that labored for a form so fine that almost any naturalness would violate it. The gross affluences and energies of the Patimkins, the crudities of Albie Pelagutti and Duke Scarpa, even the whining and wheedling of Sheldon Grossbart turned him on rather than put him off. Once, I remember, I balked. There is a scene in "Epstein" where his wife discovers his rash that they both believe is venereal, and an ugly and not very funny description follows of their fight in the nude. "Why all the *schmutz?*" I asked him. "The story is the *schmutz*," he snapped back.

Our relationship had its other ups and downs. After he dropped out of graduate school, Roth went on teaching in the college, an impressive post to me, if not to him (he was to give it up after a year and head for New York). And since he was publishing his work and looked to be making good use of his bachelor years, he seemed, at least on the surface (which was where my envy led me to look), to have the world by the tail. On the other hand, the world in those days seemed, at least on the surface, to have me by the tail. I was taking three courses at Chicago and teaching four at Indiana University Calumet Center, a glum building around which lay the oil refineries and steel mills to which most of my students returned from our discussions of Plato and Dante. On my salary of $3000 a year it was not easy to support my wife and two small boys. But, having wasted a number of years after college, I felt that I was getting somewhere. My students were challenging, to say the least, and some of the charm of scholarship had unexpectedly begun to descend upon me. Still the fact remained that Roth was visibly well off and I was visibly not, and it made certain differences. At one point I borrowed some money from him, which made us both uncomfortable until it was paid back. One evening he and his date, my wife and I, went to hear a lecture by Saul Bellow—our literary idol—and afterward went out for a beer. His girlfriend, though, ordered a scotch, and into the discussion of what Bellow had said and could have said there intruded an awkward moment at each round of drinks. Or there was a party he came to at my place to celebrate the arrival of bock beer (our version of the rites of spring). As I've suggested, Roth and I shared our past and our opinions much more than we shared our present lives. When we met, it was almost always at his place. My apartment, over in the Negro section, with its Salvation Army decor and its harassed domesticity, seemed both to touch him and make him nervous. I remember him sitting on the edge of a couch, over which I had just nailed an old shag rug to cover the holes, waiting like a social worker while my wife got our oldest son through his nightly asthma. Then the other guests arrived, the beer flowed, and we turned on with our favorite stimulant—Jewish jokes and caustic family anecdotes—dispensed principally by Roth, whose fantastic mimicry and wit soon had us rolling in our chairs.

That evening came back to mind a few years later when I was reading Roth's first novel, *Letting Go*, which is set mainly in Hyde Park and which deals with the ethos of the graduate-student/young-instructor situation during the Fifties: the "Age of Compassion," as Gabe Wallach, the protagonist, aptly puts it. The story mainly follows Wallach's involvement with Paul and Libby Herz, a needy young couple (money is only the beginning of it), and with Martha Regenhart, a voluptuous and tough-minded girl who has two children to support and who is looking for some support herself. Attracted both by Libby's frailty and by Martha's strength, and unable to make much contact with the surly Herz, Wallach, an attractive bachelor in comfortable circumstances, spends much of the novel sitting on the edge of his scruples, worrying whether too much or too little is being asked of him, a dilemma he shares with Herz, whose moral self-consciousness takes over whenever the point of view shifts to his side of the story. All of this reckoning of the wages of conscience is accompanied by cool, satirical observation, more successfully of the Jewish background of Gabe and Paul than of their professional life, which Roth used mostly to even a few scores. The best writing in the book came in the scenes in a Detroit boardinghouse when Herz's effort to push Libby through an abortion gets tangled up with the schemes of the retired shyster, Levy, to "help" the pathetic Korngold extract money from his son and to move the cases of underwear that Korngold hoards in his room, waiting for the market to improve.

Like a good many other citizens of Hyde Park, my wife and I furnished a trait here, an anecdote there, but the material was more thoroughly fictionalized in our case than in some others. What Roth was mainly drawing on, I felt, was a certain depressiveness that had been in the air: the result of those long Chicago winters, the longueurs of graduate school and composition courses, the financial strains, the disillusionment with the university (this was the period in which the Hutchins experiments were being dismantled and the administration was waging a reign of respectability in all areas), and the concomitant dullness of the society-at-large, which had reached the bottom of the Eisenhower era. But mostly this depressiveness was caused by the self-inflicted burdens of private life, which in this age of conformity often seemed to serve for politics, art, and the other avenues of youthful experience and experiment. One of the principal occupations in Hyde Park seemed to be difficult marriages: almost everyone I knew was locked into one. This penchant for early marriage and child-rearing, or for only slightly less strenuous affairs, tended to fill the vacuum of commitment for sophisticated but not especially stable young couples and fostered a rather pretentious moralism of duty, sacrifice, home therapy, experiment with domestic roles—often each other's—working things out, saving each other. It was a time when the deferred gratifications of graduate school and the climb to tenure and the problems of premature adjustment seemed the warranty of "seriousness" and "responsibility": those solemn passwords of a generation that practiced a Freudian/Jamesian concern about motives, pondered E. M. Forster's "only connect," and subscribed to Lionel Trilling's "moral realism" and "tragic sense of life." In contrast to today, everyone tried to act as though he were thirty.

Some of this Roth had caught and placed at the center of *Letting Go*. As the title suggests, the novel is a study of entangling attachments, beginning with Gabe's effort to release himself from his widowed father's possessiveness and ending with his frantic effort to complete, and thereby end, his intervention in the life of the Herzes, through helping them to adopt a child. In between, a host of characters push and pull, smother and neglect each other, usually under the guise of solicitude or obligation. At one point Wallach puts it for himself, Herz, and most of the others: "I knew it was not from my students or my colleagues or my publications, but from my private life, my secret life, that I would extract whatever joy—or whatever misery—would be mine." By "private life" he means relationships and their underlying *Realpolitik* of need, dependency, and control.

It was evident that *Letting Go* represented a major effort to move forward from *Goodbye, Columbus.* The theme of communal coerciveness and individual rights that dominates most of the stories had been opened out to deal with the more subtle perversions of loyalty and duty and creaturely feeling that flow through the ties of family, marriage, friendship. A very Jamesian theme: *The Portrait of a Lady* figures almost immediately in *Letting Go,* as a reference point for its interest in benevolent power plays. Also, in bringing his fiction more up to date with the circumstances and issues of his life, Roth had tried for a more chastened, Jamesian tone. The early chapters have some of the circumspect pace and restrained wit of the Master: well-mannered passages of nuance and implication, the main characters carefully observed, the theme tucked neatly away in the movement of action, thought, and dialogue. The book sails gracefully along for about 150 pages or so. Then it begins to turn as gray and bitter as the Chicago winter and, in time, as endless.

What went wrong? As I have indicated, the Hyde Park we had known had not been an especially chipper place, and there was plenty of reason to deal with it in terms of its grim domesticity. Still, Roth had laid it on and laid it on. If Gabe and Martha have the Herzes for dinner, the mutual strains will be as heavy as a bad Ph.D. oral, and afterward Gabe and Martha will fight about who paid for what. If Paul's passion for Libby revives at a party, it will cool before they can get around the corner. If some children are encountered at a playground with their grandmother, it is because their mother has just tried to flush herself down a toilet bowl at Billings Hospital. In this morbid world, sibling rivalry leads to homicide, intermarriage to being abandoned by both the Catholic and Jewish families, adoption proceedings to a nervous breakdown. Not even a stencil can get typed without fear and trembling.

All of which added up, I felt, not only to an exaggeration of the conditions but to an error of vision. I wondered if this *error* might have something to do with the surface view we had of each other's lives: his apparent fortune, my apparent misfortunes: clearly the germ, at least, of the Wallach-Herz relationship. As I was subsequently to realize, my view of him that year was full of misapprehensions: behind the scenery of ease and success he had been making his payments to adversity: a slipped disc, for one thing; a tense and complicated affair, some aspects of which were to figure in Gabe's relationship with Martha. On the other hand, behind

the scenery of adversity in a life like mine, there were positive purposes
and compensations that he had not taken into account, and that made
the struggle of those years tolerable and possibly significant. Though
Wallach is a scholar and Herz a novelist, they might as well be campus
watchmen for all the interest they have in their work, in ideas, even in
their careers. While this ministers to the central concerns of the novel, it
deprives both of them of force and resistance, for, stripped of any aggressive claim on the world, they have little to do but hang around their
women and guiltily talk about "working it out"—the true title of the
novel. The only character who has any beans is Martha, which is partly
owing to the fact that, having two children to support and raise, her life
intentions are to some degree objective. Otherwise there are only the
obsessive, devouring relationships and the malaise they breed: Libby per-
petually waiting to be laid, Paul reminding her to put on her scarf, Gabe
consumed by his sense of his obligations and his distrust of it, Martha
demanding that payment be made for satisfactions given. From such
characters, little natural dynamic can develop, and Roth can only forge
on and on in his relentlessly bleak way: now analytic, now satirical, now
melodramatic—giving Libby an adopted baby, Paul a religious turn, Martha a dull, dependable husband, and Gabe a wild adventure in Gary with
the extortion-minded husband of the girl who bore the baby—none of it
especially convincing, none of it quite able to lift up and justify the
burden of the pessimism.

In his essay on "Some of the Talent in the Room" Norman Mailer
wagered that the depressiveness of *Letting Go* had to do with Roth's
"working out an obsession." This seemed to me a shrewd observation,
though who in these days of obsessive fiction would 'scape hanging. In
Letting Go the obsession is with the power of women along with a male
queasiness about it that keeps both Herz and Wallach implicated, endlessly
looking for moral means to cope with their emotional vulnerability. As
Wallach, for example, remarks at one point:

> There must be some weakness in men, I thought (in Paul and myself, I
> later thought) that Libby wormed her way into. Of course I had no
> business distrusting her because of *my* weakness—and yet women have a
> certain historical advantage (all those years of being downtrodden and
> innocent and sexually compromised) which at times can turn even the
> most faithful of us against them. I turned slightly at that moment myself,
> and was repelled by the sex toward which at bottom I have a consider-
> able attachment.

This sort of observation hardly leads to insight or movement. It merely
maintains an ambivalence by shunting the anger involved off on some

courtly, literary track and letting the historical situation of women screen the personal guilt, the deep characterological misery that keeps men like Herz and Wallach in place and wide open. As the novel wears on, the anger if not guilt is more and more acknowledged in Wallach's case, as his priggishness is worn down by Martha and some of his true feelings begin to emerge. Still, the problem of coping with Libby and Martha, posited in moral terms that make it insoluble, nags away at the two men and their author. What they can't "let go" of is guilt, and it drags the book down with them.

When *Letting Go* came out, I was working at *Commentary,* a job that had come my way as the result of an essay that the *TLS* had asked me to write on Roth's recommendation. Since he hadn't liked the essay at first and since I was as touchy as Paul Herz proved to be about such matters as gratitude and pride, there had been a falling out. In New York, however, the relationship resumed, and with fewer of the disparities and diffidences that had made it tense and illusionary. As time went on, there were also reasons to level with each other: we were both separated, both in analysis, both in a state of flux. So we would get together, now and then, for dinner, and talk about problems and changes. One evening I dropped by his new place on East Tenth Street to borrow a book. It was bigger and much better furnished than mine, and he wanted me to know—screw the guilt—he intended to be comfortable here and to sink some new roots. But, for all that, the place looked as bare and provisional as mine: we might as well have both been living in tents, neither of us bachelors so much as husbands *manqué.* A portable typewriter was sitting on the dining-room table, and a lot of manuscript pages were spread around it.

"What's that?" I asked.

"It's a novel." He looked at it without much pleasure. "I've written it once, and now I'm writing it again."

It was strange to realize that he, too, got hung up. I had always assumed that he was like Chekhov, who said that he wrote "as easily as a bird sings."

Perhaps he noticed my silly smile. "You know something?" he said. "There's not a single Jew in it." He went on about the strangeness of imagining, really imagining, a family that was not a Jewish family, that was what it was by virtue of its own conditioning and conditions, just as the Jews were, but which were not just those of "the others"—the Gentiles. Something like that—though he put it, as always, more concretely—acting out, with that gift of mimicry that was always on tap, the speech and the slant of some small-town citizen of middle America.

The novel, of course, turned out to be *When She Was Good,* two years, and several more revisions, later. It was easy to see why the book had been a trial for Roth to write. Liberty Center is so far from his line of territory that everything had to be played by ear, so to speak. The town hardly exists as a place, as something seen in its physical actuality; it is rather the spirit of the American Protestant ethic circa 1948, whose people and mores, interests and values, emerge from the impersonation of idiom and tone: Liberty Center as it might have been presented not by Sinclair Lewis but by Ruth Draper. In order to bring this off, Roth had had to put aside his wit, color, and élan, keep his satirical tendency tightly in check, and write the novel in a language of scrupulous banality. This impersonality was far removed from the display of temperament that animated "Goodbye, Columbus" as the life of the bitchy heroine, Lucy Nelson, so meager and so arduous, is from that of the bitchy Brenda Patimkin.

Yet, for all the improvisation and guesswork, the surface of *When She Was Good* is solid and real, and though true to the dullness of Liberty Center's days and ways, it is beautifully constructed to take on momentum and direction and to hit its target with shattering impact, like some bland-looking object in the sky that turns out to be a guided missile. As in *Letting Go,* the theme is the wages of possessiveness and self-righteousness, but as embodied by and embedded in Lucy Nelson's raging, ball-breaking ego, it takes on a focus and power that had dissolved in the miasmic male earnestness of the previous novel. There is no false gallantry or temporizing about Lucy. Any ambivalence has been burned away, and Roth presents her and her will to power dead-to-rights. Because of this sureness of feeling, he can also present her in the round—terrible when crossed but touching in her aspirations and inexperience, her baffled need for a fathering trust, the victim as well as the avenger of her grandfather's wishy-washy Good Samaritanism, of her parasitic father's disgrace and her mother's passivity, of the family's stalled drive for respectability, and, eventually, of her husband's arrested adolescence. But from the moments early in the novel when Lucy turns in her drunken father to the police and then bars his way back into the family, the blind force of her aggression, screened by her faith in duty and responsibility and in her moral superiority, begins to charge the novel and to shape her destiny. She is unable to break off her romance with Roy Bassart until she has him safely installed in photography school and thereby ends up pregnant. She refuses the abortion she herself sought when it is offered by her father and when she learns that her mother had had one. She enters into a shotgun marriage with Roy, whom she has come to despise, with herself holding the gun. At each turn of her fate, skillfully paired with another and better alternative, it is Lucy's master emotion—her rage against her father—that directs her choice as surely as Nemesis. And some years later, when her father writes home from the jail he has landed in and thereby pulls her mother away from marriage to a man Lucy can finally respect, she turns it all against Roy in a climactic outburst of verbal castration, and then lets loose the furies of self-righteousness that drive her to madness and death. Like her grandfather's demented sister who had to be sent back to the state hospital because she followed Lucy to school and created a public nuisance, Lucy has been unable to understand "the most basic fact of human life, the fact that I am me and you are you."

In telling Lucy's story as circumspectly as he could, Roth has placed it within a context of cultural factors. Her grandfather had come to Liberty Center to escape from the brutality of the northern frontier, and the town stands in his mind, as it comes to stand in the reader's, as the image of his desire: "not to be rich, not to be famous, not to be mighty, not even to be happy, but to be civilized." Though Lucy rejects the tepid Protestantism on which Willard stands fast, she worships at the same shrine of propriety, which is the true religion of Liberty Center, and whose arbiters are the women. If men like her father and her husband founder in the complexities of society, it is the women who are supposed to straighten them out. They are the socializing agents, and the town's football stars and combat heroes, its reprobates and solid citizens, alike bow to their sway. When the high-school principal says to Roy and Lucy, "So this is the young lady I hear is keeping our old alum in line these days," he is referring to the community norm which Lucy will carry to an extreme.

Still, the cult of Momism in Liberty Center hardly added up to a pressing contemporary note, and the novel tended to be dismissed by most of the influential reviewers as slight, inauthentic, retrograde, or otherwise unworthy of Roth's talents. Coupled with the mixed reception of *Letting Go*, his reputation was slipping. Moreover, as much as I liked *When She Was Good*, it was further evidence that he was locked into this preoccupation with female power which was carrying his fiction into strange and relatively arid terrain. I knew that he had been writing plays in the last few years and had spent a lot of time watching the improvisations of the Second City Group—another part of our Chicago days that had accompanied us to New York—and I wondered if his own theatricality would lead him in that direction. But we seldom saw each other during this time. I was editing *Book Week* during the long newspaper strike, hadn't written anything for a year, and was going through a crisis or two of my own, and if we met at a party or something, we exchanged a word or two and looked around for more cheerful company. I remember thinking that we had both come a long way since Chicago—much of it out to sea.

A few months after *When She Was Good*, Roth published a sketch in *Esquire*. It was a memoir of a Jewish boyhood, this time told to an analyst, and written with some of his former verve and forthrightness. Even so, it ventured little beyond a vein that had been pretty well worked by now: the beleaguered provider who can't even hold a bat right; the shatteringly attentive mother; the neglected, unhappy sister; the narrator, who is the star of every grade and the messiah of the household. In short, the typical second-generation Jewish family; and after all the writers who had been wrestling with it in the past decade or two—Herbert Gold, Wallace Markfield, Bruce Jay Friedman, Arnold Wesker, Mordecai Richler, Irwin Faust, Roth himself, to name only a few—Roth's latest revelations were hardly news. Nor did a psychoanalytic setting seem necessary to elicit the facts of Jack Portnoy's constipation or Sophie's use of a breadknife to make little Alex eat. After five years of reading manuscripts at *Commentary*, such stuff was coming out of my ears. Perhaps Roth was only taking a small writer's vacation from the labor that had gone into his last novel or returning to the scene of his early success for a quick score. I hoped so.

But soon after came "Whacking Off" in *Partisan Review*: hysterical, raw, full of what Jews call self-hatred; excessive in all respects, and so funny that I had three laughing fits before I had gone five pages. All of a sudden, from out of the blue and the past, the comedian of those Chicago sessions of nostalgia, revenge, and general purgation had landed right in the middle of his own fiction, as Alex Portnoy, the thirteen-year-old sex maniac.

> Jumping up from the dinner table, I tragically clutch my belly—diarrhea! I cry, I have been stricken with diarrhea!—and once behind the locked bathroom door, slip over my head a pair of underpants that I have stolen from my sister's dresser and carry rolled in a handkerchief in my pocket. So galvanic is the effect of cotton panties against my mouth—so galvanic is the *word* "panties"—that the trajectory of my ejaculation reaches startling new heights: leaving my joint like a rocket it makes right for the light bulb overhead, where to my wonderment and horror, it hits and hangs. Wildly in the first moment I cover my head, expecting an explosion of glass, a burst of flames—disaster, you see, is never far from my mind. Then quietly as I can I climb the radiator and remove the sizzling gob with a wad of toilet paper. I begin a scrupulous search of the shower curtain, the tub, the tile floor, the four toothbrushes—God forbid!—and just as I am about to unlock the door, imagining I have covered my tracks, my heart lurches at the sight of what is hanging like

snot to the toe of my shoe. I am the Raskolnikov of jerking off—the sticky evidence is everywhere! Is it on my cuffs too? In my *hair*? my *ear*? All this I wonder even as I come back to the kitchen table, scowling and cranky, to grumble self-righteously at my father when he opens his mouth full of red jello and says, "I don't understand what you have to lock the door about. That to me is beyond comprehension. What is this, a home or a Grand Central station?" ". . . privacy . . . a human being . . . around here *never*," I reply, then push aside my dessert to scream "I don't feel well—*will everybody leave me alone?*"

And so on. A few minutes later Alex is back in his kingdom, doubled over his flying fist, his sister's bra stretched before him, while his parents stand outside:

"Alex, I want an answer from you. Did you eat French fries after school? Is that why you're sick like this?"

"Nuhhh, nuhhh."

"Alex, are you in pain? Do you want me to call the doctor? Are you in pain, or aren't you? I want to know exactly where it hurts. *Answer me.*"

"Yuhh, yuhhh—"

"Alex, I don't want you to flush the toilet," says my mother sternly. "I want to see what you've done in there. I don't like the sound of this at all."

"And me," says my father, touched as he always was by my accomplishments—as much awe as envy—"I haven't moved my bowels in a week." . . .

This was new, all right, at least in American fiction—and, like the discovery of fresh material in *Goodbye, Columbus*, right in front of everyone's eyes. Particularly, I suppose, guess, of the "Jewish" writers' with all that heavily funded Oedipal energy and curiosity to be worked off in adolescence—and beyond. And having used his comic sense to carry him past the shame that surrounds the subject of masturbation, and to enter it more fully than I can suggest here, Roth appeared to gain great dividends of emotional candor and wit in dealing with the other matters in "Whacking Off." The first sketch maintained a distance of wry description between Portnoy and his parents, but here his feelings—rage, tenderness, contempt, despair, and so on—bring everything up close and fully alive. And aided by the hard-working comedy team of Jack and Sophie Portnoy, the familiar counters of Jewish anxiety (eating hamburgers and french fries outside the home leads directly to a colostomy; polio is never more than a sore throat away; study an instrument, you never know; take shorthand in school, look what it did for Billy Rose; don't oppose your father, he may be suffering from a brain tumor) become almost as hilarious as Alex's solo

flights of passion. Against the enveloping cloud of their fear and possessiveness, his guilt, and their mutual hysteria, still unremitting twenty
years later, Alex has only his sarcasm and, expressive phrase, private
parts. He summons the memories of his love as well as of his hate for
them, but this only opens up his sense of his vulnerability and, from that,
of his maddening typicality:

> Doctor Spielvogel, this is my life, my only life, and I'm living it in the
> middle of a Jewish joke! I am the son in the Jewish joke—*only it ain't no
> joke!* Please, who crippled us like this? Who made us so morbid and
> hysterical and weak? . . . Is this the Jewish suffering I used to hear so
> much about? Is this what has come down to me from the pogroms and
> the persecutions? Oh my secrets, my shame, my palpitations, my flushes,
> my sweats! . . . Bless me with manhood! Make me brave, make me
> strong! Make me *whole!* Enough being a nice Jewish boy, publicly
> pleasing my parents while privately pulling my putz! Enough!

But Portnoy had only begun to come clean. Once having fully entered his
"Modern Museum of Gripes and Grievances," there was no stopping him.
Or Roth. Having discovered that Portnoy's sexual feelings and his "Jewish" feelings were just around the corner from each other and that both
were so rich in loot, he pressed on like a man who has found a stream full
of gold—and running right into it, another one. Moreover, the psychoanalytic setting had given him now the freedom and energy of language to
sluice out the material: the natural internal monologue of comedy and
pain in which the id speaks to the ego and vice versa, while the superego
goes on with its kibitzing. At the same time, Portnoy could be punched
out of the analytic framework like a figure enclosed in cardboard and
perform in his true role and vocation, which is that of a great stand-up
comic. Further, those nagging concerns with close relationships, with
male guilt and female maneuvering, from his two novels could now be
grasped by the roots of Portnoy's experience of them and could be presented, not as standard realistic fare, but in a mode that was right
up-to-date. If the background of *Portnoy's Complaint* is a classical Freudian
one, the foreground is the contemporary, winging art and humor of
improvisation and release, perhaps most notably that of Lenny Bruce.

    In short, lots of things had come together and they had turned
Roth loose. The rest of *Portnoy* was written in the same way—as series of
"takes"—the next two of which were published in *New American Review,*
the periodical which I was now editing. It may be no more than editorial
bias speaking here, but I think these are the two richest sections of the
book. "The Jewish Blues" is a sort of "coming of age in Newark, New
Jersey," beginning with the erotic phenomena of the Portnoy household

and carrying through the dual issue of Alex's adolescence: maleness and rebellion. On the one hand, there are those early years of attentively following Sophie Portnoy through her guided tour of her activities and attitudes, climaxed by a memory of one afternoon when, the housework all done "with his cute little assistance," Alex, "punchy with delight" watches his shapely mother draw on her stockings, while she croons to him "Who does Mommy love more than anything in the whole wide world?" (a passage that deserves to live forever in the annals of the Oedipal Complex). On the other hand—"Thank God," breathes Portnoy— there are the visits with his father to the local bathhouse, the world of Jewish male animal nature, "a place without *goyim* and women [where] I lose touch instantaneously with that ass-licking little boy who runs home after school with his A's in his hand. . . ." On the one hand, there is the synagogue, another version of the dismal constraints and clutchiness of home; on the other, there is center field, where anything that comes your way is yours and where Alex, in his masterful imitation of Duke Snider, knows exactly how to conduct himself, standing out there "as loose and as easy, as happy as I will ever be. . . ." This is beautiful material: so exact in its details, so right in its feeling. And, finally, there is the story of his cousin Heshie, the muscular track star, who was mad about Alice Dembrowsky, the leggy drum majorette of Weequahic High, and whose disgraceful romance with this daughter of a Polish janitor finally has to be ended by his father, who informs Alice that Heshie has an incurable blood disease that prevents him from marrying and that must be kept secret from him. After his Samson-like rage is spent, Heshie submits to his father, and subsequently goes into the Army and is killed in action. But Alex adds his cause to his other manifold grounds of revolt, rises to heights of denunciation in the anti-Bar Mitzvah speech he delivers to Spielvogel ("instead of wailing for he-who has turned his back on the saga of *his people*, weep for your pathetic selves, why don't you, sucking and sucking on that sour grape of a religion"); but then is reminded by his sister of "the six million" and ends pretty much where he began.

Still circling back upon other scenes from his throbbing youth, as though the next burst of anger or grief or hysterical joking will allow him finally to touch bottom, Portnoy forges on into his past and his psyche, turning increasingly to his relations with the mysterious creatures called "shiksas" as his life moves on and the present hang-ups emerge. His occupation is that of Assistant Commissioner of Human Opportunity in the Lindsay Administration, but his preoccupations are always with that one thing his mother didn't give him back when he was four years old, and all of his sweet young Wasps, for all of their sociological interest, turn out to be only an extension of the fantasies of curiosity and self-excitement and shame that drove Alex on in the bathroom. Even "the Monkey," the glamorous fashion model and fellow sex maniac, the walking version of his adolescent dream of "Thereal McCoy," provides mostly more grist for the relentless mill of his narcissism and masochism. All of which Portnoy is perfectly aware of, he is the hippest analysand since Freud himself; but it still doesn't help him to give up the maddeningly seductive voice inside his head that goes on calling "Big Boy." And so, laughing and anguishing and analyzing away, he goes down the road to his breakdown, which sets in when he comes to Israel and finds that he is impotent.

I could go on writing about *Portnoy*, but it would be mostly amplification of the points I've made. It's a marvelously entertaining book and one that mines a narrow but central vein more deeply than it has ever been done before. You don't have to be Jewish to be vastly amused and touched and instructed by *Portnoy's Complaint*, though it helps. Also you don't have to know Philip Roth to appreciate the personal triumph that it represents, though that helps too.

ALLEN GUTTMANN

Philip Roth and the Rabbis

It is no surprise that the most famous of the stories of conversion is by Philip Roth. Of Jewish writers a generation younger than Saul Bellow and Norman Mailer, he is the most talented, the most controversial, and the most sensitive to the complexities of assimilation and the question of identity. Roth's first collection of a novella and five stories, *Goodbye, Columbus* (1960), received the National Book Award, the praises of those writers generally associated with *Partisan Review* and *Commentary,* and considerable abuse from men institutionally involved in the Jewish community. Two stories were the focus of resentment: "The Conversion of the Jews" and "The Defender of the Faith."

Ozzie Freedman, the inquisitive hero of "The Conversion of the Jews," asks the questions that any intelligent boy wants to ask, questions like those young Mary Antin put to her teachers. How can Jews be the Chosen People if the Declaration of Independence affirms that all men are created equal? How can an omnipotent God who made the heavens and the earth be *unable* to "let a woman have a baby without having intercourse"? Rabbi Marvin Binder cannot handle questions of this sort. He sends for Mrs. Freedman. When Rabbi Binder attempts to explain to Ozzie why it is that "some of his relations" consider airplane crashes tragic in proportion to the number of Jews killed in them, Ozzie shouts "that he wished all fifty-eight were Jews." Mrs. Freedman is summoned again.

Ozzie is punished and becomes prudent, but Rabbi Binder feels an unacknowledged urge to force another confrontation with his recalcitrant pupil. Forced by Binder's nagging demands, Ozzie drops his reticence and re-asks his question: "Why can't He make anything He wants to make!"

From *The Jewish Writer in America.* Copyright © 1971 by Oxford University Press, Inc.

While Rabbi Binder prepares his answer, another child causes a distur-
bance and Ozzie takes advantage of the commotion:

> "You don't know! You don't know anything about God!"
>> The rabbi spun back towards Ozzie. "What?"
>> "You don't know—you don't—"
>> "Apologize, Oscar, apologize!" It was a threat.
>> "You don't—"
> Rabbi Binder's hand flicked out at Ozzie's cheek. Perhaps it had
> only been meant to clamp the boy's mouth shut, but Ozzie ducked and
> the palm caught him squarely on the nose.

Ozzie flees from the room and climbs to the building's roof and locks the
door. The crowd gathers, the rabbi begs him from the street not to be a
martyr, and his schoolmates—eager for sensation—urge him, "Be a Martin, be a Martin!" His mother comes and the child becomes the teacher.
Ozzie catechizes from the rooftop:

> "Do you believe God can do Anything?" Ozzie leaned his head out into
> the darkness. "Anything?"
>> "Oscar, I think—"
>> "Tell me you believe God can do Anything."
> There was a second's hesitation. Then: "God can do Anything."
>> "Tell me you believe God can make a child without intercourse."
>> "He can."
>> "Tell me!"
> "God," Rabbi Binder admitted, "can make a child without
> intercourse."

Mrs. Freedman agrees and Ozzie leaps into a safety net. Although one
critic has assured us that Ozzie's leap "becomes paradoxically a moral
symbol of his conversion to Judaism and to life," the form of the cate-
chism and the imagery are unmistakably Christian: ". . . right into the
center of the yellow net that glowed in the evening's edge like an
overgrown halo." It is a doubly parabolic descent. The economy of
characterization and the simplicity of the fable make the allegorical implications unavoidable. Was it not written that a child shall teach them?

   In Roth's collection, Ozzie's story was followed by "The Defender
of the Faith," in which the protagonists are Sergeant Nathan Marx, a
veteran of World War II, and Sheldon Grossbart, a trainee under Sergeant
Marx's care. Sheldon Grossbart, ironically named "Big Beard," begs cra-
venly for special treatment on the basis of the ethnic bond between him
and the sergeant. Although military tradition sanctifies Friday nights to
"G.I. parties" (i.e. everyone scrubs the barracks and prepares for Saturday
morning inspection), Sheldon points out that Jews must attend religious

services. Sergeant Marx allows the request and goes, another night, to attend the services he hasn't gone to for years. Then he thinks he hears Sheldon cackle, "Let the goyim clean the floors!" The sergeant begins to worry. When the captain in charge of the company informs him that Sheldon's congressman has called the general to complain about the Army's non-kosher foods, Sergeant Marx's ambivalence increases. The captain's outrage is deftly captured:

> Look, Grossbart, Marx here is a good man, a goddam *hero*. When you were sitting on your sweet ass in high school, Sergeant Marx was killing Germans. Who does more for the Jews, you by throwing up over a lousy piece of sausage, a piece of firstcut meat—or Marx by killing those Nazi bastards? If I was a Jew, Grossbart, I'd kiss this man's feet. He's a goddam hero, you know that? And *he* eats what we give him.

It turns out that Sheldon himself, not his father, wrote the letter to the congressman, that Sheldon will use his Jewishness to draw advantage for himself from the persecutions of others, that Sheldon does not even have the excuse of sincerely held faith. Given a chance to go to town for Passover, he heads for a Chinese restaurant. The penultimate turn of the screw comes when Sheldon arranges, with a Jewish acquaintance at headquarters, to be removed from orders that send him to the Pacific, where the war has not yet ended. At this moment, Sergeant Marx decides to defend the faith; he has the orders changed so that Sheldon Grossbart goes with the rest. Sheldon shrieks, "There's no limit to your anti-Semitism, is there!" Sergeant Marx calls himself vindictive, but he may also be seen as the defender of a democratic theory by which the accidents of birth give no exemption from our common fate. He acts from a sense of justice that is, finally, humanistic in its universality.

Given only these two stories, an unsympathetic reader might suspect that Roth holds a wholly negative view of Jewishness and of Judaism, but the first and final stories of *Goodbye, Columbus* and Roth's first novel, *Letting Go* (1962), are longer and more complex. The long title story plays with names. Although the story is certainly about the country discovered by the Genoese explorer, the words are from a phonograph record dedicated to memories of Ohio State University, located at Columbus, Ohio. The record is owned and utilized as a devotional aid by Ronald Patimkin, an athletic young man who is about to enter his father's business, where he will "start at two hundred a week and then work himself up." Through sales of kitchen sinks, phenomenally good during the war years, the Patimkins have risen to suburban wealth. Is not cleanliness more profitable than godliness?

The Patimkin family has whatever goods the world calls good. Their refrigerators burst with fruit; their trees are hung with sporting goods. Beefy Ronald Patimkin is a type unrelated to the pale scholar of the *shtetl* and the exploited needle-trades worker of the ghetto. Harvey Swados has noted this with characteristic acuteness:

> We might measure the distance that has been traveled by contrasting Hemingway's Jewish athlete of the Twenties, Robert Cohn, the boxer, forever attempting with fists or flattery to join the club, the expatriate Americans who exclude him, to Philip Roth's Jewish athlete of the Fifties, Ronald Patimkin, who hangs his jockstrap from the shower faucet while he sings the latest pop tunes, and is so completely the self-satisfied muscle-bound numskull that notions of Jewish alienation are entirely "foreign" to him.

Brenda Patimkin, the family's older daughter, is a paragon of Olympic virtues; she plays tennis, she runs, she rides, she swims. In the pool, she is a far cry from the *Yiddishe Momma* of yesteryear. "I went," says her boy friend,

> to pull her towards me just as she started fluttering up; my hand hooked on to the front of her suit and the cloth pulled away from her. Her breasts swam towards me like two pink-nosed fish and she let me hold them. Then, in a moment, it was the sun who kissed us both, and we were out of the water, too pleased with each other to smile.

And, as Leonard Baskin lamented in a recent symposium, "For every poor and huddled *mikvah* [ritual bath], there is a tenhundred of swimming pools." In this suburban world, the past seems passé indeed.

Brenda Patimkin stands on the magic casement of a world sharply contrasted to that of Neil Klugman's Aunt Gladys, a woman of the immigrant generation. Immediately after the first poolside scene, Roth shows us the milieu from which Neil Klugman (i.e. "wise man") wants to rise:

> That night, before dinner, I called her.
> "Who are you calling?" my Aunt Gladys asked.
> "Some girl I met today."
> "Doris introduced you?"
> "Doris wouldn't introduce me to the guy who drains the pool, Aunt Gladys."
> "Don't criticize all the time. A cousin's a cousin. How did you meet her?"
> "I didn't really meet her. I saw her."
> "Who is she?"
> "Her last name is Patimkin."
> "Patimkin, I don't know," Aunt Gladys said . . .

Aunt Gladys does know that a growing boy should eat. But Neil is not about to be satisfied with the food she makes the center of her life.

Neil has his chance. He dates Brenda, watches her at tennis, runs around a track (that may or may not symbolize the final futility of his efforts), basks in the hard sunshine of her father's wealth. He is accepted as her fiancé, as a future worker in the porcelain vineyard of Patimkin sinks.

The marvels of money, and simple physical beauty, are counterpointed by the vision of Gauguin's Tahiti. In the downtown library where Neil works, a little Negro boy comes daily to stare at a book of reproductions of Gauguin. His moan of pleasure is poignant: "Man, that's the fuckin life. . . . *Look, look,* look here at this one. Ain't that the fuckin *life?*" But the breadfruit-and-wild-flower life is unobtainable for the little Negro boy, except in fantasy; Neil's dream of classless, creedless hedonism turns out to be equally unobtainable. He bullies Brenda until she purchases a contraceptive diaphragm, but when he goes up to Boston to spend the Jewish holidays in unholy union with her, he learns that she has left the diaphragm behind, where her mother discovers it. The affair is over. Neil is convinced that the discovery was intentional, Brenda's way out. He goes off and stares into the glass that walls Harvard's Lamont Library and asks himself questions that Roth leaves to the reader's imagination. Then he takes "a train that got me into Newark just as the sun was rising on the first day of the Jewish New Year. I was back in plenty of time for work." The days he meant to spend in carnival he spends at work. He cannot join the Patimkins, cannot use Brenda to rise up "those lousy hundred and eighty feet that make summer nights so much cooler in Short Hills than they are in Newark," but he cannot remain in the world of Aunt Gladys either.

The suburbs that Neil Klugman aspires to are the ones that Eli Peck, inhabitant of Woodenton, lives in. The last story of *Goodbye, Columbus,* "Eli, the Fanatic," is the most complex and difficult to interpret. (It has certainly drawn the most contradictory interpretations.) The contrasts in this story are extreme, for the highly assimilated "successful" Jews of Woodenton are suddenly confronted by a group of Jews more strange and Orthodox than Neil's Aunt Gladys. The newcomers are from Eastern Europe, refugees from unnamed but clearly suggested persecutions; they open a *yeshiva* in pastoral Woodenton, whose name indicates both its forested environments and its hardness of heart.

Eli is the tragic go-between. Standard critical opinion holds that the "demarcation [in the story] between good and evil is absolutely clear," but this is simplification. In truth, both sides in the suburban dispute are equally rigid. With a comedy painfully true to life, Roth demonstrates how far the nominal Jews of Woodenton are from their ancestral faith. One of Eli's friends argues with him on the telephone:

> Sunday mornings I have to drive my kid all the way to Scarsdale to learn Bible stories? And you know what she comes up with, Eli—that this Abraham in the Bible was going to kill his own kid for a *sacrifice!* You call that religion, Eli? I call it sick. Today a guy like that they'd lock him up.

From this position, an Orthodox *yeshiva* is simply incomprehensible. But the caftan-clad Jews of the *yeshiva* are equally unable to understand the Americans or to realize why Eli and his neighbors are upset. Eli's desperation is intensified by his pregnant wife's devotion to the dogma of the followers of Sigmund Freud. Eli pats his wife's belly and says, "You know what your mother brought to this marriage— . . . a sling chair, three months to go on a *New Yorker* subscription, and *An Introduction to Psychoanalysis.*" His wife answers, "Eli, must you be aggressive?" There is no comfort for him.

When *Weltanschauungen* collide, it is Orthodoxy that yields. Although Eli prevails on Mr. Tzuref (i.e. troubles) to dress his assistant in one of Eli's greenish tweed suits, Eli cannot stand the sight of the "greenie" dressed in his clothing, like a vision of another self. Tormented, guilty, unable to withstand the pressures from every side, torn apart by conflicts of identity, Eli breaks down, dons the black clothing deposited by the Orthodox at his door, and wanders through the town like the Last of the Just. He goes to the hospital to see his newborn son and tells him,

> . . . I'll keep the suit at home, and I'll wear it again. I promise. Every year on the nineteenth of May, I'll wear it. I promise. All day. I won't work, I won't talk, I won't do anything but walk around with this black suit. And when you're old enough, I'll get you one, and you'll walk with me. . . .

Eli is interrupted by the men in white with needles in their hands.

It has been argued that Eli's transformation is a "conversion into the essential Jew," whose essence is to suffer for the truth; it has also been argued that Eli has been touched by "the strange power of an authentic religion." A third view is that

> Eli's grotesque attempt at atonement is doomed to failure: it cannot be understood or accepted by his neighbors, for it is private and also dishonest in the sense that Eli can no more own the experiences that make orthodox dress a truthful expression of the Greenie's identity, than he can disown that part of himself which belongs to Woodenton.

The third version seems closer to the truth, but Eli's fanatical act is pathetic rather than dishonest. There is only one path across the psychic abyss that separates Woodenton from the *yeshiva*—madness. Eli's fate is truly a tragedy and not an expiatory aberration. He has been driven to insanity, at least for the moment, by the hardness of the zealots who have treated him as a fanatic.

Support for this interpretation can be found in an extraordinary response made by Roth to a symposium conducted by *Commentary*: asked about his sense of identity, he answered with a statement and a question serious almost to solemnity:

> I cannot find a true and honest place in the history of believers that begins with Abraham, Isaac, and Jacob on the basis of the heroism of these believers, or of their humiliations and anguish. I can only connect with them . . . as I apprehend their God. And until such time as I do apprehend him, there will continue to exist between myself and those others who seek his presence, a question . . . which for all the pain and longing it may engender, for all the disappointment and bewilderment it may produce, cannot be swept away by nostalgia or sentimentality or even by blind and valiant effort of the will: how are you connected to me as another man is not?

To put the matter more abstractly, martyrdom proves the martyr's commitment to his beliefs but cannot validate them. It seems improbable that Roth intended Eli Peck to affirm an apprehension that he himself was unable to achieve.

Like Neil Klugman and Eli Peck, like Ozzie Freedman and Sergeant Marx, the hero of Roth's first (and best) novel is caught in the middle, but the dilemmas confronted by Gabe Wallach are less specifically Jewish and more easily universalized. *Letting Go* (1962) is a series of episodes in which Gabe Wallach becomes increasingly involved with people to whom he is not emotionally committed.

While doing graduate work at the University of Iowa, Gabe receives the impetuous embraces of Marjorie Howells, a *shikse* from Kenosha, Wisconsin, who revolts "against Kenosha as though Caligula himself were city manager." In her eyes he is the exotic outsider; to please her, he proclaims himself her Trotsky, her Einstein, her Moses Maimonides, but he knows that he's none of these and was not meant to be. In Chicago, where he takes a job in the university, he becomes involved with Martha Regenhart, a divorcée with two children, but the affair has an air of impermanence, and Gabe's admiration for his departmental chairman is, to speak mildly, limited:

Spigliano is a member of that great horde of young anagramists and manure-spreaders who, finding a good deal more ambiguity in letters than in their own ambiguous lives, each year walk through classroom doors and lay siege to the minds of the young, revealing to them Zoroaster in Sam Clemens and the hidden phallus in the lines of our most timid lady poets.

And Christ in the work of every Jewish writer?

Gabe's rootlessness has tragic consequences for others. In a grotesque and horrible disaster, one of Martha Regenhart's children kills the other. The moment is followed by the climax of a crazy situation in which Gabe acts as go-between for a couple who attempt illegally to adopt the baby of a girl whom Martha had encountered at work. The girl turns out to be married to a brutal and stupid man appropriately named Harry Bigoness. Gabe rushes back and forth until, at last, he decisively seizes the baby and brings it to his childless friends.

In contrast to Gabe, Roth sets forth a circle of characters committed to adjustment. Claire Herz, once known as "hot Claire Herz," has become "an outstanding mother." Dora and Maury Horvitz lead lives dictated by the *New Yorker*. Of him she says, "Maury is a very Jewish fella." The one possible affirmative contrast to Gabe and Martha is the intermarried couple, Paul and Libby Herz.

The Herzes are almost as important within the structure of the novel as narrator-hero Gabe Wallach. They had married against the will of their parents: Libby's conversion to Judaism, she explains to Gabe, was "switching loyalties": it

> somehow proved to them [the Herz family] I didn't have any to begin with. I read six thick books on the plights and flights of the Jews, I met with this cerebral rabbi in Ann Arbor once a week and finally there was a laying on of hands. I was a daughter of Ruth, the rabbi told me. In Brooklyn . . . no one was much moved by the news. Paul called and they hung up. I might be Ruth's daughter—that didn't make me theirs. . . . And my father wrote us a little note to say that he had obligations to a daughter in school, but none to Jewish housewives in Detroit.

Nonetheless, their marriage, economic difficulties, quarrels and reconciliations, suggest a way of life that is neither aimless nor complacent. It is for them that Gabe secures the illegitimate baby—for the intermarried couple, an adopted girl.

From this book, Roth went on to write a novel without Jews, almost without urban scenes, a novel that rivals and perhaps surpasses *Main Street* and *Winesburg, Ohio* as portraits of small-town America, but *When She Was Good* (1967) falls outside the bounds of this study—except insofar as it proves what everyone should have known: Philip Roth is a thoroughly assimilated American writer. Roth's next book was quite another matter.

Alexander Portnoy, the desperately comic narrator of *Portnoy's Complaint* (1969), is derived from the same sociological sources as Neil Klugman and Eli Peck and Gabe Wallach, but the literary mode in which he grotesquely lives and suffers is the novelized joke, the night-club gagster's ethnic line drawn out to nearly three hundred pages. In the hot pursuit of the blonde *shikse* by the Jewish libertine, Leslie Fiedler has seen the myth of Samson and Delilah, which allegedly underlies American Jewish fiction to the end of the 1920s. Whether or not the argument holds for Abraham Cahan and Ludwig Lewisohn, none can doubt that Alexander Portnoy's sexual adventure is freighted with social significance:

> I don't seem to stick my dick up these girls, as much as I stick it up their backgrounds. . . . Columbus, Captain Smith, Governor Winthrop, General Washington—now Portnoy. As though my manifest destiny is to seduce a girl from each of the forty-eight states. As for Alaskan and Hawaiian women, I really have no feeling either way, no scores to settle, no coupons to cash in, no dreams to put to rest. . . .

His conquests are a series of *shikses* (preceded by a series of *shikses* whom he failed to conquer). Kay Campbell of Iowa, "The Pumpkin," is a ludicrous version of Gabe Wallach's Marjorie Howells. With her family, among the "real" Americans who live on farms and never raise their voices in argument, Portnoy celebrates Thanksgiving. Finally, *he* rejects *her*, looks higher in the social system: "Another gentile heart broken by me belonged to The Pilgrim, Sarah Abbott Maulsby—New Canaan, Foxcroft, and Vassar . . ." And lower in the system too. His most serious affair is with an illiterate from West Virginia, Mary Jane Reed, nicknamed "The Monkey," for whom he represents the exotically Hebraic, just as Gabe Wallach did for Marjorie. Miss Reed is outrageously vulgar; en route to a party given by Mayor John Lindsay, Portnoy appeals to her, "Don't make a grab for Big John's *shlong* until we've been there at least half an hour, okay?" Portnoy abandons her in Athens, after sexually intricate escapades in New England and in Rome. In Israel, however, he is impotent. Exhilarated by a world in which everyone, even the longshoremen, is a Jew, Portnoy picks up a female lieutenant and is sexually helpless. He listens to her idealistic lectures on the superiority of Israeli socialism to American capitalism and then attempts to rape her. She is strong but he is stronger—and impotent. She tells him in a fine exchange of insults ("Tomboy," "Shlemiel") that he is a victim of the Diaspora, another Jew who hates himself.

There is no doubt that he does. There is no doubt that his childhood is an Oedipal joke: "She was so deeply imbedded in my consciousness that for the first year of school I seem to have believed that each of my teachers was my mother in disguise." Her overprotective, overabundant love and her vindictive demands for love in return combine to drown him in guilt. Portnoy's father is, of course, a failure, Freud's anal type writ large, writ grotesquely, a consumer of All-Bran and Ex-Lax and prune juice, a salesman of insurance to Negroes in the slums of Newark. His rage is related to the Boston-based insurance company that gives him stationery with his name printed beneath a picture of the *Mayflower* but makes it clear that he is forever on his way to America and can never arrive. Portnoy's own secret rebellion is a denial of Judaism; he claims to be an atheist and not a Jew.

Now, at the age of thirty-three, he is Assistant Commissioner on Mayor Lindsay's Commission on Human Opportunity, but still an undutiful child in the eyes of his ever-watchful parents. He can turn upon them and imitate their transparent nag into one of the classic parodies of the excesses of assimilation: he mimics Mother on Seymour Schmuck:

> I met his mother on the street today, and she told me that Seymour is now the biggest brain surgeon in the entire Western Hemisphere. He owns six different split-level ranch-type houses . . . and belongs to the boards of eleven synagogues, all brand-new and designed by Marc Kugel, and last year with his wife and his two little daughters, who are so beautiful that they are already under contract to Metro, and so brilliant that they should be in college—he took them all to Europe for an eighty-million-dollar tour of seven thousand countries, some of them you never even heard of, that they made them just to honor Seymour, and . . . in every single city . . . he was asked by the mayor himself to stop and do an impossible operation on a brain in hospitals that they also built for him right on the spot. . . .

Et cetera, et cetera. But what of poor Portnoy? He lies on Dr. Spielvogel's couch while the doctor, presumably, takes notes for the essay that is cited in the epigraph-in-the-form-of-an-encyclopedia-entry. He, Portnoy, is the "Puzzled Penis."

What are we to make of his puzzlement? Is the book a Jewish joke or is it a joke about Jewish jokes? If the latter, which seems more probable, then it is—like Black Humor—a kind of terminus, a suggestion that the satirist of assimilation has grown tired of the harvest he himself desired. A good place for a satirist to stop.

TONY TANNER

"Portnoy's Complaint": 'The Settling of Scores! The Pursuit of Dreams!'

At the end of Portnoy's uninterrupted complaint which makes up his book . . . when in his own way he too has passed beyond articulation, his psychiatrist is allowed the last word— ' "Now vee may perhaps to begin. Yes?" ' Both these figures, then, have reached the threshold of their particular 'beginning room' (as Purdy called it), and in both cases the novels about them concentrate on arriving at that point and not on how to pass beyond it. One condition for being able even to think about 'beginning' is some degree of liberation from the past, and Roth himself has spoken in an interview of wanting to 'kick a lot of the past'. At the same time, as is the case with Herzog, Portnoy's compulsion to re-evoke the past is so obsessive one wonders about the possibility of his achieving the desired detachment from it. And that is perhaps the most serious aspect of his complaint—that the sense of guilt has been so deeply implanted in him that there is nothing in the resources of rational consciousness or language which can disperse it. He ends his complaint with a paranoid fantasy of the police coming for him, and an abandonment of language, not, as in Herzog's case, to move into a serene if temporary silence, but to collapse into a howl—'A pure howl, without any more words between me and it!'

Just as for Cabot Wright the recovering of the ability to laugh

From *City of Words: American Fiction 1950–1970.* Copyright © 1971 by Tony Tanner. Harper and Row.

signified the beginning of freedom, so Portnoy has found that only by turning guilt into laughter can he achieve some degree of emancipation from it. As Roth himself has said, 'not until I had got hold of guilt, you see, as a comic idea, did I begin to feel myself lifting free and clear of my last book, and my old concern.' Kafka is a writer who has obsessed Roth, and *Portnoy's Complaint* could be seen as an American version of Kafka's *Letter to His Father*. Roth's novel is undeniably funny, indeed hysterically so; yet it is in some ways as painful as that strange and troubling work by Kafka, and equally fixated on the minute details of the familial and social past and the focal point at the centre of it all—the uncertain, suffering self.

At the end of one of Roth's most impressive early short stories, 'The Conversion of the Jews', the boy Ozzie Freedman, who has been bullied and penalized by his religious teacher, flees to the roof of the synagogue and stands on the edge threatening to jump. In this way he brings his mother, the rabbi and the watching crowd to their knees, and in this situation he can legislate to his legislators. From his dangerous edge he hurls down defiance and extracts concessions from them, making them promise that they will not use their authority to force their version of God on other people. It is another picture of a small American hero going out to a lonely edge to make his complaint against the subtle or brutal imposition of fixed definitions and rules. Waiting beneath him is a large net held out by firemen which looks like 'a sightless eye,' while above him is the 'unsympathetic sky'. 'Being on the roof, it turned out, was a serious thing.' For the young boy poised on the edge of so many things—manhood, society, and all the problems of future direction—the alternatives seem bleak. Having made his 'superiors' bow to his will, Ozzie jumps into the net which for a moment glows 'like an overgrown halo'. In some ways the story is a fantasy of revenge, the put-upon little boy finally finding a voice and a stance with which he can dominate the familial and social authorities who exercise such control over him. The jump too must be an exhilaration and relief—a kind of 'letting go'. At the same time the net must be ambiguous, for it is what the guardians of society hold out. It cushions the fall, yet it surely traps the faller. At the end of Roth's subsequent novel, which was actually called *Letting Go* (1962), Gabe Wallach, who has revealed some of the psychologically crippling effects of being brought up in the family net, or trap, writes a letter to a girl he has been involved with, which ends thus: '*It is only kind of you, Libby, to feel that I would want to know that I am off the hook. But I'm not, I can't be, I don't even want to be—not until I make some sense of the larger hook I'm on.*'

When Portnoy 'lets go' and allows himself to fall on to the psychoanalyst's couch—another sort of net waiting for the grown man—he is determined to bring that 'larger hook' into the open. There is no real knowing of the self until it becomes aware of the past it is impaled on. Sartre's observation that introspection is always retrospection can be extended to take in this truth, and for Roth's characters the sense of self and untranquil recollections from the past are inseparable. In the story, 'Defender of the Faith', Nathan Marx, a Jewish sergeant in the army, who resists the way some Jewish soldiers under his command try to exploit and presume on their common racial identity, nevertheless finds that 'one rumor of home and time past, and memory plunged down through all I had anesthetized and came to what I suddenly remembered to be myself.' Portnoy's memory takes such a plunge and he finds that, once started, he cannot desist 'from the settling of scores! the pursuit of dreams! from this hopeless, senseless loyalty to the long ago!' And, as he says from the psychoanalyst's couch—'My God! the stuff you uncover here!'

As Ozzie Freedman races 'crazily towards the edge of the roof' he finds himself throbbing with the question "Is it me ME ME ME ME! It has to be me—but is it!" At the end of Roth's novella, *Goodbye, Columbus* (1959), Neil Klugman stands staring at his reflection in a library window after the unpleasant conclusion of an affair.

> I was only that substance, I thought, those limbs, that face that I saw in front of me. I looked, but the outside of me gave up little information about the inside of me. I wished I could scoot around to the other side of the window . . . to get behind that image and catch whatever it was that looked through those eyes . . . I looked hard at the image of me, at that darkening of the glass, and then my gaze pushed through it, over the cool floor, to a broken wall of books, imperfectly shelved.

This shift in vision whereby a scrutiny of the image of the reflected self gives way to a perception of actual external objects is apt to Roth's work. In one form or another, the majority of his work has been preoccupied with the problem—what is this mysterious ME rushing towards the edge, or staring back at me from the glass? At the same time his real talent as a novelist has been for a meticulous observation of the familial and social scenes around him—for the books that are actually there on the other side of the window.

It is perhaps an awareness of having this talent which made him feel that the contemporary novel should stress outer reality more and self less. Yet that desire of Neil Klugman's to 'get behind' and find some 'inside' information about the self is there from the start in Roth's work. It is arguable that this tension between social observation and self-exploration had an effect on his two following novels. There is no mistaking Roth's ability to evoke the abrasions and lacerations of intra-familial rows and discords in *Letting Go* and *When She Was Good* (1967), and his social eye is amazingly acute. At the same time there is something rather laboured about these novels, particularly *When She Was Good*, in which Roth offers a study of a desperately neurotic woman in the distinctly non-Jewish society of the Protestant Midwest. The prose in which the book is written is uncharacteristic: rather flat, remote, dispassionate, at times somewhat lifeless. It was almost as though in a valiant attempt to write a coolly objective book about an American world removed from the self of the writer, Roth had produced rather a mask of a book.

Portnoy's Complaint (1969) is by contrast unmistakably a face, and the unhindered flow of the book must owe something to the fact that at last Roth's interest in the social scene and his feeling for the obsessed self coalesced in the writing. Everything is allowed to emerge in this mono-logue of a man who is insatiably avid for sex but incapable of relation-ships, and who sets out to retrace the steps of his childhood to find out why. This particular type of man—carnal and selfish, guilty yet incorrigible— has been there from the start of Roth's work, but he has never explored himself, or been explored, to any great depth. Nor did he dominate the foreground of the novels to the exclusion of other characters. But in *Portnoy's Complaint*, Portnoy holds the stage, indeed he is the stage. If he is some sort of psychological cripple with all kinds of emotional retarda-tions and 'hang-ups' (Roth's image of the hook prompts one to use the current colloquialism), then all that too is going to be exposed and explored. He is determined to 'let it all hang out', in the terms of another suitable colloquialism. The result is indeed the return of the repressed, and guilt, which is usually employed as an internalized agent of inhibition and retention, is paradoxically forced to promote a degree of uncensored revelation which is unusual even in recent American fiction.

Nothing is treated as sacred or taboo: everything, certainly every-thing physical, is brought to the level of speech—whether it is his mother's concern about his excrement, his childhood masturbatory prac-tices or the particular forms of sexual gratification he seeks from the *shikse* girls who obsess him. All the doors on all the rooms of his childhood are opened and while this permits us to see the comic-desperate strategies of the sexually maturing child, it also enables us to hear the cacophony of conflicting imperatives which beset him, and to become aware of all the irrational rules and emotional bullyings which were visited on the bewil-dered child. It is in this way that self-obsession merges with social observa-tion, for what Portnoy does is re-evoke scene after scene and situation after situation from his past so that environment and other characters appear vividly before us even while—and just because—he is conducting an inquiry into the determinants of his present sickness. Even the compulsive recalling of these scenes is part of the 'complaint' (as much disease as reproach); what Portnoy tries to do is to turn the complaint into an exorcism and make the concluding and inevitable howl of pain and need a howl of laughter as well.

'Doctor, maybe other patients dream—with me, everything happens. I have a life without latent content. The dream thing *happens!*' Portnoy's book is also without latent content precisely because he is able and determined to bring everything to the surface. But his unresting consciousness of himself and the resourcefulness of his vocabulary do nothing to mitigate his distress and confusion. At least, not apparently. From one point of view they too are part of the complaint inasmuch as he is constantly demonstrating that competence of terminology cannot do anything to remedy defects of temperament. Unlike Whitman's animal he certainly does moan and whine about his condition, and he knows it. 'Whew! Have I got grievances! Do I harbor hatreds I didn't even know were there! Is it the process, Doctor, or is it what we call "the material"? All I do is complain, the repugnance seems bottomless, and I'm beginning to wonder if maybe enough isn't enough.' Again: 'Is this truth I'm delivering up, or is it just plain kvetching? Or is *kvetching* for people like me a *form* of truth?' One could as readily answer in the affirmative to such questions, or not answer at all, for all the help it is to the man so helplessly launched on the flood of his own rhetoric. The questions are really aimed at himself. 'Oh, why go on? Why be so obsessed like this?' Here indeed is a question which gets to the heart of the complaint. At the same time it seems that only *by* going on like this can he alleviate some of the weight of the past which presses so damagingly on his present life. Everyone has problems in balancing conscience and appetite, but Portnoy has been submitted to so many prohibitions, warnings, taboos and hysterical laws laid down by his family that he has to have recourse to the momentary relief of comic exaggeration. 'I am marked like a road map from head to toe with my repressions. You can travel the length and breadth of my body over superhighways of shame and inhibition and fear.'

There is brilliant comic exaggeration throughout, and the nervous inventiveness of the rhetoric seems to be at once both consolation and symptom. For the complaint is still real. The weight of his family is still heavy upon him—'fighting off my family, still!'—and he reiterates his appeal to the silent Dr. Spielvogel: 'Doctor, get these people off my ass, will you please?' Like the monologist comedian, the late Lenny Bruce, to whom Portnoy has been compared, he gives the impression at times of talking for his life, of fending away continuous threats and pressures by the arresting brilliance of his loquacity. What he really yearns for is some clean, uncluttered space, like most other American heroes. This dream is implicit in his recollection of how much he enjoyed playing 'center field' in baseball games. 'Doctor, you can't imagine how truly glorious it is out there, so alone in all that space . . .' 'Center field' is the blissful opposite of home.

While *Portnoy's Complaint* can readily be appreciated and enjoyed by anyone who can recall anything of the awesome mystery and humiliating farce called growing up, it obviously does have a specifically contemporary relevance for American Jews. Portnoy is obsessed with the whole WASP American world, not just WASP girls, and he is bent on full assimilation, away from ghetto identity and towards American identity with its much wider horizons of possibility. Yet if he has left the ghetto he has not yet arrived at a place where he can have a confident new identity. If in some ways he is a 'success' there has been a heavy price to pay, as his moaning presence on the psychoanalyst's couch attests. And, as Dan Yergin pointed out in his review of the book, although there is a general idea in the Jewish family that each son will be more successful, more liberated, than the father, Portnoy's job of mediating between poor minorities and established WASP society (as Assistant Commissioner for Human Opportunity) is basically similar to his father's job of peddling insurance to the poor blacks on behalf of a rich WASP firm. Portnoy is not really 'free', and yet after a visit to Israel he realizes that, in spite of the validity of the Israeli girl's criticism of American Jews, he is nevertheless irremediably American. He is a transitional figure, like so many other Jewish figures in recent American fiction, neither quite in nor wholly out of the established society.

Perhaps it is because of Portnoy's transitional position that Roth really doesn't know how to finish the book. In the last scene that Portnoy recalls, he depicts himself 'whimpering on the floor with MY MEMORIES' after his comic-squalid failure with the Israeli girl. He knows now that he is 'a patriot in another place (where I also don't feel at home!)'. This does not represent any great progress in self-knowledge, nor the achievement of a new state of mind. Any new beginning will have to come after the end of the book—as usual. And although Portnoy recalls a lot he does not delve very deeply; there is no real opening up of hitherto sealed-off areas of the self, no attempt to establish some communication with the unconscious level. One does get the feeling that Roth did not carry his inquiry into the nature and origin of Portnoy's 'complaint' as far as he might have done. The question Portnoy asks near the end of the book is indeed a crucial one. 'How have I come to be such an enemy and flayer of myself? And so alone! Oh, so alone. Nothing but *self*! Locked up in *me*!' The state of self-incarceration which the book reveals is a condition quite prevalent among recent American characters; indeed the tremendous popularity of the book is probably related to the kind of unreachable privacy of self it finally exposes and as such it may well indicate that this is an exceedingly common condition for its readers too. But the question is not answered and the listening Dr. Spielvogel opens his mouth only to close the book.

Roth had once considered doing a series of Spielvogel stories, with the mysterious doctor at the centre of a group of New York patients. Only two were published and one, 'The Psychoanalytic Special', has a revealing twist to it. The woman who is the patient is gradually trained to resist her impulses to sexual promiscuity. But the self-restraint is also experienced as a deprivation. 'Truly, it was awful if this was what it was going to be like, being better.' It is a truism by now that to attempt to 'adjust' someone to the prevailing society might be to rob him of his most distinctive individuating qualities, and that one's neuroses might be related to the most valuable energies of the self. It may well be that Portnoy does not really want to be 'cured', nor even 'analysed' in any profound way. What he does want to do is talk without restriction about himself. Roth himself has said 'The book is *about* talking about yourself . . . The method is the subject.' He has arranged the book as though it were a series of what he calls 'blocks of consciousness', an arrangement of clusters of associations released with a pace and vitality which make them seem like the direct effusions of stream-of-consciousness; although in fact the blocks of consciousness are of course cunningly arranged in a sequence which leads finally to the point at which the monologue began—the psychoanalyst's couch. Since the book is about monologizing ('the method is the subject'), it was obviously crucial to abandon the idea of writing stories which centred around the doctor, and to allow the first-person voice complete dominion over the whole book and as much verbal space as it requires to fill with its recollections. Part of the liberating feeling in the book comes from the speaker's abandoning all pretence at dialogue: even if the compulsion to monologize is part of Portnoy's 'complaint', the unhindered freedom to do so for the duration of the book is part of Portnoy's delight.

IRVING HOWE

Philip Roth Reconsidered

. . . the will takes pleasures in begetting its own image.
—J. V. CUNNINGHAM

W̲hen Philip Roth published his col-
lection of stories, *Goodbye, Columbus*, in 1959, the book was generously
praised and I was among the reviewers who praised it. Whatever modula-
tions of judgment one might want now to propose, it is not hard to see
why Roth should have won approval. The work of a newcomer still in his
twenties, *Goodbye, Columbus* bristled with a literary self-confidence such
as few writers two or three decades older than Roth could command. His
stories were immediately recognizable as his own, distinctive in voice,
attitude, and subject; they possessed the lucidities of definition, though I
would now add, lucidities harsh and grimacing in their over-focus. None
of the fiction Roth has since published approaches this first collection in
literary interest; yet, by no very surprising turn of events, his reputation
has steadily grown these past few years, he now stands close to the center
of our culture (if that is anything for him to be pleased about), and he is
accorded serious attention both by a number of literary critics and those
rabbis and Jewish communal leaders who can hardly wait to repay the
animus he has lavished upon them. At least for a moment or two, until
the next fashion appears, we are in the presence not only of an interesting
writer but also a cultural "case."

From *Commentary* 6, vol. 54 (December 1972). Copyright © 1972 by the American Jewish
Committee.

II

The stories in *Goodbye, Columbus* are of a special kind. They are neither probings through strategic incident to reach the inner folds of character nor affectionate renderings of regional, class, or ethnic behavior. They are not the work of a writer absorbed in human experience as it is, mirroring his time with self-effacing objectivity. Nor is Roth the kind of writer who takes pleasure in discovering the world's body, yielding himself to the richness of its surfaces and the mysteries of its ultimate course. If one recalls some of the motives that have moved our novelists—a hunger to absorb and render varieties of social experience, a respect for the plenitude of the mind, a sense of awe induced by contemplation of the curve of heroic fate, a passion for moral scrutiny—none of these seems crucially to operate in Roth's work. It is, in fact, a little comic to invoke such high motifs in discussing that work, and not because Roth is a minor writer but because he is a writer who has denied himself, programmatically, the vision of major possibilities.

What one senses nevertheless in the stories of *Goodbye, Columbus* is an enormous thrust of personal and ideological assertiveness. In the clash which, like Jacob with his angel, the writer must undertake with the world around him—and, unlike Jacob, must learn when and how to lose—there can be little doubt that Roth will steadily pin his opponent to the ground. His great need is for a stance of superiority, the pleasure, as Madison Avenue puts it, of always being "on top of it." (Perhaps he should have been a literary critic.) Only rarely do his fictions risk the uncharted regions of imaginative discovery; almost all his work drives a narrative toward cognitive ends fixed in advance. Roth appears indifferent to the Keatsian persuasion that a writer should be "capable of being in uncertainties, mysteries, doubts," since that would require a discipline of patience; nor does he pay much heed to the Coleridgean persuasion that "tragedy depends on a sense of the mind's greatness," since that would mean to acknowledge the powers of *another* mind, to soften his clattering voice, and to ease himself into that receptivity to experience which is one mark of the creative imagination.

For good or bad, both in the stories that succeed and those that fail, *Goodbye, Columbus* rests in the grip of an imperious will prepared to wrench, twist, and claw at its materials in order to leave upon them the scar of its presence—as if the work of fiction were a package that needed constantly to be stamped with a signature of self. With expectations of being misunderstood I am tempted to add that, despite their severe and even notorious criticisms of Jewish life in America, Roth's stories are marked by a quintessentially "Jewish will," the kind that first makes its historical appearance in the autobiography of Solomon Maimon, where the intellectual aspirant sees himself as a solitary antagonist to the world of culture which, in consequence, he must conquer and reduce to acknowledgment.

The will dominating *Goodbye, Columbus* clamors to impose itself—in part through an exclusion of inconvenient perceptions—upon whatever portions of imagined life are being presented. And that is one reason these stories become a little tiresome upon rereading: one grows weary of a writer who keeps nagging and prodding and beating us over the head with the poker of his intentions. What is almost always central in Roth's stories is their "point," their hammering of idea, and once that "point" is clear, usually well before a story's end, the portrayal starts to pale, for not enough autonomous life remains and too much of the matter seems a mere reflex of the will's "begetting."

Even in regard to details of milieu and manners, for which Roth has been frequently praised, the will takes over and distorts. In his title novella, "Goodbye, Columbus," there are some keen notations—the refrigerator in the basement bulging with fruit, the turgidities of the wedding—which help to characterize the newly-rich Patimkins in their suburban home. And there are moments of tenderness—a quality not abundant in Roth's work—during the romance between Neil Klugman, the poor Newark boy, and Brenda Patimkin, the self-assured Radcliffe girl (though nothing she says or does could persuade one that she would ever have been admitted to Radcliffe). Yet if the novella is read with any care at all, it becomes clear that Roth is not precise and certainly not scrupulous enough in his use of social evidence. The Patimkins are easily placed—what could be easier for a Jewish writer than to elicit disdain for middle-class Jews?—but the elements of what is new in their experience are grossly manipulated. Their history is invoked for the passing of adverse judgment, at least part of which seems to me warranted, but their history is not allowed to emerge so as to make them understandable as human beings. Their vulgarity is put on blazing display but little or nothing that might locate or complicate that vulgarity is shown: little of the weight of their past, whether sustaining or sentimental; nothing of the Jewish mania for culture, whether honorable or foolish; nothing of the fearful self-consciousness which the events of the mid-20th century thrust upon the Patimkins of this world. Ripped out of the historical context that might help to define them, the Patimkins are vivid enough, but as lampoon or caricature in a novella that clearly aims for more than lampoon or caricature. (There is, for example, a placing reference to Mrs. Patimkin's membership in Hadassah, employed as a cue for easy laughs in the way watermelons once were for Southern blacks—it is an instance of how a thrust against vulgarity can itself become vulgar, and by no means the only one in Roth's work.)

On the other side of the social spectrum Roth places Aunt Gladys, still poor, fretting absurdly over her nephew's health and, quite as if she were a stand-in for the Mrs. Portnoy yet to come, rattling off one-liners about the fruit in her icebox. Aunt Gladys, we learn, is preparing for a Workmen's Circle picnic; and for a reader with even a little knowledge of Jewish immigrant life, that raises certain expectations, since the Workmen's Circle signifies a socialist and Yiddishist commitment which time, no doubt, has dimmed but which still has left some impact of sensibility on people like Aunt Gladys. But while named, as if to signal familiarity with her background, this aspect of Aunt Gladys's experience is never allowed to color Roth's portrait, never allowed to affect either the ridicule to which she is subjected nor the simplistic fable—so self-serving in its essential softness—of a poor but honorable Jewish boy withstanding suburban-Jewish vulgarity and thereupon left without any moral option in his world.

The price Roth pays for immobilizing the Patimkins into lampoon and Aunt Gladys into vaudeville is that none of the social or moral forces supposedly acting upon Neil Klugman can be dramatically marshaled. And Neil Klugman himself—poor cipher that he is, neither very *klug* nor very *man*—can never engage himself in the risks and temptations that are supposed to constitute his dilemma, if only because Roth is out there running interference, straight-arming all the other characters in behalf of this vapid alter ego. Even so extreme an admirer of Roth's work as Theodore Solotaroff acknowledges the "abstractness that Neil takes on. He . . . is too far along the path he is supposed to be traveling in the story. One could wish that he were more his aunt's nephew, more troubled and attracted by the life of the Patimkins, and more willing to test it and himself."

Now the issue is not, I had better emphasize, whether newly-rich suburban Jews are vulgar—a certain number, perhaps many, surely are—nor whether they are proper targets of satire—everyone is. What I am saying is that it is prefabricated counterpositions "Goodbye, Columbus" draws not upon a fresh encounter with the post-war experience of suburban Jews but upon literary hand-me-downs of American-Jewish fiction, popularizing styles of rebellion from an earlier moment and thereby draining them of their rebellious content.

I doubt, in any case, that Roth is really interested in a close and scrupulous observance of social life. He came to the literary scene at a moment when the dominant kind of critical talk was to dismiss "mere realism," as if that were a commodity so easily come by, and to praise "the imagination," as if that were a faculty which could operate apart from a bruising involvement with social existence. And this critical ideology served to reinforce Roth's own temperament as a writer, which is inclined to be impatient, snappish, and dismissive, all qualities hardly disposing him to strive for an objective (objective: to see the object as it is) perception of contemporary life.

Defending himself several years ago against the rather feckless attacks of outraged rabbis, some of whom complained that he did not provide a "balanced portrayal" of Jewish life, Roth wrote that "to confuse a 'balanced portrayal' with a novel is . . . to be led into absurdities." Absurdities, he continued, like supposing a group of 19th-century Russian students sending off a complaint to Dostoevsky that Raskolnikov is not a "typical student." Well, that's amusing, though I think it would be quite possible to show that, in some sense, Dostoevsky *does* present a "balanced portrayal" of Russian life. In any case, Roth in his defense, as in his fiction, makes things a little too easy for himself. For the critical issue is not whether he has given a "balanced portrayal" of the Jews as a whole or even the suburban Jews, but whether his portrayal of the Patimkins as the kind of people they are is characterized by fullness and precision. After all, no fictional portrait is merely idiosyncratic, every novel or story aspires to some element of representativeness or at least reverberation—and indeed, at a crucial point in "Goodbye, Columbus," when Neil Klugman is reflecting upon what his fate would be if he were to marry Brenda, he at least takes the Patimkins to be representative of a way of life. It will not do to say that the Patimkins are "unique," for if they were they could have no interest other than as an oddity. What is at stake here is Roth's faithfulness to *his own materials*, the justice and largesse of his imaginative treatment.

There remains another line of defense against such criticism, which Roth's admirers frequently man: that he writes satire and therefore cannot be expected to hew closely to realistic detail. This is a defense that quite fails to apprehend what the nature of good satire is. To compose a satire is not at all to free oneself from the obligation to social accuracy; it is only to order that accuracy in a particular way. If it can be shown that the targets of the satirist are imprecisely located or that he is shooting wild, the consequences may be more damaging than if the same were shown for a conventional realist. And if it can be shown that the satire is self-serving—poor Neil, poor Alex . . . —then it becomes—well, imagine how absurd *Gulliver's Travels* would seem if we became persuaded that the satiric barrage against mankind allows for one little exception, a young hero troubled by the burdens of being English and resembling Jonathan Swift.

Roth's stories begin, characteristically, with a spectacular array of details in the representation of milieu, speech, and manners and thereby we are led to expect a kind of fiction strong in verisimilitude. But then, at crucial points in the stories, there follow a series of substitutions, elements of incident or speech inserted not because they follow from the logic of the narrative but because they underscore the point Roth wishes to extract from the narrative. In "The Conversion of the Jews" a bright if obnoxious Jewish boy becomes so enraged with the sniffling pieties of his Hebrew-school teacher, Rabbi Bender, that he races out of the classroom and up to the roof, threatening to jump unless the rabbi admits that "God can do anything" and "can make a child without intercourse." The plot may seem a bit fanciful and the story, as Mr. Solotaroff justly remarks, "inflated to get in the message"—but no matter, at least our attention is being held. Then, however, comes the breaking point, when the writer's will crushes his fiction: Ozzie "made them all say they believed in Jesus Christ—first one at a time, then all together." Given the sort of tough-grained Jewish urchin Ozzie is shown to be, this declamation strains our credence; it is Roth who has taken over, shouldering aside his characters and performing on his own, just as it is Roth who ends the story with the maudlin touch of Ozzie crying out, "Mamma. You should never hit anybody about God. . . ." Scratch an Ozzie, and you find a Rabbi Bender.

A richer and more ambitious story, "Eli the Fanatic" suffers from the same kind of flaws. An exotic yeshivah sponsored by a Hasidic sect settles in Woodenton, a comfortable suburb. The local Jews feel hostile, tension follows, and Eli Peck, a vulnerable Woodenton Jew, undergoes a kind of moral conversion in which he identifies or hallucinates himself as a victim in kaftan. It is difficult, if one bears in mind Roth's entire work, to take at face value this solemn espousal of yeshivah Orthodoxy as the positive force in the story; I cannot believe that the yeshivah and all it represents has been brought into play for any reason other than as a stick with which to beat Woodenton. Tzuref, the yeshivah principal, is well-drawn and allowed to speak for his outlook, as Aunt Gladys in "Goodbye, Columbus" is not: which is one reason this story builds up a certain dramatic tension. But again Roth feels obliged to drop a heavy thumb on the scales by making his suburbanites so benighted, indeed, so merely stupid, that the story finally comes apart. Here is a Woodenton Jew speaking:

Look, I don't even know about this Sunday school business. Sundays I drive my oldest kid all the way to Scarsdale to learn Bible stories . . . and you know what she comes up with? This Abraham in the Bible was going to kill his own *kid* for a sacrifice. She gets nightmares from it, for God's sake. You call that religion? Today a guy like that they'd lock him up.

Now, even a philistine character has certain rights, if not as a philistine then as a character in whose "reality" we are being asked to believe. To write as if this middle-class Jewish suburbanite were unfamiliar with "this Abraham" or shocked by the story of the near-sacrifice of Isaac, is simply preposterous. Roth is putting into the character's mouth, not what he could plausibly say, but what Roth thinks his "real" sentiments are. He is not revealing the character, but "exposing" him. It is a crucial failure in literary tact, one of several in the story that rouse the suspicion Roth is not behaving with good faith toward the objects of his assault.

This kind of tendentiousness mars a number of Roth's fictions, especially those in which a first-person narrator—Neil Klugman, Alex Portnoy—swarms all over the turf of his imaginary world, blotting out the possibility of multiple perspective. It is a weakness of fictions told in the first person that the limits of the narrator's perception tend to become the limits of the work itself. Through an "unreliable" first-person narrator it is, of course, possible to plant bits of crucial evidence that call his version of things into question, but that requires a good deal of technical sophistication and still more, a portion of self-doubt such as our culture has not greatly encouraged these past two decades. There usually follows in such first-person narratives a spilling-out of the narrator which it becomes hard to suppose is not also the spilling-out of the author. Such literary narcissism is especially notable among minor satirists, with whom it frequently takes the form of self-exemptive attacks on the shamefulness of humanity. In some of Mary McCarthy's novels, for example, all the characters are shown as deceitful and venomous, all but a heroine pure in heart and close to the heart of the author. Neither Klugman nor Portnoy is exactly pure in heart, but as a man at ease with our moment, Portnoy has learned that "sincerity" can pay substantial dividends by soliciting admiration for the candor with which it proclaims impurities. And as for those of Roth's stories that avoid the looseness of the first-person narrative, his own authorial voice quickly takes over, becoming all but indistinguishable from a first-person narrator, raucous, self-aggrandizing, and damned sure that the denouement of his story will not escape the grip of his will.

To these strictures I would offer one exception, the Roth story that, oddly, was most attacked by his rabbinical critics: "Defender of the

Faith." This seems to me a distinguished performance, the example of what Roth might have made of his talent had he been stricter in his demands upon himself. Roth's description of the story is acute: "It is about one man who uses his own religion, and another's uncertain conscience, for selfish ends; but mostly it is about this other man, the narrator, who because of the ambiguities of being a member of a particular religion, is involved in a taxing, if mistaken, conflict of loyalties." This conflict is at once urgent for those caught up in it and serious in its larger moral implications. Nathan Marx, back from combat duty in Germany, is made First Sergeant of a training company in Missouri; he is a decent, thought-ful fellow whose sense of being Jewish, important though it is to him, he cannot articulate clearly. A few recruits in his company, led by Sheldon Grossbart, attach themselves to Marx, presumably out of common feeling toward the problem of being Jews in an alien setting, but actually because Grossbart means to exploit this sense of solidarity in behalf of private ends—he looks forward to the crucial favor of not being sent overseas to combat. As Roth comments, Grossbart is "a man whose lapses of integrity seem to him so necessary to his survival as to convince him that such lapses are actually committed in the name of integrity." At the end of the story, Sergeant Marx, incensed at the manipulation to which he has been subjected, makes certain that Grossbart is indeed shipped overseas, while he, Marx, braces himself to face the consequences of an act he admits to be "vindictive."

The power of this story derives from presenting a moral entangle-ment so as to draw out, yet not easily resolve, its inherent difficulties. Unattractive as Grossbart may be, his cunning use of whatever weapons come to hand in order to protect his skin seems entirely real; one would have to be thoroughly locked into self-righteousness not to be drawn a little, however shamefacedly, to Grossbart's urgency. The willingness of Marx to bend the rules in behalf of the Jewish recruits is plausible, perhaps even admirable; after all, he shares their loneliness and vulnerability. Established thereby as a figure of humaneness, Marx commits an act that seems shocking, even to himself, so that he must then try to resist "with all my will an impulse to turn back and seek pardon for my vindictiveness." If it is right to punish Grossbart, Marx also knows the punishment is cruel, a result, perhaps, of the same Jewish uneasiness that had first made him susceptible to Grossbart's designs.

The story does not allow any blunt distribution of moral sympa-thies, nor can the reader yield his heart to one character. Before the painfulness of the situation, Roth's usual habit of rapid dismissal must melt away. We are left with the texture of reality as, once in a while, a writer can summon it.

Neither before nor after "Defender of the Faith" has Roth written anything approaching it in compositional rigor and moral seriousness. It may, however, have been the presence of this story in *Goodbye, Columbus* that led reviewers, including myself, to assume that this gifted new writer was working in the tradition of Jewish self-criticism and satire—a substantial tradition extending in Yiddish from Mendele to Isaac Bashevis Singer and in English from Abraham Cahan to Malamud and Bellow. In these kinds of writing, the assault upon Jewish philistinism and the mockery of Jewish social pretension are both familiar and unrelenting. Beside Mendele, Roth seems soft; beside Cahan, imprecise. But now, from the vantage point of additional years, I think it clear that Roth, despite his concentration on Jewish settings and his acerbity of tone, has not really been involved in this tradition. For he is one of the first American-Jewish writers who finds that it yields him no sustenance, no norms or values from which to launch his attacks on middle-class complacence.

This deficiency, if deficiency it be, need not be a fatal one for a Jewish writer, provided he can find sustenance elsewhere, in other cultures, other traditions. But I do not see that Roth has—his relation to the mainstream of American culture, in its great sweep of democratic idealism and romanticism, is decidedly meager. There is no lack of critical attitude, or attitudinizing, in Roth's stories, but much of it consists of the frayed remnants of cultural modernism, once revolutionary in significance but now reduced to little more than the commonplace "shock" of middlebrow culture. And there is a parasitic relation to the embattled sentiments and postures of older Jewish writers in America—though without any recognition that, by now, simply to launch attacks on middle-class suburbia is to put oneself at the head of the suburban parade, just as to mock the uptightness of immigrant Jews is to become the darling of their "liberated" suburban children.

One reason Roth's stories are unsatisfactory is that they come out of a thin personal culture. That he can quote Yeats and Rilke is hardly to the point. When we speak of a writer's personal culture we have in mind the ways in which a tradition, if absorbed into his work, can both release and control his creative energies. A vital culture can yield a writer those details of manners, customs, and morals which give the illusion of reality to his work. More important, *a vital culture talks back, so to say, within the writer's work*, holding in check his eccentricities, notions, and egocentrisms, providing a dialectic between what he has received and what he has willed—one can see this in novelists as various as Tolstoy, Haw-thorne, Verga, and Sholem Aleichem.

When we say, consequently, that a writer betrays a thin personal culture we mean, among other possibilities, that he comes at the end of a tradition which can no longer nourish his imagination or that he has, through an act of fiat, chosen to tear himself away from that tradition— many American writers of the late 19th and early 20th centuries, for example, could no longer continue with firm conviction in the line of transcendental idealism which had been so liberating fifty or sixty years earlier. It is, of course, a severe predicament for a writer to find himself in this situation; it forces him into self-consciousness, improvisation, and false starts; but if he is genuinely serious, he will try, like a farmer determined to get what he can from poor soil, to make a usable theme of his dilemmas.

Perhaps this thinness of culture has some connection with that tone of *ressentiment,* that free-floating contempt and animus, which begins to appear in Roth's early stories and grows more noticeable in his later work. Unfocused hostility often derives from unexamined depression, and the latter, which I take to be the ground-note of Roth's sensibility, fully emerges only in the two novels he wrote after *Goodbye, Columbus.* But even in the early stories one begins to hear a grind of exasperation, an assault without precise object, an irritable wish to pull down the creatures of his own imagination which can hardly be explained by anything happening within the stories themselves. If sentimentality is defined as emotion in excess of what a given situation warrants, what are we to say about irritability in excess? As one of Roth's critics, Baruch Hochman, has sharply noticed:

> The energy informing [Roth's] stories is scarcely more than the energy of irritation, an irritation so great that it makes the exposure of inanity seem a meaningful moral act. For Roth does not seem really to be concerned with the substance of the values he shows being eroded. It is not at all clear how Neil Klugman, who is so offended at the Patimkins, stands for anything substantially different from what they stand for— setting aside the fact that he is poorer than they, which he cannot help. His differences with them lie elsewhere than in the moral realm. . . .

At times the note of disgust is sounded in full, as in "Epstein," a nasty joke about a middle-aged man's hapless effort to revive his sexuality. Reading the last paragraphs of this story, arranged as a pratfall for the poor slob Epstein (and how pleasurable it is for "us," the cultivated ones, to sneer at those slobs, with their little box houses, their spreading wives, their mucky kids, their uncreative jobs), one is reminded of D. H. Lawrence's jibe about writers who "do dirt" on their characters.

II

The standard opinion of Roth's critics has been that his two novels, *Letting Go* and *When She Was Good,* add slight luster to his reputation, and there is not much use in arguing against this view. Yet it should be noticed that there are patches of genuine achievement in both books, sometimes a stumbling, gasping honesty. They are not novels that yield much pleasure or grip one despite its absence, but both are marked by tokens of struggle with the materials of American life. And there are moments that come off well—the persistence of the battered divorcee, Martha Reganhart (*Letting Go*), in raising her children decently, the precocious eeriness of little Cynthia Reganhart, the struggle of Lucy (*When She Was Good*) to raise herself above the maudlin stupor of her family. Conventional achievements all of these are, and of a kind novelists have often managed in the past—of a kind, also, they will have to manage in the future if the novel is to survive. But right now, in our present cultural situation, this is hardly the sort of achievement likely to win much attention, as Roth evidently came to see.

Roth is not a "natural" novelist at all, the kind who loves to tell stories, chronicle social life, pile on characters, and if in his early fiction he seems willfully bent on scoring "points," in the novels his will exhausts itself from the sheer need to get on with things. He is an exceedingly joyless writer, even when being very funny. The reviewers of his novels, many of them sympathetic, noticed his need to rub our noses in the muck of squalid daily existence, his mania for annotating at punitive length the bickerings of his characters. Good clean hatred that might burn through, naturalistic determinism with a grandeur of design if not detail, the fury of social rebellion—any of these would be more *interesting* than the vindictive bleakness of Roth's novels.

What, one wonders, does he really have against these unhappy creatures of his? Why does he keep pecking away at them? I think the answer might furnish a key to Roth's work. Perhaps as a leftover from the culture of modernism and perhaps as a consequence of personal temperament, Roth's two novels betray a swelling nausea before the ordinariness of human existence, its seepage of spirit and rotting of flesh. This is a response that any sensitive or even insensitive person is likely to share at some point and to some extent, but it simply does not allow a writer to sustain or provide internal complications of tone in a large-scale work. It starts as a fastidious hesitation before the unseemliness of our minds and unsightliness of our bodies; it ends as a vibration of horror before the sewage of the quotidian. Men grow paunches, women's breasts sag, the breath of the aged reeks, varicose veins bulge. It all seems insufferable, an affront to our most cherished images of self, so much so that ordinary life must be pushed away, a disorder to be despised and assaulted. It is as if, in nagging at his characters, Roth were venting some deep and unmanageable frustration with our common fate.

III

The cruelest thing anyone can do with *Portnoy's Complaint* is to read it twice. An assemblage of gags strung onto the outcry of an analytic patient, the book thrives best on casual responses; it demands little more from the reader than a nightclub performer demands: a rapid exchange of laugh for punchline, a breath or two of rest, some variations on the first response, and a quick exit. Such might be the most generous way of discussing *Portnoy's Complaint* were it not for the solemn ecstasies the book has elicited, in line with Roth's own feeling that it constitutes a liberating act for himself, his generation, and maybe the whole culture.

The basic structural unit of *Portnoy's Complaint* is the skit, the stand-up comedian's shuffle and patter that come to climax with a smashing one-liner—indeed, it is worth noticing that a good many of our more "advanced" writers during the last two decades have found themselves turning to the skit as a form well-suited to the requirements of "swinging" and their rejection of sustained coherence of form. The controlling tone of the book is a shriek of excess, the jokester's manic wail, although, because it must slide from skit to skit with some pretense of continuity, this tone declines now and again into a whine of self-exculpation or sententiousness. And the controlling sensibility of the book derives from a well-grounded tradition of feeling within immigrant Jewish life: the coarse provincial "worldliness" flourishing in corner candy-stores and garment centers, at cafeterias and pinochle games, a sort of hard, cynical mockery of ideal claims and pretensions, all that remains to people scraped raw by the struggle for success. (This sensibility finds a "sophisticated" analogue in the smart-aleck nastiness of Jules Feiffer's film, *Carnal Knowledge*, which cannot really be understood without some reference to the undersides of Jewish immigrant life, not as these have affected the subject-matter of the film but as they have affected the vision of the people who made it.)

Much of what is funny in Roth's book—the Monkey's monologues, some rhetorical flourishes accompanying Alex's masturbation, Sophie Portnoy's amusement at chancing upon her son's sexual beginnings—rests on the fragile structure of the skit. All the skit requires or can manage is a single broad stroke: shrewd, gross, recognizable, playing on the audience's embarrassment yet not hurting it too much, so that finally its aggression can be passed off as good-fellowship. (We all have Jewish mamas, we're all henpecked husbands, we all pretend to greater sexual prowess than. . . .) The skit stakes everything on brashness and energy, both of which Roth has or simulates in abundance. Among writers of the past Dickens and Céline have used the skit brilliantly, but Dickens always and Céline sometimes understood that in a book of any length the skit—as well as its sole legitimate issue, the caricature—must be put to the service of situations, themes, stories allowing for complication and development. (A lovely example of this point can be seen in the skits that Peter Sellers performs in the movie version of *Lolita*.)

It is on the problem of continuity that Portnoy—or, actually, Roth himself—trips up. For once we are persuaded to see his complaints as more than the stuff of a few minutes of entertainment, once we are led to suppose that they derive from some serious idea or coherent view of existence, the book quickly falls to pieces and its much-admired energy (praised by some critics as if energy were a value regardless of the ends to which it is put) serves mainly to blur its flimsiness. Technically this means that, brief as it is, the book seems half again too long, since there can be very little surprise or development in the second half, only a recapitulation of motifs already torn to shreds in the first.

It is worth looking at a few of the book's incoherences, venial for a skit, fatal for a novel. Alex is allowed the human attribute of a history within the narrative space of the book, presumably so that he can undergo change and growth, but none of the characters set up as his foils, except perhaps the Monkey, is granted a similar privilege. Alex speaks for imposed-upon, vulnerable, twisted, yet self-liberating humanity; the other characters, reduced to a function of his need, an echo of his cry, cannot speak or speak back as autonomous voices but simply go through their paces like straight-men mechanically feeding lines to a comic. Even more than in Roth's earlier work, the result is claustrophobia of voice and vision: *he never shuts up*, this darling Alex, nor does Roth detach himself sufficiently to gain some ironic distance. The psychic afflictions of his character Roth would surely want to pass up, but who can doubt that

Portnoy's cry from the heart—enough of Jewish guilt, enough of the burdens of history, enough of inhibition and repression, it is time to "let go" and soar to the horizons of pleasure—speaks in some sense for Roth?

The difficulty that follows from this claustrophobic vision is not whether Mrs. Portnoy can be judged a true rendering, even as caricature, of Jewish mothers—only chuckleheads can suppose that to be a serious question!—but whether characters like Mr. and Mrs. Portnoy have much reality or persuasiveness within the fictional boundaries set by Roth himself. Sophie Portnoy has a little, because there are moments when Alex, or Roth, can't help liking her, and because the conventional lampoon of the Jewish mother is by now so well established in our folklore it has almost become an object of realistic portraiture in its own right. As for Mr. Portnoy, a comparison suggests itself between this constipated *nudnik* whom Alex would pass off as his father and "Mr. Fumfotch" in Daniel Fuchs's novel *Homage to Blenholt*. Fuchs's character is also a henpecked husband, also worn down by the struggle for bread, but he is drawn with an ironic compassion that rises to something better than itself: to an objectivity that transcends either affection or derision. In his last novel Fuchs remarks, while writing about figures somewhat like those in Roth's work, "It was not enough to call them low company and pass on"—and if this can be said about Depression Jews in Brighton Beach, why not also about more or less affluent ones in the Jersey suburbs?

We notice, again, that Portnoy attributes his sexual troubles to the guilt-soaked Jewish tradition as it has been carried down to him by his mother. Perhaps; who knows? But if we are to accept this simplistic determinism, why does it never occur to him, our Assistant Commissioner of Human Opportunity who once supped with John Lindsay in the flesh, that by the same token the intelligence on which he preens himself must also be attributed to the tradition he finds so repugnant—so that his yowl of revulsion against "my people," that they should "stick your suffering heritage up your suffering ass," becomes, let us say, a little ungenerous, even a little dopey.

And we notice, again, that while Portnoy knows that his sexual difficulties stem from his Jewishness, the patrician New England girl with whom he has an affair also turns out to be something of a sexual failure: she will not deliver him from the coils of Jewish guilt through the magic of fellatio. But if both Jewishness and Protestantism have deeply inhibiting effects on sexual performance—and as for Catholicism, well, we know those Irish girls!—what then happens to this crucial flake of Portnoy's wisdom, which the book invites us to take with some seriousness? As for other possible beliefs, from Ethical Culture to Hare Krishna, there can surely be little reason to suppose they will deliver us from the troubles of life which, for all we know, may be lodged in the very nature of things or, at the least, in those constraints of civilization which hardly encircle Jewish loins exclusively.

There is something suspect about Portnoy's complaining. From what he tells us one might reasonably conclude that, in a far from perfect world, he is not making out so badly; the boys on his block, sexual realists that they are, would put it more pungently. Only in Israel does he have serious difficulties, and for that there are simple geographical solutions. What seems really to be bothering Portnoy is a wish to sever his sexuality from his moral sensibilities, to cut it away from his self as historical creature. It's as if he really supposed the super-ego, or *post coitum triste,* were a Jewish invention. This wish—Norman O. Brown as a *yingele*—strikes me as rather foolish, an adolescent fantasy carrying within itself an inherent negation; but it is a fantasy that has accumulated a great deal of power in contemporary culture. And it helps explain, I think, what Roth's true feelings about, or relation to, Jewishness are. *Portnoy's Complaint* is not, as enraged critics have charged, an anti-Semitic book, though it contains plenty of contempt for Jewish life. Nor does Roth write out of traditional Jewish self-hatred, for the true agent of such self-hatred is always indissolubly linked with Jewish past and present, quite as closely as those who find in Jewishness moral or transcendent sanctions. What the book speaks for is a yearning to undo the fate of birth; there is no wish to do the Jews any harm (a little nastiness is something else), nor any desire to engage with them as a fevered antagonist; Portnoy is simply crying out to be left alone, to be released from the claims of distinctiveness and the burdens of the past, so that, out of his own nothingness, he may create himself as a "human being." Who, born a Jew in the 20th century, has been so lofty in spirit never to have shared this fantasy? But who, born a Jew in the 20th century, has been so foolish in mind as to dally with it for more than a moment?

What, in any case, is *Portnoy's Complaint*—a case-history burlesqued, which we are invited to laugh at, or a struggle of an afflicted man to achieve his liberation, which we are invited to cheer on? Dr. Bruno Bettelheim has written a straight-faced essay purporting to be the case notes of Alex's psychoanalyst, Dr. O. Spielvogel, who can barely restrain his impatience with Alex's effort to mask his true problems with "all the clichés of a spoiled Jewish childhood."

> A few times I [Dr. Spielvogel] indicated the wish to say something, but he only talked on the more furiously. . . . This extremely intelligent young Jew does not recognize that what he is trying to do, by reversing

the Oedipal situation, is to make fun of me, as he does of everyone, thus asserting his superiority. . . . His overpowering love for his mother is turned into a negative projection, so that what becomes overpowering is the mother's love for him. . . . While consciously he experienced every-thing she did as destructive, behind it is an incredible wish for more, more, more. . . .

Now this is amusing, though not as amusing as the fact that it often constitutes the line of defense to which Roth's admirers fall back when the book's incoherence is revealed ("after all, it's a patient on the couch, everyone knows you can't take what he says at face value. . . ."). But to see the book in this light, as the mere comic record of a very sick man, is radically to undercut its claims for expressing radical new truths. Roth, never unwary, anticipates the problem by having Portnoy say, "Is this truth I'm delivering up, or is it just plain *kvetching*? Or is *kvetching* for people like me a *form* of truth?" Well there's *kvetching* and *kvetching*. At times it can be a form of truth, but when the gap is so enormous between manifest content and what Dr. Spielvogel *cum* Bettelheim takes to be its inner meaning, then *kvetching* becomes at best an untruth from which the truth must be violently wrenched.

It seems hard to believe that Roth would accept the view that his book consists merely of comic griping; certainly the many readers who saw it as a banner behind which to rally would not accept that view. For, in a curious way, *Portnoy's Complaint* has become a cultural document of some importance. Younger Jews, weary or bored with all the talk about their heritage, have taken the book as a signal for "letting go" of both their past and perhaps themselves, a guide to swinging in good conscience or better yet, without troubling about conscience. For some Gentile readers the book seems to have played an even more important role. After the Second World War, as a consequence of certain unpleasantnesses that occurred during the war, a wave of philo-Semitism swept through our culture. This wave lasted for all of two decades, in the course of which books by Jewish writers were often praised (in truth, overpraised) and a fuss made about Jewish intellectuals, critics, etc. Some literary people found this hard to bear, but they did. Once *Portnoy's Complaint* arrived, however, they could almost be heard breathing a sigh of relief, for it signaled an end to philo-Semitism in American culture, one no longer had to listen to all that talk about Jewish morality, Jewish endurance, Jewish wisdom, Jewish families. Here was Philip Roth himself, a writer who even seemed to know Yiddish, confirming what had always been suspected about those immi-grant Jews but had recently not been tactful to say.

The talent that went into *Portnoy's Complaint* and portions of

Goodbye, Columbus is real enough, but it has been put to the service of a creative vision deeply marred by vulgarity. It is very hard, I will admit, to be explicit about the concept of vulgarity: people either know what one is referring to, as part of the tacit knowledge that goes to make up a coherent culture, or the effort to explain is probably doomed in advance. Nevertheless, let me try. By vulgarity in a work of literature I am not here talking about the presence of certain kinds of words or the rendering of certain kinds of actions. I have in mind, rather, the impulse to submit the rich substance of human experience, sentiment, value, and aspiration to a radically reductive leveling or simplification; the urge to assault the validity of sustained gradings and discriminations of value, so that in some extreme instances the concept of vulgarity is dismissed as up-tight or a mere mask for repressiveness; the wish to pull down the reader in common with the characters of the work, so that he will not be tempted to suppose that any inclinations he has toward the good, the beautiful, or the ideal merit anything more than a Bronx cheer; and finally, a refusal of that disinterestedness of spirit in the depiction and judgment of other people which seems to me the writer's ultimate resource.

That I have here provided an adequate definition of vulgarity in literature I do not for a moment suppose—though I don't know of a better one. It ought, however, to serve our present purposes by helping to make clear, for example, the ways in which a book like *Portnoy's Complaint,* for all its scrim of sophistication, is spiritually linked with the usual sentimental treatment of Jewish life in the work of popular and middlebrow writers. Between *Portnoy's Complaint* and *Two Cents Plain* there is finally no great difference of sensibility.

Perhaps the matter can be clarified by a comparison. Hubert Selby's novel, *Last Exit to Brooklyn,* portrays a segment of urban life—lumpen violence, gang-bangs, rape, sheer debasement—that is utterly appalling, and the language it must record is of a kind that makes Roth seem reticent; yet as I read Selby's book there is no vulgarity in it whatever, for he takes toward his barely human figures a stance of dispassionate objectivity, writing not with "warmth" or "concern" but with a disciplined wish to see things as they are. He does not wrench, he does not patronize, he does not aggrandize. Repugnant as it often is, *Last Exit to Brooklyn* seems to me a pure-spirited book; amusing as it often is, *Portnoy's Complaint* a vulgar book.

IV

About the remainder of Roth's work I have little to say. *Our Gang*, purporting to be a satire on Richard Nixon, is a coarse-grained replica of its subject. A flaccid performance, it has some interest through embodying a strong impulse in our culture, the impulse to revert not so much to the pleasures of infantilism as to the silliness of the high-school humor column. About this book I would repeat what Henry James once said of a Trollope novel: "Our great objection . . . is that we seem to be reading a work written for children, a work prepared for minds unable to think, a work below the apprehension of the average man or woman."

The Breast, extravagantly praised by my literary betters, is a work to which, as students would say, "I cannot relate." Well-enough written and reasonably ingenious, it is finally boring—tame, neither shocking nor outrageous, and tasteless in both senses of the word. Discussions will no doubt persist as to its "meaning," but first it might be better to ask whether, as a work of literature, it exists. For simply on the plane of narrative it cannot, or ought not, hold the interest of a reasonably mature reader.

Flaubert once said that a writer must choose between an audience and readers. Evidently Roth has made his choice.

PHILIP ROTH

'I Always Wanted You to Admire My Fasting'; or, Looking at Kafka

I am looking, as I write of Kafka, at the photograph taken of him at the age of forty (my age)—it is 1924, as sweet and hopeful a year as he may ever have known as a man, and the year of his death. His face is sharp and skeletal, a burrower's face: pronounced cheekbones made even more conspicuous by the absence of sideburns; the ears shaped and angled on his head like angel wings; an intense, creaturely gaze of startled composure—enormous fears, enormous control; a black towel of Levantine hair pulled close around the skull the only sensuous feature; there is a familiar Jewish flare in the bridge of the nose, the nose itself is long and weighted slightly at the tip—the nose of half the Jewish boys who were my friends in high school. Skulls chiseled like this one were shoveled by the thousands from the ovens; had he lived, his would have been among them, along with the skulls of his three younger sisters.

Of course it is no more horrifying to think of Franz Kafka in Auschwitz than to think of anyone in Auschwitz—it is just horrifying in its own way. But he died too soon for the holocaust. Had he lived, perhaps he would have escaped with his good friend Max Brod, who found refuge in Palestine, a citizen of Israel until his death there in 1968. But *Kafka* escaping? It seems unlikely for one so fascinated by entrapment and careers that culminate in anguished death. Still, there is Karl Rossmann,

From *American Review* 17 (May 1973). Copyright © 1973 by Philip Roth.

his American greenhorn. Having imagined Karl's escape to America and his mixed luck here, could not Kafka have found a way to execute an escape for himself? The New School for Social Research in New York becoming *his* Great Nature Theatre of Oklahoma? Or perhaps, through the influence of Thomas Mann, a position in the German department at Princeton. . . . But then, had Kafka lived, it is not at all certain that the books of his which Mann celebrated from *his* refuge in New Jersey would ever have been published; eventually Kafka might either have destroyed those manuscripts that he had once bid Max Brod to dispose of at his death, or, at the least, continued to keep them his secret. The Jewish refugee arriving in America in 1938 would not then have been Mann's "religious humorist" but a frail and bookish fifty-five-year-old bachelor, formerly a lawyer for a government insurance firm in Prague, retired on a pension in Berlin at the time of Hitler's rise to power—an author, yes, but of a few eccentric stories, mostly about animals, stories no one in America had ever heard of and only a handful in Europe had read; a homeless K., but without K.'s willfulness and purpose, a homeless Karl, but without Karl's youthful spirit and resilience; just a Jew lucky enough to have escaped with his life, in his possession a suitcase containing some clothes, some family photos, some Prague mementos, and the manuscripts, still unpublished and in pieces, of *Amerika, The Trial, The Castle*, and (stranger things happen) three more fragmented novels, no less remarkable than the bizarre masterworks that he keeps to himself out of oedipal timidity, perfectionist madness, and insatiable longings for solitude and spiritual purity.

July 1923

Eleven months before he will die in a Vienna sanatorium, Kafka somehow finds the resolve to leave Prague and his father's home for good. Never before has he even remotely succeeded in living apart, independent of his mother, his sisters, and his father, nor has he been a writer other than in those few hours when he is not working in the legal department of the Workers' Accident Insurance Office in Prague; since taking his law degree at the university, he has been by all reports the most dutiful and scrupulous of employees, though he finds the work tedious and enervating. But in June of 1923—having some months earlier been pensioned from his job because of his illness—he meets a young Jewish girl of nineteen at a seaside resort in Germany, Dora Dymant, an employee at the vacation camp of the Jewish People's Home of Berlin. Dora has left her Orthodox Polish family to make a life of her own (at half Kafka's age); she and

Kafka—who has just turned forty—fall in love . . . Kafka has by now been engaged to two somewhat more conventional Jewish girls—twice to one of them—hectic, anguished engagements wrecked largely by his fears. "I am mentally incapable of marrying," he writes his father in the forty-five-page letter he gave to his mother to deliver. ". . . the moment I make up my mind to marry I can no longer sleep, my head burns day and night, life can no longer be called life." He explains why. "Marrying is barred to me," he tells his father, "because it is your domain. Sometimes I imagine the map of the world spread out and you stretched diagonally across it. And I feel as if I could consider living in only those regions that are not covered by you or are not within your reach. And in keeping with the conception I have of your magnitude, these are not many and not very comforting regions—and marriage is not among them." The letter explaining what is wrong between this father and this son is dated November 1919; the mother thought it best not even to deliver it, perhaps for lack of courage, probably, like the son, for lack of hope.

During the following two years, Kafka attempts to wage an affair with Milena Jesenká-Pollak, an intense young woman of twenty-four who has translated a few of his stories into Czech and is most unhappily married in Vienna; his affair with Milena, conducted feverishly, but by and large through the mails, is even more demoralizing to Kafka than the fearsome engagements to the nice Jewish girls. They aroused only the paterfamilias longings that he dared not indulge, longings inhibited by his exaggerated awe of his father—"spellbound," says Brod, "in the family circle"—and the hypnotic spell of his own solitude; but the Czech Milena, impetuous, frenetic, indifferent to conventional restraints, a woman of appetite and anger, arouses more elemental yearnings and more elemental fears. According to a Prague critic, Rio Preisner, Milena was "psychopathic"; according to Margaret Buber-Neumann, who lived two years beside her in the German concentration camp where Milena died following a kidney operation in 1944, she was powerfully sane, extraordinarily humane and courageous. Milena's obituary for Kafka was the only one of consequence to appear in the Prague press; the prose is strong, so are the claims she makes for Kafka's accomplishment. She is still only in her twenties, the dead man is hardly known as a writer beyond his small circle of friends—yet Milena writes: "His knowledge of the world was exceptional and deep, and he was a deep and exceptional world in himself. . . . [He had] a delicacy of feeling bordering on the miraculous and a mental clarity that was terrifyingly uncompromising, and in turn he loaded on to his illness the whole burden of his mental fear of life. . . . He wrote the most important books in recent German literature." One can imagine this vibrant young woman stretched diagonally across the bed, as awesome to Kafka as his own father spread out across the map of the world. His letters to her are disjointed, unlike anything else of his in print; the word "fear" appears on page after page. "We are both married, you in Vienna, I to my Fear in Prague." He yearns to lay his head upon her breast; he calls her "Mother Milena"; during at least one of their two brief rendezvous, he is hopelessly impotent. At last he has to tell her to leave him be, an edict that Milena honors, though it leaves her hollow with grief. "Do not write," Kafka tells her, "and let us not see each other; I ask you only to quietly fulfill this request of mine; only on those conditions is survival possible for me; everything else continues the process of destruction."

Then, in the early summer of 1923, during a visit to his sister, who is vacationing with her children by the Baltic Sea, he finds young Dora Dymant, and within a month Franz Kafka has gone off to live with her in two rooms in a suburb of Berlin, out of reach at last of the "claws" of Prague and home. How can it be? How can he, in his illness, have accomplished so swiftly and decisively the leave-taking that was beyond him in his healthiest days? The impassioned letter writer who could equivocate interminably about which train to catch to Vienna to meet with Milena (if he should meet with her for the weekend at all); the bourgeois suitor in the high collar, who, during his drawn-out agony of an engagement with the proper Fräulein Bauer, secretly draws up a memorandum for himself, countering the arguments "for" marriage with the arguments "against"; the poet of the ungraspable and the unresolved, whose belief in the immovable barrier separating the wish from its realization is at the heart of his excruciating visions of defeat; the Kafka whose fiction refutes every easy, touching, humanish daydream of salvation and justice and fulfillment with densely imagined counterdreams that mock all solutions and escapes—this Kafka *escapes*. Overnight! K. penetrates the Castle walls—Joseph K. evades his indictment—"a breaking away from it altogether, a mode of living completely outside the jurisdiction of the Court." Yes, the possibility of which Joseph K. has just a glimmering in the Cathedral, but can neither fathom nor effectuate—"not . . . some influential manipulation of the case, but . . . a circumvention of it" —Kafka realizes in the last year of his life.

Was it Dora Dymant or was it death that pointed the new way? Perhaps it could not have been one without the other. We know that the "illusory emptiness" at which K. gazed, upon first entering the village and looking up through the mist and the darkness to the Castle, was no more vast and incomprehensible than the idea of himself as husband and father was to the young Kafka; but now, it seems, the prospect of a Dora forever, of a wife, home, and children everlasting, is no longer the terrifying, bewildering prospect it would once have been, for now "everlasting" is undoubtedly not much more than a matter of months. Yes, the dying Kafka is determined to marry, and writes to Dora's Orthodox father for his daughter's hand. But the imminent death that has resolved all contradictions and uncertainties in Kafka is the very obstacle placed in his path by the young girl's father. The request of the dying man Franz Kafka to bind to him in his invalidism the healthy young girl Dora Dymant is—denied!

If there is not one father standing in Kafka's way, there is another— and another behind him. Dora's father, writes Max Brod in his biography of Kafka, "set off with [Kafka's] letter to consult the man he honored most, whose authority counted more than anything else for him, the 'Gerer Rebbe.' The rabbi read the letter, put it to one side, and said nothing more than the single syllable, 'No.' " *No.* Klamm himself could have been no more abrupt—or any more removed from the petitioner. *No.* In its harsh finality, as telling and inescapable as the curselike threat delivered by his father to Georg Bendemann, that thwarted fiancé: "Just take your bride on your arm and try getting in my way. I'll sweep her from your very side, you don't know how!" *No.* Thou shalt not have, say the fathers, and Kafka agrees that he shall not. The habit of obedience and renunciation; also, his own distaste for the diseased and reverence for strength, appetite, and health. " 'Well, clear this out now!' said the overseer, and they buried the hunger artist, straw and all. Into the cage they put a young panther. Even the most insensitive felt it refreshing to see this wild creature leaping around the cage that had so long been dreary. The panther was all right. The food he liked was brought him without hesitation by the attendants; he seemed not even to miss his freedom; his noble body, furnished almost to the bursting point with all that it needed, seemed to carry freedom around with it too; somewhere in his jaws it seemed to lurk; and the joy of life streamed with such ardent passion from his throat that for the onlookers it was not easy to stand the shock of it. But they braced themselves, crowded round the cage, and did not want ever to move away." So no is no; he knew as much himself. A healthy young girl of nineteen cannot, *should* not, be given in matrimony to a sickly man twice her age, who spits up blood ("I sentence you," cries Georg Bendemann's father, "to death by drowning!") and shakes in his bed with fevers and chills. What sort of un-Kafka-like dream had Kafka been dreaming?

And those nine months spent with Dora have still other "Kafka-esque" elements: a fierce winter in quarters inadequately heated; the inflation that makes a pittance of his own meager pension, and sends into the streets of Berlin the hungry and needy whose suffering, says Dora, turns Kafka "ash-gray"; and his tubercular lungs, flesh transformed and punished. Dora cares for the diseased writer as devotedly and tenderly as Gregor Samsa's sister does for her brother, the bug. Gregor's sister plays the violin so beautifully that Gregor "felt as if the way were opening before him to the unknown nourishment he craved"; he dreams, in his condition, of sending his gifted sister to the Conservatory! Dora's music is Hebrew, which she reads aloud to Kafka, and with such skill that, according to Brod, "Franz recognized her dramatic talent; on his advice and under his direction she later educated herself in the art . . ."

Only Kafka is hardly vermin to Dora Dymant, *or to himself*. Away from Prague and his father's home, Kafka, at forty, seems at last to have been delivered from the self-loathing, the self-doubt, and those guilt-ridden impulses to dependence and self-effacement that had nearly driven him mad throughout his twenties and thirties; all at once he seems to have shed the pervasive sense of hopeless despair that informs the great punitive fantasies of *The Trial*, "In the Penal Colony," and "The Metamorphosis." Years earlier, in Prague, he had directed Max Brod to destroy all his papers, including three unpublished novels, upon his death; now, in Berlin, when Brod introduces him to a German publisher interested in his work, Kafka consents to the publication of a volume of four stories, and consents, says Brod, "without much need of long arguments to persuade him." With Dora to help, he diligently resumes the study of Hebrew; despite his illness and the harsh winter, he travels to the Berlin Academy for Jewish Studies to attend a series of lectures on the Talmud—a very different Kafka from the estranged melancholic who once wrote in his diary, "What have I in common with the Jews? I have hardly anything in common with myself and should stand very quietly in a corner, content that I can breathe." And to further mark the change, there is ease and happiness with a woman: with this young and adoring companion, he is playful, he is pedagogical, and, one would guess, in light of his illness (*and his happiness*), he is chaste. If not a husband (such as he had striven to be to the conventional Fräulein Bauer), if not a lover (as he struggled hopelessly to be with Milena), he would seem to have become something no less miraculous in his scheme of things: a father, a kind of father to this sisterly, mothering daughter. *As Franz Kafka awoke one morning from uneasy dreams he found himself transformed in his bed into a father, a writer, and a Jew.*

"I have completed the construction of my burrow," begins the long, exquisite, and tedious story that he wrote that winter in Berlin, "and it seems to be successful. . . . Just the place where, according to my calculations, the Castle Keep should be, the soil was very loose and sandy and had literally to be hammered and pounded into a firm state to serve as a wall for the beautifully vaulted chamber. But for such tasks the only tool I possess is my forehead. So I had to run with my forehead thousands and thousands of times, for whole days and nights, against the ground, and I was glad when the blood came, for that was proof that the walls were beginning to harden; in that way, as everybody must admit, I richly paid for my Castle Keep."

"The Burrow" is the story of an animal with a keen sense of peril whose life is organized around the principle of defense, and whose deepest longings are for security and serenity; with teeth and claws—*and* forehead—the burrower constructs an elaborate and ingeniously intricate system of underground chambers and corridors that are designed to afford it some peace of mind; however, while this burrow does succeed in reducing the sense of danger from without, its maintenance and protection are equally fraught with anxiety: "these anxieties are different from ordinary ones, prouder, richer in content, often long repressed, but in their destructive effects they are perhaps much the same as the anxieties that existence in the outer world gives rise to." The story (whose ending is lost) terminates with the burrower fixated upon distant subterranean noises that cause it "to assume the existence of a great beast," itself burrowing in the direction of the Castle Keep.

Another grim tale of entrapment, and of obsession so absolute that no distinction is possible between character and predicament. Yet this fiction imagined in the last "happy" months of his life is touched by a spirit of personal reconciliation and sardonic self-acceptance, by a tolerance of one's own brand of madness, that is not apparent in "The Metamorphosis." The piercing masochistic irony of the earlier animal story—as of "The Judgment" and *The Trial*—has given way here to a critique of the self and its preoccupations that, though bordering on mockery, no longer seeks to resolve itself in images of the uttermost humiliation and defeat . . . Yet there is more here than a metaphor for the insanely defended ego, whose striving for invulnerability produces a defensive system that must in its turn become the object of perpetual concern—there is also a very unromantic and hardheaded fable about how and why art is made, a portrait of the artist in all his ingenuity, anxiety, isolation, dissatisfaction, relentlessness, obsessiveness, secretiveness, paranoia, and self-addiction, a portrait of the magical thinker at the end of his tether, Kafka's Prospero . . . It is an endlessly suggestive story, this story of life in a hole. For, finally, remember the proximity of Dora Dymant during the months that Kafka was at work on "The Burrow" in the two underheated rooms that were their illicit home. Certainly a dreamer like Kafka need never have entered the young girl's body for her tender presence to kindle in him a fantasy of a hidden orifice that promises "satisfied desire," "achieved ambition," and "profound slumber," but that, once penetrated and in one's possession, arouses the most terrifying and heartbreaking fears of retribution and loss. "For the rest I try to unriddle the beast's plans. Is it on its wanderings, or is it working on its own burrow? If it is on its wanderings then perhaps an understanding with it might be possible. If it should really break through to the burrow I shall give it some of my stores and it will go on its way again. It will go on its way again, a fine story! Lying in my heap of earth I can naturally dream of all sorts of things, even of an understanding with the beast, though I know well enough that no such thing can happen, and that at the instant when we see each other, more, at the moment when we merely guess at each other's presence, we shall blindly bare our claws and teeth . . ."

He died of tuberculosis of the lungs and larynx on June 3, 1924, a month before his forty-first birthday. Dora, inconsolable, whispers for days afterward, "My love, my love, my good one . . ."

II

1942

I am nine; my Hebrew-school teacher, Dr. Kafka, is fifty-nine. To the little boys who must attend his "four-to-five" class each afternoon, he is known—in part because of his remote and melancholy foreignness, but largely because we vent on him our resentment at having to learn an ancient calligraphy at the very hour we should be out screaming our heads off on the ball field—he is known as Dr. Kishka. Named, I confess, by me. His sour breath, spiced with intestinal juices by five in the afternoon, makes the Yiddish word for "insides" particularly telling, I think. Cruel, yes, but in truth I would have cut out my tongue had I ever imagined the name would become legend. A coddled child, I do not yet think of myself as persuasive, or, quite yet, as a literary force in the world. My jokes don't hurt, how could they, I'm so adorable. And if you don't believe me, just ask my family and the teachers in my school. Already at nine, one foot in college, the other in the Catskills. Little borscht-belt comic that I am outside the classroom, I amuse my friends Schlossman and Ratner on the dark walk home from Hebrew school with an imitation of Kishka, his precise and finicky professorial manner, his German accent, his cough, his gloom. "Doctor *Kishka!*" cries Schlossman, and hurls himself savagely against the newsstand that belongs to the candy-store owner whom Schlossman drives just a little crazier each night. "Doctor Franz—Doctor Franz—Doctor Franz—*Kishka!*" screams Ratner, and my chubby little friend who lives upstairs from me on nothing but chocolate milk and Mallomars does not stop laughing until, as is his wont (his mother has asked me "to keep an eye on him" for just this reason), he wets his pants. Schlossman takes the occasion of Ratner's humiliation to pull the little boy's paper out of his notebook and wave it in the air—it is the assignment Dr. Kafka has just returned to us, graded; we were told to make up an alphabet of our own, out of straight lines and curved lines and dots. "That is all an alphabet is," he had explained. "That is all Hebrew is. That is all English is. Straight lines and curved lines and dots." Ratner's alphabet, for which he received a C, looks like twenty-six skulls strung in a row. I received my A for a curlicued alphabet, inspired largely (as Dr. Kafka seems to have surmised, given his comment at the top of the page) by the number eight. Schlossman received an F for forgetting even to do it—and a lot he seems to care. He is content—he is *overjoyed*—with things as they are. Just waving a piece of paper in the air and screaming, "Kishka! Kishka!" makes him deliriously happy. We should all be so lucky.

At home, alone in the glow of my goose-necked "desk" lamp (plugged after dinner into an outlet in the kitchen, my study), the vision of our refugee teacher, sticklike in a fraying three-piece blue suit, is no longer very funny—particularly after the entire beginners' Hebrew class, of which I am the most studious member, takes the name Kishka to its heart. My guilt awakens redemptive fantasies of heroism, I have them often about the "Jews in Europe." I must save him. If not me, who? The demonic Schlossman? The babyish Ratner? And if not now, when? For I have learned in the ensuing weeks that Dr. Kafka lives in a room in the house of an enderly Jewish lady on the shabby lower stretch of Avon Avenue, where the trolley still runs and the poorest of Newark's Negroes shuffle meekly up and down the street, for all they seem to know, still back in Mississippi. A *room.* And *there!* My family's apartment is no palace, but it is ours at least, so long as we pay the $38.50 a month in rent; and though our neighbors are not rich, they refuse to be poor and they refuse to be meek. Tears of shame and sorrow in my eyes, I rush into the living room to tell my parents what I have heard (though not that I heard it during a quick game of "aces up" played a minute before class against the synagogue's rear wall—worse, played directly beneath a stained-glass window embossed with the names of the dead): "My Hebrew teacher lives in a *room.*"

My parents go much further than I could imagine anybody going in the real world. Invite him to dinner, my mother says. *Here?* Of course here—Friday night; I'm sure he can stand a home-cooked meal, she says, and a little pleasant company. Meanwhile, my father gets on the phone to call my Aunt Rhoda, who lives with my grandmother and tends her and her potted plants in the apartment house at the corner of our street. For nearly two decades my father has been introducing my mother's "baby" sister, now forty, to the Jewish bachelors and widowers of north Jersey. No luck so far. Aunt Rhoda, an "interior decorator" in the dry-goods depart-ment of the Big Bear, a mammoth merchandise and produce market in industrial Elizabeth, wears falsies (this information by way of my older brother) and sheer frilly blouses, and family lore has it that she spends hours in the bathroom every day applying powder and sweeping her stiffish hair up into a dramatic pile on her head; but despite all this dash and display, she is, in my father's words, "still afraid of the facts of life." He, however, is undaunted, and administers therapy regularly and gratis: "Let 'em squeeze ya, Rhoda—it *feels* good!" I am his flesh and blood, I can reconcile myself to such scandalous talk in our kitchen—*but what will Dr. Kafka think?* Oh, but it's too late to do anything now. The massive machinery of matchmaking has been set in motion by my undiscourageable father, and the smooth engines of my proud homemaking mother's hospi-tality are already purring away. To throw my body into the works in an attempt to bring it all to a halt—well, I might as well try to bring down the New Jersey Bell Telephone Company by leaving our receiver off the hook. Only Dr. Kafka can save me now. But to my muttered invitation, he replies, with a formal bow that turns me scarlet—who has ever seen a person do such a thing outside of a movie house?—he replies that he would be *honored* to be my family's dinner guest. "My aunt," I rush to tell him, "will be there too." It appears that I have just said something mildly humorous; odd to see Dr. Kafka smile. Sighing, he says, "I will be delighted to meet her." Meet her? He's supposed to *marry* her. How do I warn him? And how do I warn Aunt Rhoda (a very great admirer of me and my marks) about his sour breath, his roomer's pallor, his Old World ways, so at odds with her up-to-dateness? My face feels as if it will ignite of its own—and spark the fire that will engulf the synagogue, Torah and all—when I see Dr. Kafka scrawl our address in his notebook, and beneath it, some words *in German.* "Good night, Dr. Kafka!" "Good night, and thank you, thank you." I turn to run, I go, but not fast enough: out on the street I hear Schlossman—that fiend!—announcing to my classmates, who are punching one another under the lamplight down from the synagogue steps (where a card game is also in progress, organized by the bar mitzvah boys): "Roth invited Kishka to his *house!* To *eat!*"

Does my father do a job on Kafka! Does he make a sales pitch for familial bliss! What it means to a man to have two fine boys and a wonderful wife! Can Dr. Kafka imagine what it's like? The thrill? The satisfaction? The pride? He tells our visitor of the network of relatives on his mother's side that are joined in a "family association" of over two hundred people located in seven states, including the state of Washington! Yes, relatives even in the Far West: here are their photographs, Dr. Kafka; this is a beautiful book we published entirely on our own for five dollars a copy, pictures of every member of the family, including infants, and a family history by "Uncle" Lichtblau, the eighty-five-year-old patriarch of the clan. This is our family newsletter, which is published twice a year and distributed nationwide to all the relatives. This, in the frame, is the menu from the banquet of the family association, held last year in a ballroom of the "Y" in Newark, in honor of my father's mother on her seventy-fifth birthday. My mother, Dr. Kafka learns, has served *six consecutive years* as the secretary-treasurer of the family association. My father has served a two-year term as president, as have each of his three brothers. We now have fourteen boys in the family in uniform. Philip writes a letter on V-mail stationery to five of his cousins in the army every single month. "Religiously," my mother puts in, smoothing my hair. "I firmly believe," says my father, "that the family is the cornerstone of everything."

Dr. Kafka, who has listened with close attention to my father's spiel, handling the various documents that have been passed to him with great delicacy and poring over them with a kind of rapt absorption that reminds me of myself over the watermarks of my stamps, now for the first time expresses himself on the subject of family; softly he says, "I agree," and inspects again the pages of our family book. "Alone," says my father, in conclusion, "alone, Dr. Kafka, is a stone." Dr. Kafka, setting the book gently down upon my mother's gleaming coffee table, allows with a nod that that is so. My mother's fingers are now turning in the curls behind my ears; not that I even know it at the time, or that she does. Being stroked is my life; stroking me, my father, and my brother is hers.

My brother goes off to a Boy Scout meeting, but only after my father has him stand in his neckerchief before Dr. Kafka and describe to him the skills he has mastered to earn each of his badges. I am invited to bring my stamp album into the living room and show Dr. Kafka my set of triangular stamps from Zanzibar. "Zanzibar!" says my father rapturously, as though I, not even ten, have already been there and back. My father accompanies Dr. Kafka and me into the "sun parlor," where my tropical fish swim in the aerated, heated, and hygienic paradise I have made for them with my weekly allowance and my Hanukkah *gelt*. I am encouraged to tell Dr. Kafka what I know about the temperament of the angelfish, the function of the catfish, and the family life of the black mollie. I know quite a bit. "All on his own he does that," my father says to Kafka. "He gives me a lecture on one of those fish, it's seventh heaven, Dr. Kafka." "I can imagine," Kafka replies.

Back in the living room my Aunt Rhoda suddenly launches into a rather recondite monologue on "Scotch plaids," intended, it would appear, for the edification of my mother alone. At least she looks fixedly at my mother while she delivers it. I have not yet seen her look directly at Dr. Kafka; she did not even turn his way at dinner when he asked how many employees there were at the Big Bear. "How would I know?" she had replied, and then continued right on conversing with my mother, about a butcher who would take care of her "under the counter" if she could find him nylons for his wife. It never occurs to me that she will not look at Dr. Kafka because she is shy—nobody that dolled up could, in my estimation, be shy. I can only think that she is outraged. *It's his breath. It's his accent. It's his age.*

I'm wrong—it turns out to be what Aunt Rhoda calls his "superiority complex." "Sitting there, sneering at us like that," says my aunt, somewhat superior now herself. "Sneering?" repeats my father, incredulous. "Sneering and laughing, yes!" says Aunt Rhoda. My mother shrugs. "*I* didn't think he was laughing." "Oh, don't worry, by himself there he was having a very good time—*at our expense.* I know the European-type man. Underneath they think they're all lords of the manor," Rhoda says. "You know something, Rhoda?" says my father, tilting his head and pointing a finger, "I think you fell in love." "With him? Are you *crazy?*" "He's too quiet for Rhoda," my mother says. "I think maybe he's a little bit of a wallflower. Rhoda is a very lively person, she needs lively people around her." "Wallflower? He's not a wallflower! He's a gentleman, that's all. And he's lonely," my father says assertively, glaring at my mother for going over his head like this *against* Kafka. My Aunt Rhoda is forty years old—it is not exactly a shipment of brand-new goods that he is trying to move. "He's a gentleman, he's an educated man, and I'll tell you something, he'd give his eyeteeth to have a nice home and a wife." "Well," says my Aunt Rhoda, "let him find one then, if he's so educated. Somebody who's his equal, who he doesn't have to look down his nose at with his big sad refugee eyes!" "Yep, she's in love," my father announces, squeezing Rhoda's knee in triumph. "With him?" she cries, jumping to her feet, taffeta crackling around her like a bonfire. "With *Kafka?*" she snorts. "I wouldn't give an old man like him the time of day!"

Dr. Kafka calls and takes my Aunt Rhoda to a movie. I am

astonished, both that he calls and that she goes; it seems there is more desperation in life than I have come across yet in my fish tank. Dr. Kafka takes my Aunt Rhoda to a play performed at the "Y." Dr. Kafka eats Sunday dinner with my grandmother and my Aunt Rhoda and, at the end of the afternoon, accepts with that formal bow of his the mason jar of barley soup that my grandmother pressed him to carry back to his room with him on the No. 8 bus. Apparently he was very taken with my grandmother's jungle of potted plants—and she, as a result, with him. Together they spoke in Yiddish about gardening. One Wednesday morning, only an hour after the store has opened for the day, Dr. Kafka shows up at the dry-goods department of the Big Bear; he tells Aunt Rhoda that he just wants to see where she works. That night he writes in his diary: "With the customers she is forthright and cheery, and so managerial about 'taste' that when I hear her explain to a chubby young bride why green and blue do not 'go,' I am myself ready to believe that Nature is in error and R. is correct."

One night, at ten, Dr. Kafka and Aunt Rhoda come by unexpectedly, and a small impromptu party is held in the kitchen—coffee and cake, even a thimbleful of whiskey all around, to celebrate the resumption of Aunt Rhoda's career on the stage. I have only heard tell of my aunt's theatrical ambitions. My brother says that when I was small she used to come to entertain the two of us on Sundays with her puppets—she was at that time employed by the W.P.A. to travel around New Jersey and put on marionette shows in schools and even in churches; Aunt Rhoda did all the voices and, with the help of a female assistant, manipulated the manikins on their strings. Simultaneously she had been a member of the Newark Collective Theater, a troupe organized primarily to go around to strike groups to perform *Waiting for Lefty.* Everybody in Newark (as I understood it) had had high hopes that Rhoda Pilchik would go on to Broadway—everybody except my grandmother. To me this period of history is as difficult to believe in as the era of the lake dwellers, which I am studying in school; people say it was once so, so I believe them, but nonetheless it is hard to grant such stories the status of the real, given the life I see around me.

Yet my father, a very avid realist, is in the kitchen, schnapps glass in hand, toasting Aunt Rhoda's success. She has been awarded one of the starring roles in the Russian masterpiece *The Three Sisters,* to be performed six weeks hence by the amateur group at the Newark "Y." Everything, announces Aunt Rhoda, everything she owes to Franz and his encouragement. One conversation—"One!" she cries gaily—and Dr. Kafka had apparently talked my grandmother out of her lifelong belief that actors are not serious human beings. And what an actor *he* is, in his own right, says Aunt Rhoda. How he had opened her eyes to the meaning of things, by reading her the famous Chekhov play—yes, read it to her from the opening line to the final curtain, all the parts, and actually left her in tears. Here Aunt Rhoda says, "Listen, listen—this is the first line of the play—it's the key to everything. Listen—I just think about what it was like the night Pop passed away, how I wondered and wondered what would become of us, what would we all do—and, and, *listen*—"

"We're listening," laughs my father. So am *I* listening, from my bed.

Pause; she must have walked to the center of the kitchen lino-leum. She says, sounding a little surprised, " 'It's just a year ago today that father died.' "

"Shhh," warns my mother, "you'll give the little one nightmares."

I am not alone in finding my aunt a "changed person" during the weeks of rehearsal. My mother says this is just what she was like as a little girl. "Red cheeks, always those hot, red cheeks—and everything exciting, even taking a bath." "She'll calm down, don't worry," says my father, "and then he'll pop the question." "Knock on wood," says my mother. "Come on," says my father, "he knows what side his bread is buttered on—he sets foot in this house, he sees what a family is all about, and believe me, he's licking his chops. Just look at him when he sits in that club chair. This is his dream come true." "Rhoda says that in Berlin, before Hitler, he had a young girl friend, years and years it went on, and then she left him. For somebody else. She got tired of waiting." "Don't worry," says my father, "when the times comes I'll give him a little nudge. He ain't going to live forever, either, and he knows it."

Then one weekend, as a respite from the "strain" of nightly rehearsals—which Dr. Kafka regularly visits, watching in his hat and coat at the back of the auditorium until it is time to accompany Aunt Rhoda home—they take a trip to Atlantic City. Ever since he arrived on these shores Dr. Kafka has wanted to see the famous boardwalk and the horse that dives from the high board. But in Atlantic City something happens that I am not allowed to know about; any discussion of the subject conducted in my presence is in Yiddish. Dr. Kafka sends Aunt Rhoda four letters in three days. She comes to us for dinner and sits till midnight crying in our kitchen. She calls the "Y" on our phone to tell them (weeping) that her mother is still ill and she cannot come to rehearsal again—she may even have to drop out of the play. No, she can't, she can't, her mother is too ill, she herself is too upset! goodbye! Then back to the kitchen table to cry. She wears no pink powder and no red lipstick, and her stiff brown hair, down, is thick and spiky as a new broom.

My brother and I listen from our bedroom, through the door that silently he has pushed ajar.

"Have you ever?" says Aunt Rhoda, weeping. "Have you *ever?*"

"Poor soul," says my mother.

"*Who?*" I whisper to my brother. "Aunt Rhoda or—"

"Shhhh!" he says. "Shut *up!*"

In the kitchen my father grunts. "Hmm. Hmm." I hear him getting up and walking around and sitting down again—and then grunting. I am listening so hard that I can hear the letters being folded and unfolded, stuck back into their envelopes, then removed to be puzzled over one more time.

"Well?" demands Aunt Rhoda. "*Well?*"

"Well what?" answers my father.

"Well, what do you want to say *now?*"

"He's *meshugeh,*" admits my father. "Something is wrong with him all right."

"But," sobs Aunt Rhoda, "no one would believe me when I said it!"

"Rhody, Rhody," croons my mother in that voice I know from those times that I have had to have stitches taken, or when I have awakened in tears, somehow on the floor beside my bed. "Rhody, don't be hysterical, darling. It's over, kitten, it's all over."

I reach across to my brother's twin bed and tug on the blanket. I don't think I've ever been so confused in my life, not even by death. The speed of things! Everything good undone in a moment! By what? "*What?*" I whisper. "*What is it?*"

My brother, the Boy Scout, smiles leeringly and, with a fierce hiss that is no answer and enough answer, addresses my bewilderment: "Sex!"

Years later, a junior at college, I receive an envelope from home containing Dr. Kafka's obituary, clipped from *The Jewish News*, the tabloid of Jewish affairs that is mailed each week to the homes of the Jews of Essex County. It is summer, the semester is over, but I have stayed on at school, alone in my room in the town, trying to write short stories. I am fed by a young English professor and his wife in exchange for babysitting; I tell the sympathetic couple, who are also loaning me the money for my rent, why it is I can't go home. My tearful fights with my father are all I can talk about at their dinner table. "Keep him away from me!" I scream at my mother. "But, darling," she asks me, "what is going on? What is this all about?"—the very same question with which I used to plague my older

brother, asked now of me and out of the same bewilderment and innocence. "He *loves* you," she explains.

   But that, of all things, seems to me precisely what is blocking my
way. Others are crushed by paternal criticism—I find myself oppressed by
his high opinion of me! Can it possibly be true (and can I possibly admit)
that I am coming to hate him for loving me so? praising me so? But that
makes no sense—the ingratitude! the stupidity! the contrariness! Being
loved is so obviously a blessing, *the* blessing, praise such a rare bequest.
Only listen late at night to my closest friends on the literary magazine and
in the drama society—they tell horror stories of family life to rival *The
Way of All Flesh*, they return shell-shocked from vacations, drift back to
school as though from the wars. What they would give to be in my golden
slippers! "What's going on?" my mother begs me to tell her; but how can I,
when I myself don't fully believe that this is happening to us, or that I am
the one who is making it happen. That they, who together cleared all
obstructions from my path, should seem now to be my final obstruction!
No wonder my rage must filter through a child's tears of shame, confusion,
and loss. All that we have constructed together over the course of two
century-long decades, and look how I must bring it down—in the name of
this tyrannical need that I call my "independence"! My mother, keeping
the lines of communication open, sends a note to me at school: "We miss
you"—and encloses the brief obituary notice. Across the margin at the
bottom of the clipping, she has written (in the same hand with which she
wrote notes to my teachers and signed my report cards, in that very same
handwriting that once eased my way in the world), "Remember poor
Kafka, Aunt Rhoda's beau?"

   "Dr. Franz Kafka," the notice reads, "a Hebrew teacher at the
Talmud Torah of the Schley Street Synagogue from 1939 to 1948, died on
June 3 in the Deborah Heart and Lung Center in Browns Mills, New
Jersey. Dr. Kafka had been a patient there since 1950. He was 70 years
old. Dr. Kafka was born in Prague, Czechoslovakia, and was a refugee
from the Nazis. He leaves no survivors."

   He also leaves no books: no *Trial*, no *Castle*, no Diaries. The dead
man's papers are claimed by no one, and disappear—all except those four
"*meshugeneh*" letters that are, to this day, as far as I know, still somewhere
in among the memorabilia accumulated by my spinster aunt, along with a
collection of Broadway Playbills, sales citations from the Big Bear, and
transatlantic steamship stickers.

   Thus all trace of Dr. Kafka disappears. Destiny being destiny, how
could it be otherwise? Does the Land Surveyor reach the Castle? Does K.
escape the judgment of the Court, or Georg Bendemann the judgment of

his father? " 'Well, clear this out now!' said the overseer, and they buried the hunger artist, straw and all." No, it simply is not in the cards for Kafka ever to become *the* Kafka—why, that would be stranger even than a man turning into an insect. No one would believe it, Kafka least of all.

———————

"I always wanted you to admire my fasting," said the hunger artist. "We do admire it," said the overseer, affably. "But you shouldn't admire it," said the hunger artist. "Well then we don't admire it," said the overseer, "but why shouldn't we admire it?" "Because I have to fast, I can't help it," said the hunger artist. "What a fellow you are," said the overseer, "and why can't you help it?" "Because," said the hunger artist, lifting his head a little and speaking, with his lips pursed, as if for a kiss, right into the overseer's ear, so that no syllable might be lost, "because I couldn't find the food I liked. If I had found it, believe me, I should have made no fuss and stuffed myself like you or anyone else." These were his last words, but in his dimming eyes remained the firm though no longer proud persuasion that he was still continuing to fast.

(Franz Kafka, "A Hunger Artist")

JOHN N. McDANIEL

Distinctive Features
of Roth's Artistic Vision

$\mathbf{I}$n examining the "circumstances of
ordinary life," Roth has employed a wide range of artistic techniques
resulting in a fictional canon notable for its variety. In fact, the diversity
of Roth's fiction has generated evident difficulty in assessing Roth's intention and achievement as a writer of fiction. Certainly most critics acknowledge Philip Roth as a major talent, as one who has been keenly
responsive to the human condition as it is revealed in contemporary
American experience. Richard Locke, in a recent review of Updike's
Rabbit Redux, makes this point succinctly:

> Who are the novelists who have tried to keep a grip on our experience as
> we've wobbled along in the past decade or two, the writers to whom we
> turn to find out something of where we are and what we're feeling, the
> writers who give the secular news report? I'd suggest that there are five:
> Saul Bellow, Norman Mailer, Bernard Malamud, Philip Roth—and John
> Updike himself.

Despite such acknowledgment, however, the critical community has been
divided in its response to Roth as a significant contemporary author.
Critics have taken stances toward his achievement that are as diverse as
the fiction itself: he has been called an anti-semite and a Jewish moralist, a
romantic writer and a realistic writer, a polemicist, a satirist, a mannerist,
a sentimentalist, and a liar; he has been praised for having "a clear and
critical social vision," condemned for having a "distorted" view of society,

From *The Fiction of Philip Roth.* Copyright © 1974 by John N. McDaniel. Haddonfield
House.

and accused of entertaining an "exclusively personal" vision of life that does not include society at all. Whereas Alfred Kazin recently spoke so confidently of what he calls Saul Bellow's "signature," it seems that from the collective viewpoint of the critical community Roth's mark has been something of an indecipherable scrawl.

Some attempts have been made to place Roth in relation to other contemporary American writers, but such attempts have often been accompanied by a distortion of clearly observable facts emerging from Roth's fiction and artistic creed; too, such attempts have resulted in a blurring of Roth's most distinctive characteristics as a writer of fiction. For example, Theodore Solotaroff joins Roth with Bellow and Malamud under the banner of Jewish moralists—writers who "feel and think with their Jewishness and [who] use the thick concreteness of Jewish moral experience to get at the dilemmas and decisions of the heart generally." The difficulty with Solotaroff's assessment, however, is that it was made on the basis of only one collection of Roth's fiction, *Goodbye, Columbus*; furthermore, Solotaroff's assertion is vitiated by Roth's subsequent "non-Jewish" fiction and his expressed uncertainty about Jewish values, Jewish morality, and his indebtedness to the Jewish heritage. Moving away from a Jewish point of reference, Helen Weinberg, David L. Stevenson, and Albert J. Guerard suggest that Roth can be viewed, along with Mailer, Malamud, Salinger, and Gold, as a disciple of Saul Bellow, or at least as one who writes in the activist mode initiated in America by Bellow. Although this assessment is helpful in pointing out a shared concern for the plight of the self in the American experience, such a view does not account for Roth's strong commitment to social and political concerns, nor does it account for the shift in Roth's fiction *toward* the victim-hero and *away* from the activist hero—a shift that is the reverse of the stages of development through which Bellow, Malamud, Gold, and Salinger have gone. Certainly Irving and Harriet Deer are correct in saying, "If Roth had to make a choice, he would side with Ralph Ellison as opposed to Salinger, Malamud, Bellow, and Gold. . . ."

Despite general affinities among Roth, Salinger, Malamud, Bellow, and Gold, one can approach Roth's "signature" most effectively by contrasting him to these contemporaries. Such an approach is suggested by the perceptible shift toward victimization, absurdity, and satire in Roth's presentation of character. Weinberg has argued persuasively that the pattern of development in the fiction of Bellow, Malamud, Mailer, and Gold is from the closed-structure tale to the open-structure tale and from the victim-hero to the activist hero. "The turning is away from the cognitive victim-hero in a world unavailable to reasonable minds, toward the activist hero, the seeker open to all life-mysteries." But to suggest, as Weinberg, Stevenson, and Guerard do, that Roth's fiction has taken such a turn or that he is under the influence of Bellow's activist hero is to fly in the teeth of Roth's own statements and of his emphatic if not total shift toward victimization and absurdity in his fiction. Roth has indeed responded favorably to some of Bellow's fiction, but on the basis of Roth's public statements about Bellow's work, we might well assume that the early, realistic presentations in *Dangling Man* and *The Victim,* not the activist stance that Bellow takes in *The Adventures of Augie March* and *Henderson the Rain King,* most appeal to Roth. Although Roth has disparaged the latter two activist works, he goes so far as to say that "*The Victim* is a book which isn't as well-known as it should be, but I think it's perhaps one of the great books written in America in the 20th century." M. Gilbert Porter has recently said, "Saul Bellow's Herzog seems to speak for the representative new hero in American fiction when he exclaims to the lawyer handling his divorce case, 'I'm not going to be a victim. I hate the victim bit.' " If, as Porter says, "The movement away from the 'victim bit' seems clearly the direction of the recent American novel," one might conclude that Roth has been swimming upstream, against the main current of contemporary American fiction. Such a conclusion at least has the advantage of clarifying the outlines of Roth's fiction, outlines that have been unfortunately blurred by a facile inclusion of Roth in the coterie of Jewish-American writers led by Bellow, Malamud, Salinger, Mailer and Gold.

    The uniqueness of Roth's "signature" is intimately associated with his commitment to social realism, to a willingness to confront the community—its manners and its mores—as subject for his art. The confrontation between the hero (activist or victim) and world, between private and public realms, between "un-isolated" individuals and the shaping forces of general life, is the confrontation that is central to the realistic mode—and the fiction of Philip Roth. Certainly many critics have detected in Roth's fiction a noticeable attention to manners, to moral issues, and to literary realism; too often, however, Roth's most characteristic mode has been dismissed in the cavalier manner of Irving Malin, who complained that Roth's "loyalty to social realism is unfortunate," and that, "unlike Malamud, Roth is also comfortable, too comfortable, with . . . realism." It is my contention that we can best assess Roth's artistry by viewing him, rather broadly, as a writer whose artistic intentions are "moral," whose method is realistic, and whose subject is the self in society.

    Given Solotaroff's contention that Roth's sensibility is embedded in a Jamesian concern for motives and for what Trilling calls "moral realism," it is altogether possible to think that Roth writes, in part, to fill a void that Trilling pointed out in 1948:

> Perhaps at no other time has the enterprise of moral realism ever been so much needed, for at no other time have so many people committed themselves to moral righteousness. We have the books that point out the bad conditions, that praise us for taking progressive attitudes. We have no books that raise questions in our minds not only about conditions but about ourselves, that lead us to refine our motives and ask what might lie behind our good impulses.

As our examination of Roth's fiction has shown, the question of what lies behind "good impulses" is one that virtually every major character in his fiction asks. The crises depicted in Roth's fiction are not so much ontological as they are moral, for although the character may begin with the question of identity and selfhood, he is likely to conclude with the questions of Neil Klugman, Gabe Wallach, and Peter Tarnopol: what do I owe to my fellow man, and how do I explain my actions toward him? What is my relation to society, and what are the dangers of the moral life? To what extent have I been victimized by false ideals and self-deceptions grounded in the society of which I am an ineluctable part?

Inevitably, when we hear such questions we think immediately of Tolstoy, Conrad, Dostoevski, Gogol—the great European novelists—and Henry James, America's most prominent novelist of manners and moral realism; nor is it surprising that allusions to these novelists and their works appear frequently in Roth's fiction. For example, Henry James plays an important role in *Letting Go*. Gabe Wallach spends a good part of his graduate school life writing a dissertation on James—so much so that when the novel opens, Gabe declares that his "one connection with the world of feeling was not the world itself but Henry James." In fact, James's *The Portrait of a Lady* serves as a link between Gabe and the Herzes (Gabe meets Libby as a consequence of loaning the novel to the Herzes, and the affinities between Libby Herz and Isabel Archer lead Gabe into a long discussion of the realistic technique and moral concern of James's work). Certainly Murray Kempton is correct in seeing a Jamesian essence brooding over *Letting Go*, but one might go even further to say that the novel presents characters who are engaged in a Jamesian "ordeal of consciousness" (to use Dorothea Krook's phrase for James's fiction), and that Roth is clearly interested in the working out of moral and psychological problems involved in such an ordeal. The burdens of responsibility, the clash between the actual world and the "invented reality" that grows out of what one "sees and feels," the moral difficulties of "letting go" (a phrase that Roth borrowed from Mrs. Gereth in *The Spoils of Poynton,* who tells Fleda Vetch, "Only let yourself go, darling—only let yourself go!")—all these are concerns that Roth has in common not only with James but with other European novelists of manners and moral realism as well. Roth underscores this point when he declares,

> As for a moral concern, that I feel is certainly central to the novel I wrote and I care most about—*Letting Go.* Is that Jewish? I do not know. I feel that two writers whom I care a good deal about, and who have influenced me considerably, although it may not be apparent, are Tolstoy and Henry James. The center of both seems to me to be a very strong moral concern. Neither is a Jew. So whether the moral concern in my work comes from the fact that it is fiction, or the fact that I am Jewish, I simply do not know. It is very difficult for a writer to speak about his own sources, and one winds up either being wrong or sounding terribly pretentious. I do know that there are certain writers, like Gogol and Dostoievski, to whom I respond with a lot of feeling. . . .

The moral concerns in Roth's fiction, its attempts to get at the truths of the heart generally, have been pointed out by several critics. I should only like to add that Roth gives the basis of the central moral problem that recurs in his fiction when he says that the condition of men is that they are strangers to one another, and "because *that* is our condition . . . it is incumbent upon us not to love one another—which is to deny the truth about ourselves—but to practice no violence and no treachery upon one another, which is to struggle with the darkest forces within ourselves." Here is a touchstone with which we can evaluate the moral condition of virtually every character in Roth's fiction—from the "soul-battered" Ozzie Freedman to the treacherous Tricky Dixon.

Perhaps the most significant aspect of Roth's moral interests is that they extend clearly into his conception of art (and here the affinity between Roth and such writers as Henry James is at its strongest). In Roth's view, "It is the job of fiction to redeem [the] stereotype and give it its proper weight and balance in the world." He goes on to assert:

> I do not think that literature, certainly not in my country and in my time, has direct social and political consequences. I think that it alters consciousness and I think that its goal is to alter consciousness, not to alter the housing problem or Jewish-Gentile relations and so on. Its task and its purpose is to create shifts in what one thinks is reality and what the reader does. When the reader then goes on to act differently in his life, as a result of reading your story, I do not know how responsible you are for his actions. I think that what you are responsible for is the

> honesty of the portrayal, for the authenticity of your vision. If that is
> distorted you are a bad artist. To sum up, I do not think that literature is
> a call to action; it speaks for the consciousness.

Roth clearly embraces James's belief that fictional experience "is our apprehension and our measure of what happens to us as social creatures." Furthermore, Roth ventures the hope that "literary investigation may even be a way to redeem the facts, to give them the weight and value that they should have in the world, rather than the disproportionate significance they probably have for some misguided or vicious people"—an observation that illuminates not only the stereotypic attitudes Roth attacks in his early fiction but also the satiric thrusts in his later fiction. In speaking of the satire in *Portnoy's Complaint*, "On the Air" and *Our Gang*, Roth insisted that "writing satire is essentially a literary, not a political, act," for, in his thinking, "satire is moral rage transformed into comic art." After all, asks Roth, isn't "challenging moral certainties a good part of what literature aspires to do?"

Literature as a call to consciousness is, of course, precisely the note struck by James and Conrad. Roth has brought a similar notion to bear when critics from the Jewish community state that he is doing the Jews a disservice or when other critics recoil from the pointed social and political satire in his fiction:

> . . . At this point in human history, when power seems the ultimate end
> of government, and "success" the goal of individual lives; when the value
> of humility is in doubt, and the nerve to fail hardly to be seen at all;
> when a willful blindness to man's condition can only precipitate further
> anguishes and miseries—at this point, with the murder of six million
> people fixed forever in our imaginations, I cannot help but believe that
> there is a higher moral purpose for the Jewish writer . . . than the
> improvement of public relations.

For Roth, as for James, fiction not only treats moral issues, but has the purpose of elevating and liberating the reader's social and moral consciousness through realistic examination of "man's condition." Just as "those of us who are willing to be taught, and who needed to be, have been made by *Invisible Man* less stupid than we were about Negro lives," so can the stereotypes of Jewish malingerers, Jewish mothers, Jewish family life, and Protestant Midwestern fathers, mothers, sons and daughters be put into new perspectives—for "the stereotype as often arises from ignorance as from malice."

A strong social and moral consciousness, coupled with a readily evident persuasion toward a realistic portrayal of man in society, points toward Roth's distinctiveness as a contemporary American author, for it is the prevailing opinion that such concerns have never been central to the American literary tradition. In 1948 Lionel Trilling asserted, "The fact is that American writers of genius have not turned their minds to society. . . . In America in the nineteenth century, Henry James was alone in knowing that to scale the moral and aesthetic heights in the novel one had to use the ladder of social observation." Trilling's contention that "Americans have a kind of resistance to looking closely at society" is not a startling observation, most critics of the American novel would agree. Walter Allen maintains that "The classic American novels have dealt not so much with the lives of men in society as with the life of solitary man, man alone and wrestling with himself." R. W. B. Lewis sees in writers like Bellow, Salinger, and Mailer a continuation of what Walt Whitman called the "principle of individuality, the pride and centripetal isolation of a human being in himself—identity—personalism." Mark Schorer speaks of the representative American novel as the "evocative novel," one that, in opposition to the social novel, demonstrates that the "gap between the individual human being and the social circumstances in which he exists has become hazardously wide." The point to be made here is that the American novelistic tradition, unlike the European tradition, has not sustained a concern for man in society, and as Jonathan Baumbach says, "The novel of manners has always been, with the notable exception of Henry James, a secondary and somewhat artificial tradition in American literature. . . ." Certainly Roth is not a proponent of the documentary social novel or a novel of manners in the European sense of the term (for, as Trilling persuasively argues in "Art and Fortune," such a novel is not possible in America); nonetheless, Roth's relation to his contemporaries is more sharply defined if we consider him as a social realist—as a writer, that is, who does not yield to the romantic impulse as defined by Chase, Allen, Lewis, and others. Roth has been characteristically associated with such Jewish-American writers as Mailer, Salinger, Bellow, Malamud, and Gold, when in fact his closest associates among American authors are Sinclair Lewis, F. Scott Fitzgerald, John O'Hara, John P. Marquand— writers who, as James Tuttleton demonstrates, are primarily "concerned with social conventions as they impinge upon character."

Although Roth has been tantalized by the figure of the essentially romantic activist hero—as is suggested by his presentation of Neil Klugman and Gabe Wallach—he ultimately cannot accept the hero who quests for selfhood outside the boundaries of society and its manifold pressures. If this is so, we might suspect that Roth rejects the typical heroes of contemporary literature—heroes that Joseph Waldmeir describes in his essay "Quest Without Faith":

> Whether by force or by choice (since a too great concern with the problems of existence in an age of conformity can push one willy-nilly outside the pale) the heroes of the new American novel are disaffiliates. Saul Bellow's Augie March and Henderson are both irrevocably separated from society. So too are Norman Mailer's Sergius O'Shaugnessy and Mikey Lovett, Nelson Algren's Frankie Machine and Dove Linkhorn, Bernard Malamud's Frank Alpine, J. D. Salinger's Holden Caulfield, William Styron's Cass Kinsolving and Peyton and Milton Loftis, Herbert Gold's Bud Williams. . . .

When we look at Roth's criticisms of his contemporaries, what we discover is that it is precisely this disaffiliated hero who earns Roth's displeasure. Bellow is right in stating that a writer reads the fiction of his contemporaries "with a special attitude," but in Roth's case the attitude itself is of interest, for it emphasizes the most salient features of his artistic creed. In "Writing American Fiction," Roth undertakes a casual but nonetheless illuminating examination of Bellow, Malamud, Salinger, Mailer, Gold, and Styron, and in so doing he places his own distinctive artistic concerns in bold relief.

Of these six writers, Roth feels the greatest affinity with Salinger, primarily because Salinger's fictional world, "in all its endless and marvelous detail, is decidedly credible." Roth is often touched by the lovingness that is attributed to Seymour Glass, and he feels that the note of despair in Salinger's fiction, dramatized by Seymour's committing suicide and Holden's being institutionalized, is an understandable one. Ultimately, however, Roth is at odds with Salinger's fictional heroes and with his fictional strategy. His major complaint against Salinger is that he avoids confronting the recognizable social world. Salinger's conception of mysticism—which, in Roth's view, is based on the premise that the deeper one goes into the world the further one gets away from it—is symptomatic of Salinger's turning away from the community: "For all the loving handling of the world's objects, for all the reverence of life and feeling, there seems to me, in the Glass family stories as in *The Catcher*, a spurning of life as it is lived in this world, in this reality. . . ." This spurning of life, in Roth's view, is conveyed by Salinger's fictional heroes, who have learned to live in this world by not living in it. Roth concludes, "Since madness is undesirable and sainthood, for most of us, out of the question, the problem of how to live *in* this world is by no means answered; unless the answer is that one cannot."

Roth feels that the spurning of life as it is actually lived in society is evident, too, in the fiction of Bernard Malamud. *The Natural* is a book about baseball, but "it is not baseball as it is played in Yankee Stadium," just as the Jews of *The Magic Barrel* and *The Assistant* "are not the Jews of New York City or Chicago." Roth discovers in Malamud's fiction a world "which has a kind of historical relationship to our own, but is by no means a replica of it." To clarify his point, Roth goes on to say that the Jews in Malamud's fiction

> are a kind of invention, a metaphor to stand for certain human possibilities and certain human promises, and I find myself further inclined to believe this when I read of a statement attributed to Malamud which goes, "All men are Jews." In fact we know this is not so; even the men who are Jews aren't sure they're Jews. But Malamud, as a writer of fiction, has not shown specific interest in the anxieties and dilemmas and corruptions of the modern American Jew, the Jew we think of as characteristic of our times; rather, his people live in a timeless depression and a placeless Lower East Side; their society is not affluent, their predicament not cultural.

Roth does not mean to say that Malamud has avoided moral issues or turned away from the problems of being human; in fact, the contrary is true. But Roth insists that Malamud has not engaged the recognizable social life that the realistic writer thrives on, for Malamud "does not—or has not yet—found the contemporary scene a proper or sufficient backdrop for his tales of heartlessness and heartache, of suffering and regeneration."

In Roth's view, Salinger and Malamud are two of America's best authors, yet their works seem to be curiously out of touch with the actual world. Neither writer "has managed to put his finger on what is most significant in the struggle going on today between the self (all selves, not just the writer's) and the culture." In the fiction of Saul Bellow and William Styron Roth finds a similar inability or unwillingness to confront the social world in all of its recognizable aspects. In Roth's opinion, the fiction of Bellow and Styron, peopled by heroes who affirm life in foreign and unrealistic climes, is further evidence that our best writers have avoided examining American public life. The end of *Henderson the Rain King* (where Henderson is pictured galloping around a Newfoundland airfield) makes a deep impression on Roth, for here he sees "a man who finds energy and joy in an imagined Africa, and celebrates it on an unpeopled, icebound vastness." Roth complains of a similar, if somewhat more muted ending in Styron's *Set This House on Fire*. ". . . At the end of the book, for all his disgust with what the American public life does to a man's private life, Kinsolving, like Henderson, has come back to America, having opted for existence." But, Roth goes on to say, "the America that we find him in seems to me to be the America of his childhood, and, if only in a metaphoric way, of all our childhoods." Roth is right in saying that "using a writer for one's own purposes is of course to be unfair to him"; nevertheless, Roth's objection to the novelistic strategies of Bellow and Styron certainly places his own attitudes clearly in front of us: the author must confront the social world squarely if he is to describe human character faithfully, and affirmation achieved through geographic displacement or metaphoric evasion is, finally, no affirmation at all.

Herbert Gold and Norman Mailer demonstrate a quite different "spurning of life" in their fiction, for what one discovers, Roth argues, is that both writers adopt a pose—with the result that elation and affirmation, on the one hand, and anger and disgust, on the other, arise from the personality of the artist rather than from the fiction itself. In Gold Roth perceives a writer whose concern is with his own individuality rather than with the individuality of his fictional characters, and there is "a good deal of delight in the work of his own hand. And, I think, with the hand itself." Hence, in works like Gold's *Therefore Be Bold* and *Love and Like* the reader is confronted with "a writer in competition with his own fiction," with the result that "reality" is replaced by personality—"and not the personality of the character described, but of the writer who is doing the describing." Roth detects in Salinger's novelistic strategy a similar inclination to place the writer's persona (Buddy Glass) in the reader's line of vision—but in Gold's fiction the technique is employed not as an act of desperation but rather as an act of willful and mannered euphoria that has little to do with the reality of Gold's fictional realm. In his recent work, Norman Mailer, like Gold, has employed "life as a substitute for fiction"—particularly in *Advertisements for Myself*, "an infuriating, self-indulgent, boisterous, mean book." Roth maintains that the novelistic strategy adopted by Mailer is indicative of the contemporary author's plight, for just as Salinger, Malamud, Styron, and Gold have in various ways spurned life as it is actually lived, so does Mailer give up on making an imaginative assault on the American experience.

Roth's remarks about his contemporaries are quite revealing and, in light of his artistic creed, certainly understandable. In "Writing American Fiction" Roth is ostensibly pressing home the thesis that the present social world is not as manageable or suitable as it once may have been, a thesis that underscores Roth's awareness of social and political absurdity. Equally revealing, however, is Roth's charge that some of our best American writers have rejected the moral, social, and realistic requirements of art that he himself is committed to—a point that, perhaps ironically,

Bellow also makes: "American novelists are not ungenerous, far from it, but as their view of society is fairly shallow, their moral indignation is non-specific. What seems to be lacking is a firm sense of a common world, a coherent community. . . ." Despite this concern for a lack of moral and social commitment by American artists, however, Bellow, in a 1968 response to "Writing American Fiction," suggests where the writers of activist fiction and Roth part company:

> The modern writer specialises in grotesque facts, and he cannot compete with the news, with "life itself." Perhaps he should begin to think of interesting himself in something other than the grotesque. There is good reason to think that absurdities are traveling in two directions, from art into life and from life into art. We cannot continue to ignore Oscar Wilde's law. "Nature imitates art." Roth is right if—and only if—fiction cannot leave current events without withering away.

In contending that modern writers cannot compete with current events, with "life itself," Bellow dramatizes the very real differences between the sensibility of writers of activist fiction and the sensibility of Philip Roth. Following the major American (romantic) tradition, Bellow, Mailer, Salinger, and Gold have explored the human condition through characters who have cut themselves off from the grotesque facts of the recognizable American public life; Roth, on the other hand, following the tenets of social realism, has explored the human condition through characters who have descended into the midst of the absurdities of the American experience. Roth is under no delusion, however, that social realism is either a prevailing or an easily manageable literary mode, nor does he regard the moral function of art as a light burden, easily cast aside:

> Fiction is not written to affirm the principles and beliefs that everybody seems to hold, nor does it seek to guarantee us of the appropriateness of our feelings. The world of fiction, in fact, frees us from the circumscriptions that the society places upon feeling; one of the greatnesses of the art is that it allows both the writer and the reader to respond to experience in ways not always available in day-to-day conduct. . . . We may not even know that we have such a range of feelings and responses until we have come into contact with the work of fiction. . . . Ceasing for a while to be upright citizens, we drop into another layer of consciousness. And this dropping, this expansion of moral consciousness, this exploration of moral fantasy, is of considerable value to a man and to society.

Roth's assault on the American experience—his exploration of moral fantasy, his concern for moral consciousness, his willingness to confront the grander social and political phenomena of our time—is, I think, the most significant aspect of his art. Despite the diversity of Roth's fiction, despite the variety of themes, values, and characters that emerge from his novels and short stories, we see an abiding faith beneath Roth's pessimism, a faith that leads him to answer one of his critics by saying, "I find that Mr. Liptzin's view of the universe is negative; I think of my own as positive." Roth has demonstrated a willingness to explore the limits of his artistic creed with a deeply felt concern for man and society, a concern that is detectable beneath his ponderous realistic novels and his most vitriolic satire. It is that concern, I think, that leads Roth, in his most recent fiction, to employ some of the same artistic strategies that he has criticized in his fellow writers. *Our Gang*, for example, comes perilously close to substituting "life for art," a point that is emphasized by Roth's preface to the May, 1973 "Watergate Edition" of the novel; too, works such as "On the Air," *The Breast*, and *The Great American Novel* utilize fantasy and metaphor, often at the expense of credibility (how seriously can we take a character who turns into a breast, it might be asked—and how realistic is *that?*). That much is frighteningly recognizable even in Roth's most recent fiction is, however, Roth's best defense against charges of inconsistency, and certainly Roth has remained hell-bent (*Our Gang* makes the term an irresistible one to use) on putting his finger on our cultural predicament, on sending us a secular news report, however grotesque the facts of "life itself" may be.

Writing in 1959, the year that *Goodbye, Columbus* was published, Alfred Kazin posed a challenge to which Roth has responded more sensitively than perhaps any other writer of the past decade:

> What many writers feel today is that reality is not much more than what *they* say it is. This is a happy discovery only for genius. . . . There has probably never been a time when the social nature of the novel was so much at odds with the felt lack of order in the world about us. In the absence of what used to be *given*, the novelist must create a wholly imaginary world—or else he must have the courage, in an age when personal willfulness rules in every sphere, to say that we are *not* alone, that the individual does not have to invent human values but only to rediscover them. The novel as a form will always demand a common-sense respect for life and interest in society.

The shape of Roth's future fiction is as indeterminate and unpredictable as the shape of our future society, but one can say, with assurance, that in the past decade Roth has maintained an abiding respect for life and an unyielding interest in society. Above all, he has had the courage, in an age of personal willfulness, to say that we are not alone.

SANFORD PINSKER

The Comedy That 'Hoits':
"The Breast"

 T *he Breast* is a static novel, one even
more severely limited by its controlling gimmick than *Our Gang*. But this
time the initial premise is literary rather than political, and the result is
comic allegory rather than satirical invective. As the book jacket baldly
declares: "It is the story of the man who turned into a female breast." For
all of Portnoy's wild flights into grotesque fantasy, there was enough about
him that touched common ground. In his case, the built-in constraints of
an analyst's couch struck readers as exactly the right locale for a
confession-complaint.

In *The Breast*, however, that necessary level of particularity Roth
had once insisted upon gives way to a more symbolic "hoit." By this I
mean to suggest two things: first, that *The Breast*, like *Our Gang*, is more
"exercise" than novel, and, second, that its very "symbolism" (whether
taken comically, seriously or on some ironic level in between) overwhelms
more mundane, but essential, elements like "story." Moreover, I am
convinced that prolonged discussions about *The Breast* as a contemporary
reworking of Franz Kafka's famous story "The Metamorphosis" or Nicolai
Gogol's equally famous "The Nose" will not quite do. Surely Roth means
to call our attention to them, but the recognition that he is sharing in a
highbrow allusion is not quite the same thing as critically judging the
work of art at hand. All puns aside, *The Breast* must support itself.

Besides, Roth had sounded echoes to Kafka earlier: In *Portnoy's
Complaint*, for example, one of Alex's tirades includes the following:

From *The Comedy That "Hoits."* Copyright © 1975 The Curators of the University of
Missouri; University of Missouri Press.

Say you're sorry, Alex. Say you're sorry! *Apologize!* Yeah, for what? What have I done now? Hey, I'm hiding under my bed, my back to the wall, refusing to say I'm sorry, refusing, too, to come out and take the consequences. *Refusing!* And she is after me with a broom, trying to sweep my rotten carcass into the open. Why, shades of Gregor Samsa! Hello Alex, goodbye Franz!

To be sure, Kafka's anguished, often unfinished and always puzzling fictions are a shorthand of modernity itself. His nightmares speak to an age growing accustomed to dark dreams, one burdened by bureaucracy and troubled with ill-defined guilts. In an intriguing essay entitled "Looking at Kafka," Roth broods over a photograph of Kafka taken in 1924 (when Kafka was forty) and the coincidences that draw one man, uneasily, to another. At the time the essay was written, Roth was also forty. "Looking at Kafka" is a curious hybrid: not quite literary criticism, although Roth has a deep understanding of Kafka's life and art, and not quite an impressionist memoir about himself. Both elements are there, intertwined by a complex fate and each shedding light upon the other.

Roth focuses on the Kafka of 1924 because that was the crucial year he *"found himself transformed in his bed into a father, a writer, and a Jew."* Philip Roth's latest book, My Life as a Man, is a bitter account of a similar (albeit, largely failed) transformation. Even more importantly, Roth turns to Kafka for a model of guilt metamorphosed into artful play, for sagas of "hoit" that can coexist with a comic vision. It was only when Roth realized that "this morbid preoccupation with punishment and guilt was all so funny" that a book like Portnoy's Complaint became possible. And, if an author's own words can be believed, it was Kafka, more than any other writer who made the difference:

> I was strongly influenced by this book [Portnoy's Complaint] by a sit-down comic named Franz Kafka and the very funny bit he does called "The Metamorphosis." . . . there is certainly a personal element in the book, but not until I had got hold of guilt, you see, as a *comic idea,* did I begin to feel myself lifting free and clear of my last book, and my old concerns.

In The Breast, Roth turns fabulator, giving his kinship with Kafka full comic rein. His contemporary version of Gregor Samsa's strange metamorphosis—Alan David Kepesh turning into a female breast rather than a beetle—translates the angst of one age into the self-conscious, stridently flip posture of another. The result is more an academic in-joke than a *roman à clef* as Kepesh, a professor of comparative literature, becomes the unwitting victim of too much "teaching," too intensely done. As Kepesh hypothesizes, what has happened to him

. . . might be my way of *being* a Kafka, being a Gogol, being a Swift. They could *envision* these marvelous transformations—they were artists. They had the language and those obsessive fictional brains. I didn't. So I had to live the thing.
(*The Breast*, New York: Holt, Rinehart and Winston, 1972, p. 72)

Roth has visited enough academic watering holes in the last few years (interestingly enough, "Looking at Kafka" was dedicated to his students at the University of Pennsylvania) to know the type well. If *The Breast* is, among other things, a highly ingenious way of biting the hands that have fed him, it is hardly an unusual phenomenon, given the new patronage universities provide. In any event, to Kepesh's list of impressive "theys," we must now, presumably, add the name of Philip Roth.

Granted, not all the jokes in *The Breast* are so unabashedly high-brow. There are moments when Kepesh's wit turns inward, when a capacity for black humor takes the edge off even *his* predicament:

I don't foresee a miracle . . . I suspect it's a little late for that, and so it is not with such hope beating eternally in the breast that the breast continues to want to exist.

(21)

And, too, there are the comic visits of Kepesh's father, formerly the owner of a hotel in South Fallsburg, New York, called the Hungarian Royale. Now retired, he visits his son, apparently (or is it, perhaps, *resolutely?*) oblivious to what has transpired:

. . . seated in a chair that is drawn up close to my nipple, he recounts the current adventures of people who were our guests when I was a boy. Remember Abrams the milliner? Remember Cohen the chiropodist? Remember Rosenheim with the card tricks and the Cadillac? Yes, yes, yes, I think so. Well, this one is dying, this one has moved to California, this one has a son who married an Egyptian.

(26)

All this while he, of course, has a son who turned into a breast! But it is hard to sustain the evasive smalltalk (for Roth as well as Mr. Kepesh), even in a book of less than eighty, wide-margined pages.

The real question in this book—Kafkaesque seriousness aside and bits of black humor to the contrary—is "Why a breast?" Not since that idiotic exercise in pornography called *Deep Throat* has anyone played so fast and loose with human biology. Blaming it on something called a "massive hormonal influx," Kepesh is presumably converted

. . . into a mammary gland disconnected from any human form, a mammary gland such as could only appear, one would have thought, in a

dream or a Dali painting. They tell me that I am now an organism with
the general shape of a football, or a dirigible.

(12)

At one point Kepesh speculates about the possibility of it all being
a "wish," one all too literally fulfilled. Given Portnoy's breakdown and
the psychiatric case studies to follow (Smitty in *The Great American Novel*;
Peter Tarnopol in *My Life as a Man*), Kepesh, too, looks like a prime
candidate for the looney bin. But he vigorously denies psychological
explanations of his "breast"—and advises readers to resist them as well:

> No, the victim does not subscribe to the wish-fulfillment theory, and I
> advise you not to, neat and fashionable and delightfully punitive as it
> may be. Reality is grander than that. Reality has more style. There. For
> those of you who cannot live without one, a moral to this tale. "Reality
> has style," concludes the embittered professor who became a female
> breast. Go, you sleek, self-satisfied Houhynhnms, and moralize on that!
> (34)

If I am right about *The Breast*'s mode as one of comic allegory, it is
"allegory" of a very playful, post-Modern, sort. To talk pedantically about,
say, the breast fetish in American culture (see Woody Allen's delightful
spoof in *Everything You Wanted to Know About Sex*) or about Kafkan
themes in current fiction is to miss both the pain and the wit of Roth's
novella.

What *The Breast* retains, however, is that strident voice generously
sprinkled with exclamation points. Predictably enough, it cries out for
more sex, more ingeniously performed. Not that Kepesh enjoys sex, for all
his escalating demands and kinky tastes; like other Roth protagonists, he
is grimmest in the bedroom. Moreover, as fashionable paradox would have
it (for example, those considered "insane" are, often, saner than you or I),
Kepesh insists that *he* is not the abnormal one. After all, in a world where
a person can wake up as a female breast, what could make sense? Therefore, when Kepesh suggests that a prostitute have sex with him (Claire,
his ex-mistress is, it seems, too prudish), normal assumptions about the
"grotesque" are up for grabs:

> Why shouldn't I have it [sex] if I want it! It's insane otherwise! I should
> be allowed to have it all day long! This is no longer ordinary life and I
> am not going to pretend that it is! *You* want me to be *ordinary—you*
> expect me to be *ordinary* in this condition! I'm supposed to be a sensible
> man—when I am like this! But that's crazy on your part, Doctor! . . .
> Why shouldn't I have anything and everything I can think of *every single*
> *minute of the day* if that can transport me from this miserable hell! . . .

Instead I lie here being sensible! That's the madness, Doctor, *being sensible*!

(36–37)

I suspect Roth has been itching to make such adolescent proclamations (italics and all) for some time. Instant gratifications—rather than normal operating procedures—are the only way one can respond to the mad world as it is. Given the political climate and/or the residues of societal repression, *Our Gang* and *The Breast* pass themselves off as "liberating" acts. But they are the product of writing fiction in a shoddy cultural moment, one which forgets that authentic freedom is more difficult to achieve, that even expressing the "hoit" requires deeper thought. Nonetheless, with these matters finally off his chest—*The Breast* removed as it were—Roth could begin to deal with the heart as well as the erogenous zones.

MARY ALLEN

When She Was Good
She Was Horrid

Philip Roth writes brilliantly of ob-
sessives—Eli, the fanatic, and others compelled by orthodox forms of
Jewishness; Alexander Portnoy, obsessed with masturbation to compensate
for everything his mother has outlawed and the puritanism of his heritage
generally; the bisexual hangup of Alan Kepesh, blossoming into a female
breast, metaphor of repressed desires. And in both his comic and his sober
writing Roth reveals an obsession with women's power over men. Being
intensely concerned with his characters' morality, as most Jewish writers
have been, he shows the great wrong of a woman's wielding her power in
the name of goodness. Like the characters of Kafka, who greatly influenced Roth, most of his men are so emotionally bound to those in power
that even though they hate and fear them, they do in fact believe them to
be right, and thus, good. It is through this quality of appearing "good"
that the woman obtains her power. As one of Roth's most penetrating
critics, Theodore Solotaroff, points out, Roth is preoccupied with a woman's power over a man, "by a kind of moral one-upmanship that attaches
his virtue, indeed his humanity, to his willingness to satisfy her needs,
however unending or corrupt these may be."

Portnoy's Complaint gives the super caricature of the Jewish mother,
perhaps of all mothers. This is the home-life version of the ball-breaker,
who is not unlike the middle-aged castrators of James Purdy and the
epitome of female monsters as the career woman, Nurse Ratched. All the

From *The Necessary Blankness: Women in Major American Fiction of the Sixties.* Copyright
© 1976 by the Board of Trustees of the University of Illinois. University of Illinois Press.

ugliness of the type gushes forth with Mrs. Portnoy, all from her sick son Alexander's point of view. There is clearly enough power in Roth's development of this type to indicate more than a mere literary interest in it. But through the detachment of caricature, the method of the fabulators, and the technique of allowing the analysand the couch to himself for the entire course of the book, a one-sided and prejudiced treatment of the subject of mother is granted. The revealing last line of the novel, which is the psychiatrist Dr. Spielman's only comment—" 'Now vee may perhaps to begin. Yes?' " (*Portnoy's Complaint*, New York: Bantam Books, 1970, p. 309. Further page references to this edition are included in the text.)— calls for a more complete accounting, which would necessitate a modified version of mother that is not as simplified as the stereotype which has guided Portnoy's complaint.

We realize early in his soliloquy that Portnoy has never considered the possible reasons for his mother's obsession with perfecting and possessing him. If he has been used by his mother, at this point he is no less guilty of using her as the incorporation of all that is distastefully Jewish as well as everything that is wrong with him. As Portnoy the child imagined her incapable of doing wrong, Portnoy the obsessed adult sees her incapable of doing anything right. The safe distancing of Mother Portnoy in caricature can enlist the unqualified outrage of Jew and goy alike for all wrongs committed by mothers, without the problem of considering her point of view. The caricature clarifies and thoroughly denigrates, while freeing the reader from any conflicting sympathies that might occur had she been given a more realistic treatment. The obviousness of the satire from an author who is not everywhere heavy-handed indicates Roth's awareness of the means by which such stereotypes are projected, in this case through the eyes of the self-pitying son. And while Roth treats his comic version of woman glibly and with relief, the bitch type represents a deeply felt view of women's power, which is a major concern of the two long non-comic novels preceding the story of Mrs. Portnoy.

In parodying the *Reader's Digest*'s idea of "The Most Unforgettable Character I've Met," *Portnoy's Complaint* reminds us how closely most mothers fit such a description, which is particularly ironic given the complexes Roth deals with. But by reducing mother to comic imbecility one may strike back at her for being the pervasive, guilt-producing force that she is. A comic treatment of the Oedipal obsession (suggested to Roth by Kafka's use of the absurd) is both refreshing and effective for Alexander Portnoy and for Roth, giving the appearance, through distance and exaggeration, of a control over a problem that otherwise might be overwhelming. Only through caricature, however, is Roth able to under-mine the concept of woman's power.

Portnoy's sense of his mother's omnipotence is a first sign of his own limited view, an understandable one for the inexperienced child judging his parent. All of his female teachers and all women of authority resemble his mother; from that womb he came, and to it he must return. After a time of escape with his fantasy woman, the Monkey, her sexual indulgences no longer intrigue him. Completing a cycle of escape through other types of women, he returns to his true obsession in the form of Naomi, the Jewish Pumpkin, who resembles his mother and accordingly renders him impotent. All things reside in mother, who can do anything—she, with the power to suspend peaches in jello and foretell a rainstorm by one drop in the window!

The link between mother's power and her goodness, which be-comes the downfall of a Portnoy, is created in no subtle way by Sophie Portnoy. Obvious as her methods are, the boy is too much the believer to detect any fallacy in her thinking. She invests her son with the idea that she is "too good," a term which becomes synonymous with the concept of mother and her authority. "It was my mother who could accomplish anything, who herself had to admit that it might even be that she was actually too good" (10). Her goodness manifests itself in her constant concern for others (primarily her son) and in her capacity for self-sacrifice, so righteously based on holy doctrine. The mother becomes the saint, with her perversion of selflessness and suffering the claim to her child's devotion and the means by which she develops his guilt. Portnoy's mother is so good that she even befriends the old Negro woman who works for her. Roth's facile use of this treatment of the Negro is one of his least effective touches, one which might once have been clever but which in a contemporary reading falls flat. Nor are other specific ways in which Mrs. Portnoy's narrow, obsessive soul manifests itself either original or of particular fascination. It is her cumulative effect as an absolute power and source of goodness in Portnoy's eyes that is her significance. The carica-ture, like Portnoy's obsession, is shown through necessarily repetitious effects rather than through surprising and unique ones. This is the limita-tion not only of Mrs. Portnoy but of her son, and of the novel that relates his monotonous complaint.

Not only is Sophie Portnoy good, or "too good," as she says, but "she alone is good" (12). Only she clears the weeds from the graves of her relatives; only she is a good sport when losing at Mah-Jongg. Her very being encompasses a particular definition of *good*. For the boy, who has not discovered the perversion in his mother's use of this term, he continues, no doubt in great confusion, to wonder at the meaning of such goodness. He even maintains her integrity after she holds a knife over him (the castrator at work) to persuade him to eat. And for all his later attempts to dispel his early myth, no analyst can untie for him the mother-power-goodness construct.

The reversal to masturbation, that special secret kept from Portnoy's mother (despite her attempts to get at the doings behind the bathroom door), is a triumph against her obsessive demands that he be a good little boy. The act satisfies the sexual urges she would never allow him to experience in a normal heterosexual way, and the form of satisfaction is itself a further taboo. The pornography of these activities is an exotic way of disobeying mother and doing so in her near presence, adding further titillation to the excitement Portnoy finds in masturbation. The novel's first few pages are hilarious until the act, like any obsession, becomes monotonous. Unlike most of his contemporaries, obsessed with varieties of heterosexual sex, Roth persists with onanism even in his non-comic novels. This perfectly appropriate subject of *Portnoy's Complaint* is a less appropriate activity for the cerebral, dutiful Paul Herz of *Letting Go*, who has no desire to make love to his wife or to other women, but who reverts to masturbation as a way of demonstrating his manhood.

If all that is good is Jewish, and all that is bad goyish, Portnoy's rebellion seeks the opposite of his virtuous mother in his fantasy of the deliciously wicked *shikse*. His mother might control him, but he will control this dream woman, the very embodiment of America, "a *shikse* nestling under your arm whispering love love love love love!" (165). Gone are the heavy concerns, the goodness and the guilt, the power which Portnoy and other Roth protagonists associate with "character." "But who wants character?" Portnoy asks. "I want Thereal McCoy!" . . .—Miss America . . .—this perfect, perfect-stranger, who is as smooth and shiny and cool as custard" (170). But simple bliss is not for Portnoy even when he actually meets his fantasy woman, since he is doomed to deny easy satisfactions. With his true passions linked to mother there is little left for anyone like the Monkey, whom he callously abandons with a cheerful goodbye as she prepares to leap from a hotel room in Athens.

The Monkey is a sometimes humorous caricature of Portnoy's "most lascivious adolescent dreams" (118), an amazing creature who initiates sexual perversions which equal Portnoy's own fantasies. She is never made believable, nor is she meant to be, although she shares with Roth's serious heroines an inclination to insanity and suicide, brought on by the sense of a personal void, which she in her quaint fashion attempts to fill with extravagant sexual pursuits.

The Monkey's effect is quite unlike that of the women who exert the real power in Roth's works and who are his central figures, however. For one thing, Portnoy, and any other observer of this phenomenal girl, can easily see into her wild obsessions and eventually steer clear of them. Portnoy understands her perversions because they are his own, and he scoffs at the idea of ever marrying such a person and having to pull her up from degradation. It is exactly the opposite quality—a stern moral posture (or what appears to be that)—which truly binds the Roth male to a woman, offering him the hope of being lifted from his own mire of corruption back to the blessed status of the good boy. Quite as obvious as the Monkey's perversions is her low mentality, something the Roth hero would never accept in a wife. Such a liability is made painfully clear when the Monkey is seen in social situations, such as the Mayor's party, which are so important to the conventional Portnoy. There is no way that this hillbilly from West Virginia can ever make Portnoy proud. She is "ineducable and beyond reclamation" (232), evidenced to Portnoy by her speech, her thoroughly visceral reaction to all experience, and finally by her handwriting and the illiterate note to her cleaning lady which is the decisive touch to his portrait of coarseness.

Roth's writing demonstrates a desire that his characters retain some form of the awe and dignity that inspired the Jew of the past, and the Monkey quite clearly has no capacity for refinement or noble aspirations. Public figures who represent only a slick and immoral approach to life particularly offend Roth, who writes in disgust of the way Eisenhower prayed every night, as related by Mrs. Eisenhower: " 'I muffed a few,' " he would say, and then, turning the failures over to God, he would roll on his side and sleep. The posture of talking to God as one would to a valet represents a sacrilege Roth deplores and which is related to the way his characters seek something almost divine in women. Lucky Nelson's bitchery may be the focus of attack in *When She Was Good*, but Roth does sympathize with her outrage against the vapidity of her surroundings, which offer so little color and sense of wonder. Although Roth's writing often takes the form of tedious obsessions and vulgarities, he never allows a reconciliation with the banalities which are his subject.

If *Portnoy's Complaint* is the embodiment in caricature of Roth's realized obsession with women's power, his earlier books, *Letting Go* and *When She Was Good*, are the dramatization of this concern in a more realistic and complete way. Neither of the two heroines of the books is Jewish, and it is to the author's credit as one of our most versatile writers that he accurately depicts the rhythms of their dialogue and the details of their surroundings, which are so far from his native, urban, Jewish milieu.

He does not attempt to show that all women are shrewish manipulators, as these two women are, but he does play up the fact that his conscience-stricken men seek out such women who will repeat the persecutions the men received from their mothers. Women who are not dominating do populate Roth's world, but they never hold the interest of the author, his male protagonists, or the reader. Few of them are so colorful as the Monkey, and none of them are as convincingly developed as Libby Herz and Lucy Nelson.

Libby, wife of Paul Herz in *Letting Go*, holds a special appeal for Gabe Wallach, the narrator and central character of this long account of his interaction with the painful Herz marriage. Many readers of the novel justifiably question what the two men both see in Libby. As Gabe relates, "My first impression of her had been clear and sharp: profession—student; inclinations—neurotic. She moved jerkily and had the high black stockings and the underfed look. She was thin, dark, intense, and I could not imagine that she had ever once gotten anything but pain from entertaining a room full of people." (*Letting Go*, New York: Bantam Books, 1970, p. 6. Further page references to this edition are included in the text). Nothing in this portrait indicates Libby's great appeal, and the impression of her throughout the novel does not change basically from this first account. *Letting Go* is not a love story, although it is very much a story of combinations of men and women, incapable of love, whose various obsessions draw them destructively together. Paul and Libby often refer to their "love" for each other, but their life together is a constant, nagging battle, fed by her gnawing lack of purpose and his obsession with duty. Even making love to her is a burdensome task for him. (For all Roth's pornography his men are squeamish about heterosexual lovemaking.) When Gabe discovers Libby's distress because her husband so seldom makes love to her (the pretext for his abstinence is to avoid the expense of a pregnancy), Gabe weakens, just once, and kisses her. But no sexual attachment follows, which is rare considering the ease with which couples in most contemporary fiction commit their adulteries. Gabe is bound to Libby throughout this long story, but it is with a peculiar psychological, not a sexual, dependence.

Perhaps one reason why many readers have questioned the likelihood that both of these men would be attracted to Libby is that sexual attraction, which we have come to accept as inevitably leading to culmination in our fiction, is not the primary source of her power over them. In fact, most often for Roth's people it is because of men's reluctance that liaisons do not culminate sexually. Libby desperately wants her husband to make love to her, and there is a good chance that she would sleep with

Gabe if he urged her to. But both men are drawn to her for something else—a tense, demanding quality that gives her power but which also makes her vulnerable. She may be a woman of deep character whose potential is frustrated by her limited life. On the other hand, perhaps she shows only a surface promise of depth and is frantically vacant within. The men see her as the former, she herself as the latter.

The clue to Libby is in the first descriptive word Gabe applies to her, *neurotic*. She is by no means an unintelligent or an insensitive woman, and her comments regarding James's *Portrait of a Lady*, which is the issue of the first few pages of *Letting Go*, reveal a perception finer than Gabe's. Her husband Paul, who will teach the novel, has not even read it yet, and it is difficult to imagine a particularly perceptive reading coming from him, although Libby is certain that his intellect is far superior to hers. Libby's dismay at Isabel Archer's marriage to Osmond is one way of announcing her own marital problems, although as Roth's work dramatizes, modeled on James's *Portrait*, there is no simple thing one wants or gets from marriage. Gabe realizes, "Perhaps the truth was that Libby was a girl with desires *nobody* could satisfy; perhaps they weren't even 'desires' but the manifestations of some cellular disorder, some physiochemical imbalance that fated her to a life of agonized yearning in our particular world of flora and fauna, amongst our breed of humanity" (239). While he senses these qualities in her and is harshly critical, Gabe is attracted to her despite (or perhaps because of) them, drawn beyond his will to just such neuroticism as hers.

Paul's Uncle Asher has warned him that Jewish girls devour, but Libby, a Catholic, proves to be as devouring as any of them. The author frees himself of any Jewish stereotype in the creation of *shikse* bitches, but it is likely that they retain something of a Jewish quality that Asher refers to. Roth clearly despises the domination of women, but he is so well aware of this attitude, and of the weaknesses of men which make such domination possible, that the interactions of his men and women characters are truly convincing. Roth's women are by no means inferior in stature to his men, but they are less likeable. In Paul Herz's obsession with duty to his wife he is stiffly aloof, but as other of Roth's husbands, vulnerable and somewhat lovable all the same. In this the lines are drawn between Roth's men and his women, who are distasteful to most readers but who are loved by his men. Although Gabe later modifies his opinion, his first view of the Herz marriage is that "the impossible one to live with . . . was clearly the wife" (15). The feeling throughout the novel is that it is she who brings about the unhappiness of the marriage.

The theme of woman as the source of unhappiness in marriage is announced in the opening pages of the novel with a letter from Gabe Wallach's mother, written as she was dying: "Whatever unhappiness has been in our family springs from me. Please don't blame it on your father however I may have encouraged you over the years. Since I was a little girl I always wanted to be Very Decent to People. . . . I was always doing things for another's good. The rest of my life I could push and pull at people with a clear conscience" (2). This is an incredible statement. What woman on her deathbed or at any other time would admit to this crime, so indefinable that it need never be confessed either to herself or to others? But of course the "confession" is ironically balanced by Mrs. Wallach's reminder that what she did resulted only from her motive of doing good. To whatever degree Roth's heroines may be responsible for causing unhappiness, they are almost never dissociated with the concept of good.

Mrs. Wallach's letter reveals the fantasy of a Portnoy and perhaps of other Roth characters—the desire that mother (or her replacement) take the responsibility for their unhappiness. Roth is too perceptive an author to suggest any simple placing of blame for human misery any more than he suggests that Portnoy's complaint gives a complete picture of Mrs. Portnoy. His characters believe what they want to believe. It is peculiar that Gabe Wallach, ostensibly a perceptive intellectual and our enlight-ened narrator (perhaps an unreliable one), should never have observed any pattern of power in his own mother when he sees it so clearly in Libby. Although he appears more sophisticated than Paul and is surely more disciplined than Portnoy, like them he is obsessed with the notion of the woman as a figure of power and goodness. Thus, there is no sign that he takes his mother's confession seriously.

Libby, likewise, never loses the aura of her superior worth in the eyes of her husband, regardless of what she does. Even though Paul doubts his own manliness when he marries her, and Gabe sees him looking "as shabby and defeated as a man can who has been made a fool of by his wife" (17), neither of them is quite capable of seeing her as other than good. Nor can they do enough for her. In a perverted form of self-sacrifice Gabe goes through a torturous process to secure a baby for Libby. And among other things, Paul can never make enough money to satisfy her obsession to buy. On one occasion he comes home with a slashed hand, and her first reaction is to ask only if he was docked his afternoon's pay. Libby takes an office job for a day or so, but the sight of her over a typewriter is so pathetic to her husband and to Gabe that it seems quite out of the question for her to work.

The traditional duties of a man weigh heavily upon Paul, who is pathetically, and predictably, no freer when he leaves Libby to go to New York than he was with her, being hopelessly and unhappily bound. Even Libby's inability to have a child (due to a kidney ailment) is somehow flung back at him as his failure, perhaps for not making love to her oftener. Libby accentuates Paul's sense of guilt, but it is difficult to imagine his being much happier with anyone else. She is quite necessary to him, in great part as a focus for his unhappiness. Gabe once described him as a person who "actually found pleasure in saying to the world: Woe is me" (26).

There is more than one opportunity in *Letting Go* for Gabe to let go of his attraction for this neurotic girl who holds him with the same power she holds her husband. Gabe attracts women with no trouble, the first of these being a student named Margie who insists on moving in with him after their first night together. Like Paul, who was hastened into marriage by Libby's demands, the good-natured but weak Gabe offers no resistance, and Margie moves in with all her trappings. While she is ill he is reduced to errand boy, stalking the supermarket to collect supplies for her. He soon realizes how little difference it makes whether or not she is sick, however, and gathers the nerve to escape "this sweet empty-headed girl" (28), who is not powerful enough to dominate him. His allegiance once again turns to the neurotic Libby.

Gabe's most promising alliance is with Martha Regenhart, a divorcée with two children, among whose squalor an almost successful love affair takes place. Martha is the sanest and the sloppiest person in the novel, capable of love, and healthy-minded particularly in contrast to the other characters. Her lack of self-consciousness is refreshing in view of the tedious vanities of the unhappy trio, each with a crippling sense of his own problems. Paul, Libby, and Gabe are more intelligent and literate than Martha is, but there is a sterility in the men's studies as there is in their lives. For all three of them existence is unduly grim. Martha is much the better for being less cerebral than they, but we know from her earthy simplicity that Gabe will not be attracted to her for long. Perhaps he is incapable of involvement to the point of marriage, but if he were to marry, the girl would probably be someone more like Libby. His rationale for breaking with Martha is epitomized in the way he sees her medicine cabinet, which is such a wreck he considers the perpetrator of it insane. "I flung open the medicine chest to be confronted again by that skull and crossbones. Big as life it said: DANGER. But *she* didn't seem to know there were children in the house! *She* apparently didn't read in the papers about all the poisoned kids! A mess! An unexcusable mess!" (281). Gabe, of course, is not as worried about the danger to the children as he is about the threat of involvement to himself.

Martha is what the other women in *Letting Go* are not: motherly, frowzy, earthy, and large. Gabe sarcastically alludes to her size: " 'It's great you're five nine, Martha, it's perfect you're hefty. The bigger they are the better they can enjoy the fall' " (385). Her fleshiness is the too obvious reminder to him of the sexual nature of their union. But it is not the sexual bond or a sexual trap that is the nemesis for Roth's men. They soon weary of the mere sex object. Their lives might be easier with the simpler, more physical women, but they always turn back to the complicated, suffering ones whose very misery suggests something noble. Such women are seen as saviors who in turn must be protected and labored for. The affection and devotion of Roth's protagonists appear to be proportional to the demands of the woman, and since Libby's demands are almost impossible to fulfill she continues to exert a fascination for both her husband and Gabe. They strain themselves with efforts for her as if in doing so they might free themselves of the guilt and coldness which characterize them both.

Martha makes her demands as well, but they are in more concrete and realizable terms: she wants Gabe to pay the rent, buy the food, and stay with her, marry her. Much has been said in praise of Martha, but it is more by contrast with Libby that her humanity appears in so favorable a light than that her actions are particularly noteworthy. She hassles Gabe about money, about the Herzes, about her children, and soon their affair takes on the sordid and monotonous quality of the Herzes' continuous arguments, in a book which excels in the lifelike dialogue of people who repeat their tedious quarrels for a lifetime. But there are choices offered to all of the main characters—if the story is patterned on James there must be—and especially with Gabe we are kept wondering if or how he will let go of his old ways and take hold of something new. The various women in his life offer choices in the same way Isabel Archer's suitors offer different lives for her. But instead of choosing one of them, Gabe remains a Lambert Strether, observing and helping others to fulfill their lives in preference to dealing with his own.

In light of the abuses of parenthood that abound in *Letting Go*, Martha's generous affection for her children is particularly meaningful. " 'I love those kids. I'm glad I've got them, overwhelmingly glad. I work nights and I hate it—you don't *know* how I hate it. But I'm glad I've got those kids. They're *something*, damn it' " (321). Martha's honorable motherhood weakens, however. Apparently as a way of favoring the relationship with Gabe, she eventually allows the children she so ardently cares for to go with her former husband, a man she describes as crude and cruel, an unlikely replacement to offer the children a good home. And it follows that after the children have moved in with him a tragic accident takes the younger child's life, an act which serves as a punishment for Martha for relinquishing her responsibility as a parent. The sacrifice of her children is further a foolish move for Martha because they were never the source of her problems with Gabe in the first place. In fact, he rather admired the way she handled them. Until she gives up her children, Martha is the only exemplary parent in a novel which has for a main concern the abuses of parenthood. But no longer the fully dedicated mother, Martha realizes that she has lost Gabe's respect without increasing her chances of marrying him. He is never explicit about his dwindling interest in her, but she suspects it is related to his idea of a woman's nobility, and she has now lost hers. " 'You don't feel the same, Gabe. I think you liked me noble better' " (465–66).

Roth attempts to create in Martha Regenhart the kind of woman, in contrast to Libby, whom both his protagonist and the reader will like and admire. She is warmer, more spontaneous, and more loving than anyone in the book. But Roth betrays his own distaste for her and his preference for more neurotic but intelligent women. The statement by Paul's Uncle Asher that he prefers women who are uncluttered by education, keeping "the thing in a pure state" (429), parodies a kind of purity which holds no charm for Roth. Martha embodies such an uninteresting purity. Perhaps she is not bright enough, too big, or too vulgar. Roth shows keen attention to the details of dress, that shell of a person which, as one James character points out, is indeed an essential part of the human being. Roth's men want women to be ladies, and they grimace at the discrepancies in a woman's style of dress and manner of speaking which indicate more than a surface disarray. This kind of clutter *is* significantly damning. Nothing about Martha disturbs Gabe so much as the way she dresses when the Herzes come to dinner: "When she rushed past me to answer the knock at the front door, it was not a woman that moved by but a circus—a burst of color and a clattering of ornaments" (308). Like her sloppy medicine cabinet, Martha is messy in a way that cannot be dismissed. Even her natural blond hair let loose and floating below her waist is repellent to Gabe, who prefers Libby's stark hairdo, pulled tightly back. Whether the appeal is to propriety, dignity, or discipline, the neurotic woman, who is neater and more delicate physically, is the one who holds the limelight. Just as Martha could not be at the center of a James novel, she cannot be a focal character for Roth, who tries to make her likeable but does not succeed.

Gabe's obsessive efforts to help the Herzes adopt a child are a way of projecting the worthiness of motherhood onto Libby as well as being an eerie projection of his own thwarted sense of family. His bizarre pursuit of the baby is merely melodramatic if seen only as an attempt to bring about the adoption for the sake of his friends. But when seen as a form of do-gooding to ease his own conscience and as a projection of a halo for Libby as a mother, the frantic chase to the child's home on New Year's Eve becomes a more symbolic quest. (Presenting Libby with a child may also be a symbolic form of the adultery that never took place.)

Motherhood when viewed from Libby's point of view is an obsession of another sort, a primarily materialistic one. It is no loss to her that she is advised not to attempt a second pregnancy (she had an abortion early in her marriage), for she is not willing to take that kind of a risk to become a mother. However, she would gladly purchase a child and possess it. Such a concept further defines Libby as less than the "good" woman her men imagine her to be. Nor is she "good" if the term has anything to do with a benevolent concern for other people; by her own admission, "out of the clear blue sky she began to hate people" (325).

The women in Letting Go all let go of their children: Libby through abortion, Martha when she turns her children over to their father, and Theresa Haug, who gives her child up for adoption by the Herzes. The reasons for abdication of motherhood are different in each case, but they add up to a general malaise affecting the bond between parent and child. Early in the novel distortions of this bond are shown in the relationships of the three main characters with their parents: Paul visits his dying father, who has never forgiven him for marrying Libby, and is so disgusted by the man that he almost stays away from his funeral; Libby's parents have blotted her name out of the family because of the marriage, a fact announced to her in a chilling letter of denunciation; and Gabe's father clings to his son, compulsively nagging at him to come home for visits. Mr. Wallach finally decides to marry a gaudy woman named Fay Silberman, a doomed alliance from its beginning, sheerly as a compensation for his not having Gabe nearby. Parents and children infect each others' lives, but Roth's primary attack is aimed at parents for the suffering they inflict. And Libby's destructive powers in marriage are a sign of her destructive potential as a parent.

Roth is equally adept at relating the states of mind of his male and his female characters. While at times we see his image of women only as his own fantasy or that of his characters, he keeps us aware that it is just that, and he has enough concern for his women to examine their minds for a necessarily different viewpoint. Gabe, as he narrates the story, sympathizes first with Paul and then with Libby. Roth takes us into the daily life of a woman alone at home—what she thinks about and what she does while her husband is at work. Most housewives in literature are notoriously bored, and few of them must any longer spend the day doing housework. When the husband goes the wife is faced with a desperate vacancy, and the activities she manufactures are usually meaningless repetitions to kill time until her husband returns. One favorite pastime is the shopping trip. The neurotic Libby, miserable as a housewife, is plagued by her craving for expensive things she cannot afford. After her husband leaves she nervously recites to herself, *"But I am sweet and good. I deserve as much as anybody—"* (355), which is what her husband believes her to be and what she imagines she should be, but far from what her feelings tell her she is. With all of the hours of the morning lying ahead, should she get dressed? Make the bed? What can she do after that? She lies down and hides her head in the pillowcase, one of the many suicidal impulses of the idle housewife.

Libby does not generally lack insight, but she convinces herself of an inferiority to her husband, the scholar and writer of the family. She only dabbles at bad poetry. In such a view of a woman's concept of herself Roth does not necessarily project a desire that women be incompetent but a realistic and sympathetic view of their actual *sense* of incompetency, particularly as they measure themselves in relation to the activities of men. Libby is awed by her hard-working husband (although she is oblivious to his lack of intellectual passion for his studies). Their days always begin with the important announcement that he must be off to his job. And what is she going to do? Paul even fixes her breakfast in his zealous attempts at duty, and as Libby sees her plate laid out in the morning (she makes no attempt to fix breakfast herself), she feels more useless than ever. It does not offend her that Paul takes over the duties usually expected of the wife, for she has no feeling for her role as homemaker. She must force herself to prepare dinner as if it were a major hardship; her thin little hands grating potatoes make a sad sight indeed. She says to her husband, " 'I don't want to stay at home! What's at home? What's at home but a lot of crappy furniture! . . . Oh I want a baby or something . . . a dog or a TV. Paulie, I can't do anything' " (246). The same sentiment is reflected in her reply to the question asked her by the representative from the adoption agency, what does she do?: " 'I don't do anything' " (346), the usual dismal comment of women. Roth is unusually sensitive to this question put to a woman and of demeaning answers. The scenes with Libby at home during the day, doing nothing, are among the most painful and effective moments of this or any other recent novel that deals with the consciousness of a woman.

With the dread empty hours on her hands Libby looks forward to her appointment with a psychiatrist. After a traumatic afternoon in his office, she is hysterical by the time her husband comes home in the evening. We hear very little about his day, but we know how bad hers has been. Roth does not suggest that Libby or anyone else escape through a job any more than he suggests simple answers to other complex problems, but his documentation of what happens to a high-strung, intelligent woman who remains idle certainly suggests that some occupation is in order. While the adoption of a child for Libby is a central issue of the novel, it is obviously only an illusion of the three main characters that this or any other form of parenthood will be a cure for her despair. Libby is delighted when she finally gets a baby, but her pleasure is demonstrated in an abnormal obsession with the child—too much running to the baby's room to see if she is still there, with the same brittle tension that is her reaction to other things. Since the truest satisfaction in Libby's life comes from owning things, she would be better off making money than raising children. But Roth, the humanist, could hardly suggest this. Becoming a mother is surely the conventional answer to what Libby might do with her life, but it does not represent a choice that has anything to do with her understanding of our suitability for motherhood.

The main characters in *Letting Go* are all locked in their own obsessions, but Libby's misery is shown the most vividly. Her husband and Gabe are both involved in work they presumably have chosen for certain expected satisfactions, although these are never demonstrated. Paul at least has the pride of doing his duty by his wife, and if that does not bring pleasure, he never expected that it would. Gabe has a life free of the painful marriages he sees around him and is in demand as a lover and as a friend. But Libby is narrowed into a style of life that offers nothing particularly suited to her, except perhaps that it gives her a position of some power over her husband. Her admiration of him, however, makes her despise herself by comparison. With little to do all day but contemplate her own condition, she sinks toward madness. She tells the psychiatrist she is "nuts" and demonstrates it by screaming that she will have only him as her analyst, even though she cannot pay. Eventually she attempts suicide.

In showing the neuroticism that festers in idleness, particularly as Libby feels increasingly inferior to the men around her and lashes out more spitefully, Roth takes a closer look at the *creation* of the bitch than most writers do, those who merely show her devastating effects on others.

Readers who know only of Roth's caricature of Mrs. Portnoy, where no insight into her is given because her son is so thoroughly obsessed with his own problems, should look at *Letting Go* to see that he does attempt to get at causes and complexities of the manipulating woman. It makes Libby no less a shrew if we learn how she came to be one, but Roth, while he exploits the type, at least makes us aware that there are processes which lead to her condition.

Gabe's mother was not unlike Libby, someone difficult to live with and impossible for her husband to know: "Anna had been more than he could handle or understand, but he had asked her to marry him; maybe that was *why* he had asked her. He did not know. He had thought at the time and he thought still that he had loved Anna" (503). The pattern of female dominance changes little from one generation to the next; Libby carries on with the same mysterious power that Anna possessed. And as a sign that the future is to repeat a similar process, Martha Regenhart's seven-year-old daughter Cynthia pushes her brother to his death from the top bunk of their bed, where he has crawled in with her. With more than a sexual innuendo the incident suggests women's power to effect men's ultimate destruction. Surprisingly, considering the constant tensions seen here between men and women, sexual problems are only secondary. Even with Paul and Libby, the fact that he rarely makes love to her is not the source of their arguments. In fact, Roth is unique among current writers for giving so little time, in his non-comic works, to explicit scenes of lovemaking. His heroes are not so easily satisfied. They seek the domination of women, which eventually may lead to total destruction as it does for Martha's unassuming young son. No one casts the slightest suspicion on Cynthia for the "accident"; they sympathize with her for having gone through such a traumatic event. After all, how could a little girl be anything but good?

When She Was Good presents the epitome of female self-righteousness in Lucy Nelson, a product of Liberty Center, a small town in the Midwest. This novel also emphasizes a noticeable contrast between leading male and female figures in the fiction of the sixties: the men are usually gentler, weaker, and more sensitive, while the women are rigid and dominating. As with Paul's attitude toward his wife Libby, Roy Bassart sees Lucy as "good" no matter what she does or how much he suffers because of her. Although he finally denounces her, he makes this statement from a distance, impulsively, and we rather expect to see him fall back into his irrational belief in her goodness. Roy may be less masochistic than his counterpart Paul Herz, for he does enjoy his pleasures, but both men have a weakness for the same kind of woman.

The lightness signified in Lucy's name, and she is a blonde, is translated in Roy's initial concept of her to the title of "Angel." He meets her as a friend of his cousin Ellie, and drawn to the "character" in her face he immediately offers to take her picture. Roy could find more perfect faces for his pictures any time, those with the look of fashion models, but typically of the Roth male he has little interest in shallow, pretty girls. He sees courage and strength in Lucy, especially in her suffering, knowing like everyone else in town of her drunken father and of how she daringly took steps against him. Above all, he is convinced of her worthiness. This image of Lucy is set immediately as Roy meets her (before she has talked to him), idealized by his concept of woman as angel, an image he joyfully imagines he can capture in a photograph. Under the effect of this illusion of Lucy as angel he is oblivious to the nastiness she soon displays. When he playfully asks her if she wants her picture taken she abrasively blurts out *no*, a prophetic reaction to him. Moments later she glares at him: " 'Just who do you think you're talking to, you!' " (*When She Was Good*, New York: Bantam Books, 1970, p. 99. Further page references to this edition are included in the text.) To anyone but this idealistic man she is no angel.

Lucy's obsession with her own dignity is emphasized by shame of her family, as well as by a belief that women are superior to men (although she is furious that men will not take their place as *men* and be stronger). Her father's drunken uses of her mother set a pattern she refuses to forget, with the absolute rigidity that comes to characterize her. At the age of fifteen she gets the chance she has wanted, and when her father comes home drunk one night and for no apparent reason dumps his wife's Epsom salts on the floor, Lucy calls the police and has him put in jail, an act that immortalizes her. The ostensible cause of Lucy's fury is her mother's passive suffering, but she thrives on a reservoir of hatred for all that is weak and incompetent, especially in men. In marrying Roy Bassart, a kind and dreamy boy, she is in a position to demonstate fully her scorn of such weakness.

One criticism of Roth's characterization of Lucy is that he gives little hint as to the sources of her viciousness. Life is lackluster for all of these midwesterners. Why then is it that Lucy is filled with so much more hatred than anyone else? But if the author cannot fully know the source of her anger, that does not negate his portrayal of it. After all, can we ever know what in nature makes these hard hearts? Many male writers give amazingly effective portraits of women, with a credibility that admits a lack of comprehension. Lucy's hostility is not entirely inexplicable, however. Certainly ambition with no adequate outlet has something to do with it. Given the limitations of Liberty Center, and the author's antipathy to the tedium of a daily existence that offers no hint of enlightenment, Lucy's reactions are believable. In Liberty Center none of the inhabitants will advance far, but a significant and traditional difference separates Roy and Lucy: he is the male dreamer and she the female domestic. Dissatisfied with one job Roy moves on to another, always with the belief that he will find his true vocation. Lucy expects a great change to better her life as well, but she has in her past no concrete satisfactions to draw from and none to look forward to. Roy's dreams are of the past as well as of the future. After coming home from the army he strolls down to his old high school and relishes the memory of his days there. "For the hour of the day, for the time of his life, for this America where it is all peacefully and naturally happening, he feels an emotion at once so piercing and so buoyant it can only be described as love" (55).

In this thoroughly serious novel Roth intends no satire for such sentiments. This midwesterner of limited intellect but honestly developed emotions enjoys an intense pleasure that Roth grants is possible for a person of imagination, irrespective of region. (It is true that in addition to Roy's superior imagination he has also had more varied experiences than Lucy, at least making a brief escape from the town.) His dream of having a baby daughter is a delicious fantasy, although wholly unrelated to the pangs of childbirth and the effort of child-rearing, and is so lyrically communicated to Lucy that she is convinced to have another baby (as long as this time it is her decision). But she is not long to idealize the birth of a child. Her marriage came about because of an unwanted pregnancy, which meant the end of any fantasies for her.

In Lucy's case the forced marriage more than anything illustrates her particularly unbending and unimaginative nature. She refuses to have the abortion her father offers, preferring the unwanted marriage in which she can make Roy pay for what he has done. In this setting of the fifties with its courtship by car, that long and strenuous battle to get the girl to go "all the way," the threat of pregnancy is certainly of a magnitude not possible to the girl of the sixties with the Pill and other devices more readily available and acceptable. But the fact that Lucy is offered an abortion and refuses it begins to establish that she is more a victimizer than an innocent victim. Her desire for revenge along with the bleakness of her surroundings, to which she does not bring the imagination that enlivens her husband, work together to make her one of the super bitches of the sixties.

Lucy's problems are very much crystallized in her concept of the woman as a martyr-saint. She despises her mother's passive suffering, but her view of life rests upon the idea that men are responsible for women's misery and must be made to pay. Always with a lust for power, but with no specific course for her energies after her vague dream of college is abandoned for marriage, Lucy ironically magnifies in herself the very long-suffering quality she loathes in her mother. And her unsatisfied ambition, for want of a more spectacular focus, gradually centers into a supreme hostility for Liberty Center and its people. Her husband, who is at home there, never experiences her kind of ambition; his dreams are realizable within the realm of this small town. But the more Lucy tries to adjust to her occupation as a wife there, the more she detests it and sees herself as the martyr in a horrible system where she is fated to be a self-sacrificing domestic in a dull part of the world. Her attempts to live out this role righteously, for the sake of moral superiority if not for satisfaction (and Roth allows her no other possibilities), only increase her frustration and suggest an eventual breakdown.

In the first weeks of her marriage Lucy finds herself "trying with all her might to do what she was told" (193). She visits the in-laws "because that's what they were: she was his wife" (195). She detests everything about this pose of subservience, craving not only the subtle power of the wife who rules her husband (she has that) but a more outward form of control. Even full control over the movements of others does not satisfy; she is obsessed with changing people in ways that are impossible. As she imagines Roy to change she even believes that she might be in love with him—her creation, not the old Roy. Without even the flexibility to see that she has chosen an impossible task, she is frozen in her own hatred and frustration. The only thing left for her is to hound Roy to perform his duty, to be a father, which to her means a show of authority and responsibility having nothing to do with human warmth. She even at one time prays bitterly "*Make him a father!*" (292).

As Lucy conceives of a rigid role for her husband as father, she also imagines an ultimately confining life for herself as wife. She must do whatever the dreary things are that a wife and a mother do, roles that she is surely to some degree forced into. From conception onward she is antagonistic toward the life growing inside her because she did not put it there. The diaphragm she wears after her child is born is much to her liking, for she now sees herself in control. Such a desire to regulate childbirth is viewed by most male writers, Roth among them, as a callous denial of what is natural and good. At the point in the novel where we learn of Lucy's birth control methods her selfishness is already so well established that her use of a contraceptive is merely given as one more vicious fact about her. Roth does not change his tone in dealing with this

problem, offering no possibility that a woman might be justified in deciding not to have a child until she wants one. By the time Lucy has decided
to have a second child and she makes the untimely announcement of her
pregnancy, her marriage has already exploded.

Lucy is all icy letter of the law, without a drop of mercy. Her son
before long senses the tyranny even her husband has not recognized and
hides from her under the bathroom sink with a washrag over his face.
Lucy contends that the child's withdrawal is the result of Roy's inconsis-
tent behavior, his frequent "running off." But the only running off he
does is to go to work or to make an occasional call on the parents and
relatives Lucy resents, fearing that they will pull him away from her. As
Roy grows more mellow, Lucy becomes more rigid. Because most of Roth's
heroines do adhere to the letter of the law in marital fidelity, they can
flaunt this virtue in view of the marital infidelities around them, as Lucy
does when she learns of adultery in Roy's family. But while she lives out
her fidelity to perfection, she does so with an incapacity for tenderness. It
is by no means through restraint that someone like Lucy is sexually
faithful in marriage. If a love affair were possible for her we might feel
more hope for her soul. (She seems so frigid one wonders how she ever
became involved with Roy in the first place.) But Lucy will never again
slip from her high moral post and give up the claim to authority that it
gives her.

Nowhere does Roth more effectively show the alienation and
misery that come to those who opt for power instead of love than he does
with Lucy. Even when she is most effective in exerting power over her
husband and child she is intensely unhappy. Roy "had settled at last into
the daily business, whether he liked it or not, of being a father, and a
husband and a man: her child had two parents to protect him, two parents
each doing his job, and it was she alone who had made all this come
about. This battle, too, she had fought and this battle, too, she had won,
and yet it seemed that she had never in her life been miserable in the way
that she was miserable now" (228).

Lucy ostensibly maintains her worthiness, protesting too much to
convince us that even she continues to believe in it. Whether or not she is
aware of the suffering she causes is never made clear, but if thoughts of it
do occur to her she either rationalizes or represses them as effectively as
she puts away the memory of her father. One wonders why she does not
examine more closely the misery that persists even with her loyalty to
family, hard work, and clean living habits, which if they do not bring the
more spectacular victories of life do usually present quiet satisfactions. The

question one wishes to ask of Lucy is, "Why doesn't your goodness bring you relief?"

At one time in her life Lucy turns to Catholicism, but not for solace or spiritual guidance, instead for the authoritarianism which her parents do not provide, the one thing she equates with parenthood. By such a standard, her parents simply do not act like parents. Lucy's attempts to adopt Catholicism reinforce her natural bent to moral severity only briefly, however. When she wants action to bring justice to her father, since Saint Teresa is no help, she immediately calls upon the law. She balks at confession, at the priests behind dark windows looking down on her. "I am their superior in every single way! People can call me all the names they want—I don't care! I have nothing to confess, because I am right and they are wrong and I will not be destroyed!" (84).

Lucy's frigid puritanism, which would appear mainly to be the product of the narrow morality of small-town midwestern thinking, is distinctly exhibited only in her case. If what she represents is an essence of place, it takes hold with none of the other citizens of Liberty Center as it does with her. Lucy's Grandfather Will, it is announced at the book's beginning, dreams only of being "civilized," which for him means a kindly, tolerant treatment of everyone, with large doses of forgiveness for the wayward son-in-law, Whitey Nelson. Neither his daughter Myra nor her husband is afflicted with a moral rigidity. Whitey feels guilty for not doing more for his wife, but not merely because it is his duty. In his weak way he loves her. Roy, a peacemaker, is as moderate as they are. His Uncle Julian, the worldliest of them all, is the spirit of goodness itself compared to Lucy's hardhearted purity. Only Willard's wife Berta is as cold and as sneering as Lucy.

Lucy sees her honesty as one of the most important signposts of her morality. In the way of many malicious people she makes it a tool of cruelty, attempting to breed hatred by using the truth to turn people against each other. In her last drama with Roy's family she renounces Julian for his adulteries in the presence of his wife and daughter. When she defends herself to the doctor who diagnoses her first pregnancy, " 'I'm not bad! . . . I'm good!' " (144), even her rationale is based on malice: " 'I hate liars and I don't lie' " (143). Her defensiveness and her later attack on one who commits adultery reflect her own guilt and self-loathing for participating in premarital sex, and forever afterward she is out to punish others for their sins as a way of expiating her own.

It takes Roy's uncle to summarize Lucy's qualities and to attempt to make Roy see them realistically. When she arrives in the middle of the night to demand her husband's return, Julian calls her "a little ball-breaker of a bitch . . . Saint Ball-Breaker' " (279). Only a violent occasion can convince Roy that this is true. He and Lucy spend the day with his relatives while he pleads with her to make up with them, at least for her son's sake. But Lucy remains unyielding and aloof, until later she ends their visit with deafening screams in the car. That night, when the young son says he hates his mother, Roy's breaking point is reached, and with the child he goes back to Julian, the only person who can help him generate the courage to leave Lucy. With the safety of distance Roy phones his wife and delivers the epithets worthy of her. Referring to their child's terror and to the odd habits that have come of it, Roy turns the blame back on her: " 'Because of you!' she shouted. 'Not doing your job!' 'No, Lucy, because of *you!* Because of your screaming, hateful, bossy, hateful, heartless guts! Because he never wants to see your ugly, heartless face again, and neither do I! Never!' " (268).

One wonders why Roy waits so long to say these things. But even considering the provocation that leads to his denunciation, he seems more to be mouthing his uncle's words than his own. If Lucy had not run off as she does that night, to her death, he would as likely fall back into his belief in her goodness as maintain a hostility unnatural to him. On the very day before he denounces her Roy had told Lucy how especially pretty she looked and that she was superior to the attractive and richer Ellie. One of the reasons he has always remained so convinced of Lucy's worthiness is her freedom from materialism, a fatal error of judgment on his part, for she uses her lack of wealth as she does everything else—as a source of bitterness and as a means to power.

Lucy's father believes in her in the same way Roy does, although she does what she can to destroy him. She is forever his dear little girl. It is only kindness and a hope for a free life for her that prompts him to offer her an abortion, without a word of blame for an act that would have brought forth the rage of most parents of her time. Perhaps punishment would earn Lucy's respect for her father, except that his life is too flawed to make his authority count. Mr. Nelson believes in the goodness of his daughter as he believes in the goodness of his wife, who is genuinely kind and loving. Ironically, Myra's worthiness has as unfortunate an effect on him as Lucy's viciousness does, for it inspires violence through the guilt it produces. His separation from his family may be the most painful instance in the novel of the suffering which results from the idea that women are worthier than men. Whitey's days were always saddened by his difficulty in finding work during the Depression, which he saw as the cause of his failure. But the image of himself as a casualty is reinforced, not counteracted, in his own home by his daughter and even by his wife. *When She Was Good* closes with his letter to Myra, to whom he has been writing from prison for years in secret so that Lucy would not find out, establishing his own sense of moral inferiority to women: "I said years ago that without you I would slide to hell in a hurry. I guess it was a prediction that came all too true" (308).

Lucy's husband might easily have become another Whitey Nelson, except that she would never have allowed him out of her sight, let alone have carried on a correspondence with a man who had abandoned his responsibilities. Her death by freezing (the body is recovered as rigid and intact as her life had been) symbolizes the inevitable result for one of her uncompromising nature. Insanity overcomes her in her final moments of terrified aloneness, and she runs from everyone out into the snow. Only her death makes it possible for Roy and her son Edward at last to be free of her domination.

In American literature Lucy Nelson ranks as one of the most monstrous bitches in a tradition made up of too many weak and bland women. She is trapped with a passion that devours, but it is a grand passion. Roth grants her near-tragic dimensions, which is in a perverse way a tribute to women, who in his fiction are superior to his men in their dramatic intensity. He never suggests that they lack intelligence or perception, as so many writers do, and he is painfully aware of their sense of limitations in a world which, as he shows it, offers few alternatives for them. Not all of his women are powerful beings, but only those who are ever truly capture his imagination and that of his heroes. Typical of the Roth position is the reaction of Roy to Lucy when he says that other girls are merely pretty, but *"her* face had character in it" (101).

And yet Roth's heroines do lack the quality that seems most important to him—genuine goodness. His capacity to produce primarily the negative as he develops his heroines' unyielding cruelty, however convincingly it is presented, not only results in a damning version of women but operates as a serious limitation to his art. If he were able to envision something of the noble in his powerful women, that which is so desired, he might create some magnificent characters. But the absence of generous qualities keeps them from eliciting our deepest sympathies. The extreme degree of their hardness at the same time makes it impossible to regard them as representative of the American woman. There is a certain clarity and obviousness in the inhumanity of Roth's women that makes them a less insidious influence than those created by the writer who projects a more likeable image but who humors his women along with affection and never allows them to think or to have real passions.

Roth never denies the masochism in his men that allies them with women who are destructive. It is directly through their selection of such women that we are led to his powerful heroines. The stress throughout Roth's work on the male concept of goodness is to some degree an attack upon a kind of idealism that ironically brings about disastrous results. But in another respect the same concept is the crucial area in dealing with Roth's vision of women, for he suggests that the "goodness" so desired in them is *altogether* a construct of the male mind. It is not unlikely that an author would place a diabolical woman at the center of his fiction for dramatic purposes. But because Roth shows his heroes specifically questing for goodness in women, and never finding it, he suggests that it is virtually impossible for it to exist there. Again and again—for Alexander Portnoy, for Gabe Wallach, for Paul Herz, for Roy Bassart—the idea of goodness is their creation (although only the reader is aware of this), something impossible actually to find in women.

If woman was at one time in literature designated as man's moral guardian, for Roth she no longer has even the possibility of containing that which is moral. There is no evidence that he wishes such a condition to be true, or that it benefits him as an artist to succumb to his obsession with women's inhumane power, which he quite honestly does, when he might fashion far more acceptable portraits of women. But instead, in his creation of heroines he projects his enormous rage and disappointment with womankind, writing with power and conviction, but as a man who rails at the world because he has never found in it a woman who is both strong and good.

HERMIONE LEE

'You Must Change Your Life': Mentors, Doubles and Literary Influences in the Search for Self

Political coercion and obstruction are public visions of family, marital and psychological struggles. The question of who or what shall have influence over the self applies to every area of Roth's work, and quite as much to narrative modes as to subject-matter. I have [previously] said that his novels describe various forms of opposition between discipline and freedom, and it is already apparent that in his treatment of this opposition Roth is highly literary, referential and self-conscious. Moreover, each of his books explicitly relates the predicament of his characters to the writer's narrative choices and solutions. And so his spokesmen are frequently writers or teachers of literature, as self-conscious as their author about the influence of books on their lives. 'Literature got me into this,' says Tarnopol, 'and literature is gonna have to get me out.'

This explicit relationship between influence in life and in literature is clearly but awkwardly embodied in *When She Was Good* (1967), a long, miserable 'American tragedy' of a girl in a small Midwest town in the 1950s, Lucy Nelson, who despises and all but destroys her liberal, over-protective grandfather, her alcoholic father, her helplessly feminine mother, and the nice but stupid boy who gets her pregnant at the age of 18. Lucy's savage insistence on duty ('You have to do what's *right*'), her

From *Philip Roth*. Copyright © 1982 by Hermione Lee. Methuen & Co., Ltd.

conviction that everyone is at fault except herself, her rage at the smalltown life which traps her, end in frantic self-destruction. Though this is his only novel with a Gentile and provincial setting, and with a woman at its centre, Roth insists on its relation to his other work. Lucy's thwarted bids for freedom are, he says, another version of Portnoy's, her coercive rhetoric is like the American government's in the war with Vietnam. Even so, it is the most uncharacteristic and uninspired of his books, doggedly naturalistic, and vacillating uneasily between presenting Lucy as pitiful victim and portraying her as tyrannical monster. The parallel, though, between the restrictions imposed on and enforced by Lucy, and the restrictions Roth places on himself in writing this novel, is a typical one. Roth is trying to write the big, Gentile, American naturalist novel in the tradition of Wolfe, Dreiser or Sinclair Lewis:

> 'Town' meant Iron City, where the logs were brought to be milled and the ore to be dumped into boxcars, the clanging, buzzing, swarming, dusty frontier town to which he walked each schoolday—or in winter, when he went off in a raw morning dimness, ran—through woods aswarm with bear and wolf. So at the sight of Liberty Center, its quiet beauty, its serene order, its gentle summery calm, all that had been held in check in him, all that tenderness of heart that had been for eighteen years his secret burden, even at times his shame, came streaming forth.

The uncomfortable syntax, the embarrassing archaisms ('aswarm', 'streaming forth'), the dull choice of words ('swarming', 'summary', 'serene'), reveal the straitjacketed writer. This is a mode that suits Roth no better than Lucy's family, town and marriage suit her.

Lucy Nelson does not admit to her literary mentors. She is never to be found reading *Main Street,* or *An American Tragedy,* or *You Can't Go Home Again.* (In fact she reads 'Ozymandias', useful for its image of the desolation wreaked by a 'sneer of cold command'.) Elsewhere, Roth allows himself to be more playful and explicit with 'the question of influence'. At the beginning of *Letting Go,* Gabe Wallach and Libby Herz have a long conversation about James's *The Portrait of a Lady* ('That book . . . is really full of people pushing and pulling at each other'), which alerts us to specifically 'Jamesian' traits in the characters—Libby's romantic aspirations, Gabe's 'hanging fire'—and, more generally, to the crucial subject of self-defining choices, crucial not just for *Letting Go* but for all Roth's work. If you are what you have chosen to be, then you must live with it—like Isabel Archer at the end of *The Portrait of a Lady.* But that moral, Jamesian desire of Roth's characters to come to terms with their chosen selves is balked by impenetrable obstacles which owe more to Kafka than to James. What Roth calls 'a deeply vexing sense of characterological enslavement'—Portnoy's complaint, and that of all the Kepeshes and Zuckermans—is almost always described in literary as well as psychoanalytical terms. In his comments on *My Life as a Man*, Roth refers to the scene in *The Trial*, where K., in the cathedral, hopes that the priest will come down from his pulpit and point him to 'a mode of living completely outside the jurisdiction of the Court'. As Roth sees it, the man in the pulpit is oneself, and the court 'is of one's own devising': the only possible existence, in the world according to Kafka, is an ironic toleration of that trap. Roth's novels describe different versions of 'characterological enslavement' either accepted or resisted, and each version invokes one, or several, literary authorities for the predicament.

When Roth turns David Kepesh, professor of literature, into a breast (*The Breast*, 1972), he makes literary influence into an explicit part of Kepesh's 'enslavement': 'I got it from fiction,' the professor tells his analyst. 'The books I've been teaching—they put the idea in my head. . . . Teaching Gogol and Kafka every year—teaching "The Nose" and "Metamorphosis".' 'I have out-Kafkaed Kafka.' But Dr Klinger is there to tell him that 'hormones are hormones and art is art', to make him accept himself as *real*. (It is usual for Roth's psychoanalysts to oppose or belittle their patients' *literary* analyses of their problems.) Kepesh's task is to accept that 'It is only life, and I am only human.'

> For him there is no way out of the monstrous situation, not even through literary interpretation. There is only the unrelenting education in his own misfortune. What he learns by the end is that, whatever else it is, it is the real thing: he *is* a breast, and must act accordingly.

Kepesh's last words, addressed to 'my fellow mammalians', are a quotation from Rilke ('You must change your life'). In this extreme parable of 'characterological enslavement' Kepesh has progressed from literary explanations, fantasies, frustration and disbelief, to an acceptance of his grotesque self, an acceptance he finds it easiest to express, however, in a quotation.

Kepesh in *The Breast* succeeds where Portnoy leaves off and where Tarnopol fails. The writer and teacher in *My Life as a Man* is compelled to explain his breakdown through a series of fictions that make his life into texts for interpretation. The more his fictional Zuckerman protests that he is 'real', not a character out of *The Trial*, the less Tarnopol finds it possible to accept that 'this is me who is me being me and none other.' He cannot write himself out of his predicament. Tarnopol's self-conscious blockage makes for a frantically energetic, garrulous, funny novel—Roth's equivalent to Bellow's *Herzog*—which is (necessarily) repetitive and self-indulgent.

More shapely and assured versions of literary influence as an explicit part of 'characterological enslavement' are found in *The Professor of Desire* and *The Ghost Writer.*

The Professor of Desire (1977) is a realist—as opposed to surreal—portrait of David Kepesh (written five years after *The Breast*) which makes elegant, complex use of Chekhov and Kafka as authorities for Kepesh's predicament while he is still living 'as a man'. Kepesh is torn between reckless erotic ambitions and conscientious intellectual dedication. Peripheral characters line up from childhood onwards as 'secret sharers' of his two selves: first, his anxious hotelier parents and the vulgar comedian Herbert Bratasky; then the two Swedish girls he lives with in London (while writing his thesis on Arthurian legends), the affectionate Elizabeth and the debauched Birgitta; later, his responsible, chivalrous department head 'Arthur' Schonbrunn and the libidinous poet Baumgarten. His marriage to the sexy, sloppy Helen Baird makes the conflict unmanageable: erotic pleasures are driven out by the professor's need for responsible order; the result is anxiety and impotence. His mother's death seems a judgement on his inability to sustain 'steady, dedicated living.' The commonsensical Dr Klinger tries to close the gap between libido and conscience, but the real, if temporary, cure comes from Claire Ovington, who is erotic, innocent, virtuous and orderly all in one, and brings Kepesh a period of simple peace and satisfaction.

He celebrates by returning to his abandoned book on Chekhov, whose stories tenderly express the 'humiliations and failures' of 'socialized beings' who 'seek a way out of the shell of restrictions and convention.' At the end of the novel, Claire and Kepesh are visited in the country by Kepesh's widowed father and the father's old friend, who, having survived the concentration camps, says that his ambition had always been to be 'a human being . . . someone that could see and understand how we lived, and what was real.' Even though his sufferings have been so much less, Kepesh feels himself to be failing in that ambition. Sensing by now that his passion for Claire is an 'interim,' not a solution, he tells her that the comical, pathetic visit of the two old men is like a Chekhov story, and that they two are left (like the lovers at the end of 'The Lady with the Little Dog') knowing 'that the most complicated and difficult part was only just beginning.'

In Chekhov's 'The Duel,' the story that is central to Kepesh's work on that author, the 'weaseling, slovenly, intelligent, literary-minded seducer' Layevsky, imprisoned by what an analyst would call 'the libidinous fallacy,' finds his antagonist and 'secret sharer' in the rationalist zoologist Von Koren, who believes that the race should be improved by exterminating 'lepers' like Layevsky. Von Koren almost kills him in their duel in the Caucasus, but is distracted by the intervention of a man of faith. The duel releases 'a sense of shame and sinfulness' in Layevsky; he makes an honest woman of his mistress and tries to 'change his life'. Von Koren, who is leaving, apologizes to the reformed Layevsky for having misjudged him: 'Nobody knows the real truth,' he says. As Von Koren's boat disappears into a dark, stormy Black Sea, Layevsky reflects:

> In the search for truth man makes two steps forward and one step back. Suffering, mistakes, and weariness in life thrust them back, but the thirst for truth and stubborn will drive them on and on. And who knows? Perhaps they will reach the real truth at last.

Kepesh too is making two steps forward and one step back. But his acceptance of the limits to personal happiness in an unhappy world is only partly allowed to take its tone from the dignity and pathos of 'a muted Chekhov tale of ordinary human affliction.' Before this last scene, Roth boldly externalizes the professor's 'blockage' by sending Kepesh and Claire to Prague. Here, of course, Kafka is the spiritual authority. Kepesh discusses Kafka's relevance to the citizens of Prague with a Czech professor, who, sacked from his post, ironically tolerates his fate by translating *Moby Dick*, painstakingly and pointlessly, into Czech. The Jewish-American and the Czech teachers of literature salute each other's blockages, the one sexual, the other political, in terms that exactly describe what Roth's novels do with literary influence—batten on to it, consume it, use and abuse it, and finally break free of it to find their own voice and style:

> 'Well,' he says, putting a hand on my arm in a kind and fatherly way, 'to each obstructed citizen his own Kafka.'
>
> 'And to each angry man his own Melville,' I reply. 'But then what are bookish people to do with all the great prose they read—'
>
> '—but sink their teeth into it. Exactly. Into the books, instead of into the hand that throttles them.'

Kepesh and Claire visit Kafka's grave, and find it next to the graves of all those who perished in the camps. In a café, sitting next to two alluring prostitutes, he writes his next lecture (couched in the form of Kafka's 'Report to an Academy'), which sets out honestly to explain the relevance of his own libidinous history to his teaching of literature. His own desires, the professor's 'life as a man', must be acknowledged in the classroom (he will tell his students) if they are to understand how *Madame Bovary* and other great novels 'concerned with erotic desire' have any 'referential' relationship to the students' own lives and to the life of their teacher. Like Kafka's ape speaking to the Academy, the professor wishes to give to his students 'an open account of the life I formerly led as a human being. I am devoted to fiction, and I assure you that in time I will tell you whatever I may know about it, but in truth nothing lives in me like my life.' But at night he dreams of being taken (by Herbert Bratasky) to visit Kafka's whore, a decrepit old woman who offers to show him her withered cunt in the cause of scholarship. The desecration of Kafka's image in the dream violently subverts the lecture's attempt to reconcile the conscientious, dedicated life of the mind with the shameful, secret life of the body. The four Prague episodes—the professor, the cemetery, the lecture, the dream—are not explained; characteristically, they are left to jostle and overlap uncomfortably in the reader's mind. The total effect is to set Professor Kepesh in the mortifying, inexplicable, blocked world of Kafka (or Gogol) rather than the dignified, tender Chekhovian world.

But, after all, the professor is not a citizen of Prague; his relatives left Europe and were not killed in the camps; he can teach, write and speak freely (even if America in the 1970s does seem unreal and alien). What obstructs him is an internal conflict. Kafka, as Kepesh tells Claire, says to his sausage-eating colleague that 'the only fit food for a man is half a lemon'; by contrast, the lemon in the professor's fridge is replaced by his caring mother's packets of frozen food. The visit to Prague is weighted with guilt. Martin Green describes the sources of that guilt well, in his comments on Roth's essay 'Looking at Kafka' (1973). This extraordinary essay completes a study of Kafka by imagining that he has survived and come to America and is, in 1942, the 9-year-old Roth's Hebrew school-teacher, invited home by the family to be matched with Aunt Rhoda:

> The contrast . . . is between the self-denying and self-defeating Czech, spiritual athlete and ascetic, and the brash and greedy son of immigrants, the Jew who got away, whose writings embody the all-voracious culture around him, even as they bitterly criticize it.

In his own professional life, Roth's editing of the Penguin 'Writers from the Other Europe' series could be seen as an expiation of that guilt. His admiration for writers who died in the war (Bruno Schulz, the brilliant Galician author of two novels, who translated *The Trial* into Polish, and was shot by an SS agent in 1942), or who endured the camps (Tadeusz Borowski, who survived Auschwitz and Dachau and killed himself in Warsaw in 1951), or who are living under severe prohibitions in Czecho-slovakia (Milan Kundera, to whom *The Ghost Writer* is dedicated, for whose *Laughable Loves* Roth wrote an introduction, and who has also written on Kafka), or whose work has been savagely attacked by the authorities (Danilo Kiš, a Yugoslav writer for whom Bruno Schulz is 'a god'), inevitably involves self-comparisons:

I am wholly in awe of writers like Sinyavsky and Daniel, of their personal bravery and their uncompromising devotion and dedication to literature. To write in secrecy, to publish pseudonymously, to work in fear of the labor camp, to be despised, ridiculed, and insulted by the mass of writers turning out just what they're supposed to—it would be presumptuous to imagine one's *art* surviving in such a hostile environment, let alone coming through with the dignity and self-possession displayed by Sinyavsky and Daniel at their trial.

In Kepesh or Zuckerman, Roth projects a complicated attitude, not simply the Jewish-American writer's guilt for the sufferings of eastern European writers and, before that, for the Jews in Europe, but, with it, a kind of wistfulness, even envy, for the writer who has had more to sink his teeth into than books and relationships. This half-shaming sense lurks behind Kepesh's fixation on Kafka and, more comically, behind Nathan's fantasy of Anne Frank's survival in *The Ghost Writer*. Of all Roth's novels, *The Ghost Writer* is the most concentratedly about influence. It is an elegant, small-scale *Bildungsroman*, a 'rite of confirmation' in which the 23-year-old Nathan Zuckerman comes to manhood and dedicates himself to the writer's task in one night spent at the house of the reclusive Russian-Jewish novelist, E. I. Lonoff, deep in the snowy Berkshires. The novel, or rather novella, eschews the straggling, garrulous form of *My Life as a Man* or the loosely linked episodes of *The Professor of Desire* in favour of a coolly controlled structure. Nathan's evening, night and morning at the house encircle two life stories, one real (Nathan's) and one fictive. The 'fictive' story imagines the possibility of the survival of Anne Frank (a play about whose life and death, drawn from her diary, is running on Broadway). Nathan, curious about the position in the household of a mysterious, attractive fellow guest, Amy Bellette (adopted orphan? mistress? family friend? amanuensis?), identifies her as Anne Frank—an Anne Frank who had, after all, survived the camps. The two stories, his and hers, are carefully opposed: the Jewish son who angers his own loving parents by 'betraying' the Jews in the story he has written ('Higher Education') is set against the legendary, 'sainted' Jewish daughter, whom he imagines sacrificing a post-war reunion with her father in order that, through her assumed death, her art may live. Just as she has survived to see her diary immortalize the sufferings of the Jews in Europe, and now claims kinship not with her real father but with the writer Lonoff, recorder of the 'exclusion and confinement' of the race, so Nathan needs to turn to a writer-father. At first we take Anne Frank's story as literal; only gradually does it appear that it is a 'useful fiction', Nathan's fantasy (comparable to Kepesh's dream of Kafka's whore in *The Professor of*

Desire). Through this invention Nathan acts out his own anxiety about the double burden placed on the Jewish writer: disinheritance from those he must write about, responsibility to their history.

All the other parallels in this book are as carefully balanced as that between Nathan and Amy—those between the Jewish-American writers, the self-denying Lonoff and the self-publicizing Abranavel; between wife and girl in Lonoff's house, the martyred Hope and the sensual Amy; between highpowered New York and country life in the Berkshires, an old landscape of the American Transcendentalists, where the writer is thrown on his own resources; between Nathan's real father and his literary father, Lonoff. The two references pinned up in Lonoff's study (where Nathan eavesdrops, masturbates, writes to his father, inspects Lonoff's library and sleeps in the day-bed), one of them to Chopin and Byron ('tenderness, boldness, love and contempt') and the other to Henry James (restraint, renunciation, the high road of art), sum up the alternatives. The choice, as always in Roth, but most neatly diagrammed here, is between the 'hunger artist's' asceticism and anxiety, and the 'hungry panther's' appetite for full absorption in the world of sex, love and power. Can the artist have both, or must he deny himself? Lonoff's index card refers the aspiring Nathan to Henry James's story 'The Middle Years', in which a young doctor sacrifices a fortune in order to minister to the dying novelist Dencombe, a perfectionist and compulsive corrector of his own work (like Lonoff, and James) who is aware that he has just missed greatness, and whose last words bleakly describe the artist's fate: 'We work in the dark—we do what we can—we give what we have. Our doubt is our passion and our passion is our task. The rest is the madness of art.' James's austere ideal of dedication is the model for Lonoff's asceticism, which his disciple has admired in the stories of 'thwarted, secretive, imprisoned souls' and which he now sees in Lonoff's life: 'a man, his destiny, and his work—all one.' The stories are 'visions of terminal restraint'; the characters (always 'a bachelor, a widower, an orphan, a foundling, or a reluctant fiancé') are blocked in their smallest impulses towards self-surrender by those 'devoted underlings' of 'Sanity, Responsibility and Self-Respect', 'the timetable, the rainstorm, the headache, the busy signal, the traffic jam, and, most loyal of all, the last-minute doubt'. The small details of Lonoff's behaviour, closely observed by Nathan—his fussiness over the fire and the record-player, his annotation of magazine articles, the half an egg he wants for breakfast—are symptomatic of the restraint that prevents him from wanting to do anything except 'turn sentences around', least of all run off to Italy (always an idealized escape route for Roth's heroes) with the mysterious Amy. The ageing maestro renounces the temptations of young love as he has renounced those of fame, while his wife, driven berserk (a brilliantly painful comic study) by living for thirty-five years with so much 'moral fibre', tries to abdicate in favour of her rival: 'You get the creative writer—and I get to go!'

While love and despair rage around him, Lonoff (like the Czech professor) is 'kind and fatherly', if ironical, to his disciple. But Nathan has not yet chosen Lonovian, or Jamesian, completeness: there is a gap, pointed out by both his fathers, between what he writes and what he is. And Lonoff has not been his only model; earlier he had met and admired Felix Abranavel, wryly summed up by Lonoff:

> Beautiful wives, beautiful mistresses, alimony the size of the national debt, polar expeditions, war-front reportage, famous friends, famous enemies, breakdowns, public lectures, five-hundred-page novels every third year, and still . . . time and energy left over for all that self-absorption. . . . Like him? No. But impressed, oh yes. Absolutely. It's no picnic up there in the egosphere.

Lonoff and Abranavel, possible models for the aspiring Jewish-American writer, suggest composite models: Nathan compares Lonoff to Singer; his pilgrimage invokes Charlie Citrine's to Humboldt in Bellow's *Humboldt's Gift,* and Abranavel has more than a touch of Mailer. But Philip Roth is also projected, as the young beginner before *Goodbye, Columbus,* as the much-courted and famous author of *Portnoy,* as the established and private man of letters. In his 'middle years', he is ghost-writing himself as disciple and as master, so that his subject, in this grave, marvellously controlled comic novel, is at once the illusions and the deprivations of a literary vocation. Nathan Dedalus's choosing of a new father prompts him to tell his life story to Lonoff, who is described at the end as 'the picture of the chief rabbi, the archdeacon, the magisterial high priest of perpetual sorrows.' The need for an 'archdeacon' to whom the son or writer can confess, and who will tell him how to change his life, is common to Roth's characters. They fix on writers or analysts rather than on priests or rabbis, but, like K. in the cathedral, they want instruction and consolation. The novels, in their pursuit of 'who or what shall have influence over the self', are full of magus figures. They may be literary sages, 'singing masters' of the soul, like James or Kafka. They may be treacherous coaches like Tricky, or spokesmen for repressive authoritarianism, like Rabbi Binder or Judge Wapter—or Lucy Nelson. They may be cherishing but oppressive fathers, or destructively over-possessive wives or mothers. They may be 'secret sharers' (the term, from Conrad, used by Kepesh for Baumgarten and by Nathan for Alvin Pepler) who seem, however grotesquely, to enact a suppressed part of the blocked self. Or the 'blocked' hero may himself be a teacher, a mentor to others, whose courses, like Tarnopol's on 'transgression and punishment' or Kepesh's on desire, express their obsessions. Most of the mentors and *alter egos* are, as in Kafka, ominous rather than reassuring. They inspire the kind of distrust that is the basis of *Our Gang*, or the fear that is a running joke in *Zuckerman Unbound* (1981).

After the success of his novel *Carnovsky* in 1969 (the year of *Portnoy*, of course), people accost Nathan Zuckerman (thirteen years older now than he was in *The Ghost Writer*) on buses and in the street, write him abusive letters, spill out their fantasies to his answering service, report his invented affairs in the gossip columns, and take his name in vain on television. Whether he eats a snack in a café or takes a famous actress out to dinner, he is public property, and needs an armed chauffeur. Having tried to enfranchise himself by writing *Carnovsky*, he finds himself imprisoned by Fame. Reality—'le vrai' as Flaubert calls it—is taking its revenge. New York seems to consist entirely of his would-be assassins or confiding fans. Alvin Pepler, the disgruntled, loquacious scapegoat of the TV quiz scandals of the 1950s, dogs Nathan's steps, with marvelous comic insistence, his manic adulation rapidly turning to abuse, as though summoned up by Nathan's paranoia: 'This Peplerian barrage is what? Zeitgeist overspill? Newark poltergeist? Tribal retribution? Secret Sharer? P. as my pop self? . . . He who's made fantasy of others now fantasy of others.'

It is tempting to ridicule *Zuckerman Unbound*, as some critics did, for protesting too much about the painful problems of wealth and fame, though Nathan's fear of assassination in New York can strike no one as exaggerated. But, even if this novel, for all its comic brio, is self-regarding, it fits exactly into the pattern of Roth's work. Comical Nathan, the complaining self who goes in fear of his *Doppelgänger*, is also the disinherited son. In a brilliant family scene round the father's deathbed, Nathan, having tried to offer consolation with a brand-new scientific theory of the endlessly self-renewing life of the universe, hears the word 'bastard' painstakingly pronounced: it is his father's last word. Later, his brother tells him what had caused his father's death: reading *Carnovsky*. 'You killed him, Nathan, with that book. *Of course* he said "Bastard". He'd seen it! . . . You don't believe me, do you? You can't believe that what you write about people has *real consequences*.' The book ends as Nathan is driven by his armed chauffeur through the Newark streets of his childhood, now a ghetto. 'Who are you supposed to be?' the black occupant of what was his father's house asks him. ' "No one," replied Zuckerman, and that was the end of that.'

Like Portnoy, Nathan is locked inside himself, unamused by the joke ('you keep ducking when you should be smiling'), desperate for advice. His agent has his case in hand ('My concern is defusing the persecution mania, Nathan'), but it is a matter of Nathan's dislocation from 'le vrai' that, in this novel so tightly contained within the New York literary world, the literary agent should have taken over the role of analyst. Part of the originality of *Portnoy's Complaint* was its use of the analysand's monologue as a literary stratagem. It is not, though, a novel about analysis. Dr Spielvogel is silent until his punchline, and Portnoy's confession is, as Roth says, 'highly stylized'. Nor does Portnoy change his life: part of his complaint is that 'his sense of himself . . . is so *fixed.*' And, of course, the analyst cannot simply tell the patient to 'change his life'; his version of the patient may be rejected, the blockage may be impenetrable. Of all the magus figures in Roth, the analysts are the least authoritarian.

Roth uses them first as escape routes for unhappy young married women. In a story of 1963 called 'The Psychoanalytic Special' a suburban housewife hooked on clandestine affairs, who 'desperately' wants 'to be changed', commutes four times a week to tell Dr Spielvogel about her dreams, her boring marriage and her departed lover. In the end she finds that being cured is worse than the affliction. Libby, in *Letting Go*, pays a weeping visit which she can't afford to a Dr Lumin, to tell him that Paul neglects her, that she loves Gabe, and that she feels cracked. Dr Lumin is matter-of-fact: 'These are real problems. . . . But what's this cracked business? How far does it get us?'

These disheartening forays into analysis lead on to the silent reappearance of Dr Spielvogel in *Portnoy* as the reader's 'secret sharer'. After *Portnoy*, analysis becomes a central, active ingredient in the comical blockages of Tarnopol and Kepesh. Spielvogel's adage—'tolerate it'—helps Tarnopol, in *My Life as a Man*, to save himself from Maureen, but his rejection of the analyst's 'reductivism' ('Does your wife remind you of your mother?') culminates in a furious sense of betrayal when he finds that Spielvogel has, himself, 'written him up'. The analyst has published his patient's case history (with certain significant features altered) in an article called 'Creativity: The Narcissism of the Artist,' a use of himself as 'evidence' which that very narcissism renders Tarnopol quite unable to excuse. Kepesh in *The Professor of Desire* is irritated by Dr Klinger's dogged 'demythologizing' of his case. Only Kepesh as a breast begins to respond to the 'demystifying' of his predicament. 'You are not insane,' Klinger tells the breast. 'It *is* something that has happened to you . . . *this is no delusion.*' This is the only treatment that Roth's analysts can provide: the best they can do is to make people tolerate their condition, however surreal it may seem to them, as *real*—and thus their condition may become tolerable. Such 'demythologizing' is liable to be funny: Roth's scenes of analysis often take the form of comic routines, two-handers between the funny man and his stooge (roles that may alternate between patient and analyst):

> 'Your sperm? What about your sperm?'
>   'My semen—I leave it places.'
>   'Yes?'
>   'I smear it places. I go to people's houses and I leave it—places.'
>   'You break into people's houses?'
>   'No, no,' I said sharply—what did he think I was, a madman? 'I'm invited. I go to the bathroom. I leave it somewhere . . .'
>   . . . 'Speak up, please,' said the doctor.
>   'I sealed an envelope with it,' I said in a loud voice. 'My bill to the telephone company.'
>   Again Spielvogel smiled. 'Now that is an original touch, Mr Tarnopol.'
>   And again I broke into sobs. 'What does it mean!'
>   'Come now,' said Dr Spielvogel, 'what do you think it "means"? . . .'
>   'That I'm completely out of control!' I said, sobbing. 'That I don't know what I'm doing any more!'
>   'That you're angry,' he said, slapping the arm of his chair. 'That you are furious. You are not *out* of control—you are *under* control. Maureen's control. You spurt the anger everywhere, except where it belongs. There you spurt tears.'

Maureen Tarnopol is in analysis too, but her pain is not made available to us. In Tarnopol's 'life as her man' she is the monstrous 'lunatic' who traps him into marrying her by faking a pregnancy test, sabotages his professional life, goes through abortions and suicide attempts before her violent death, and leaves Tarnopol unmanned and obsessed. Of all Roth's female characters, Maureen is the most frantic and destructive. That she has her own story to tell is frequently suggested (not least by the book's epigram, taken from her diary: 'I could be his Muse, if only he'd let me'). But she is seen, in the main, as the 'unmanning' influence on Tarnopol, and thus takes her place among the pantheon of obstructors, authorities or mentors who encompass Roth's complaining heroes. He makes some early, conscientious attempts to engage with the psychology of women such as Libby and Martha in *Letting Go* or Lucy Nelson in *When She Was Good*, but the later women characters are placed in either obstructive or enfranchising relations to the son/husband/writer/complainant. They stand, in the main, as Dionysian or daemonic influences opposed to the Apollonian reason and wisdom of the male analysts and writers. Only rarely is female sexuality apprehended without guilt or dread, and then it is usually felt as consolation, something to hold on to after a bad dream:

> I awaken perspiring. . . . Then, blessedly, I find Claire, a big warm animal of my own species, my very own mate of the other gender, and encircling her with my arms—drawing her sheer creatureliness up against the length of my body—I begin to recall [the dream].

Roth's male characters overlap with each other and with Roth; his women characters can be grouped together as overprotective mothers, or as monstrously unmanning wives, or as consoling, tender, sensible girlfriends, or as recklessly libidinous sexual objects. Occasionally, like Portnoy's 'Monkey' —dressed for Mayor Lindsay's dinner like a stripper, murmuring obscenities down the Assistant Commissioner's phone, understanding 'Leda and the Swan' with her cunt—they burst through the confines of their type with a kind of vengeful comic energy. And in the last two novels there are developments: Hope Lonoff of *The Ghost Writer* and Caesara O'Shea, the ironical film star of *Zuckerman Unbound*, are unexpected and exactly seen.

Nevertheless, Roth's use of women characters as part of an examination of 'who or what shall have authority over the (male) self' does not endear him to feminist critics. Alix Kates Shulman, for example, is dissatisfied with *When She Was Good*, which, she says, like other 'male-oriented' versions of the American forties and fifties such as *Summer of '42* and *The Last Picture Show*, 'neglects' the female point of view. (A feminist antidote to the novel would be Lisa Alther's *Kinflicks*.) Sarah Cohen dislikes 'Philip Roth's Would-Be Patriarchs and their *Shikses* and Shrews'. Roth is impatient with the 'Feminist Right', as he makes clear in his review of Alan Lelchuk's *American Mischief*, which, he says, will be called sexist 'for demonstrating . . . that there are indeed women in America as broken and resentful as the women in America are coming to proclaim themselves to be.' If Roth's fiction does demean women, it can only be seen to do so paradoxically. The greediest male dreams of sexual power and gratification are felt by a man who has been turned into a breast and is completely humiliated and helpless. That literal enactment of 'breast envy' is the most extreme of Roth's subservient male fantasies; his men are vulnerable, envious and afraid of women, not domineering chauvinists. Portnoy is really no exception: his insistence that well-brought-up girls should suck him off is only skin-deep bravado. Accusations of chauvinism might be more accurately directed against the thinness with which these girls are characterized in Portnoy's narrative.

But this is ultimately more a question of fictional methods than of sexual politics. I called *Zuckerman Unbound* a self-regarding novel, because it seems to treat Roth's early fame rather solemnly. But it is at autological criticism, since Roth's novels are *about* self-regard, and their difficulty lies in reconciling 'le vrai' with the narcissistic quest for self. The mentors— literary, spiritual, sexual—who are posted around Roth's complainants are there because they play some part in the struggle towards an acceptance of

> the unalterable necessity
> of being this unalterable animal.

(The lines are from Wallace Stevens's 'Aesthétique du Mal', quoted at the start of *Letting Go*.) Rendered 'unfit', like Novotny, by some undiagnosable pain, the butt of some inexplicable joke, making complaints and appeals in all directions but essentially on their own, Roth's Kafkaesque buffoons totter towards a way of feeling *real*, of saying 'this is me who is me being me and none other'. Most of the books end (like Bellow's *Herzog*) as this process begins: no one is allowed to finish. The parallel, as Zuckerman tries to explain to his dying father, is with the universe, which, according to the big-bang theory, is 'being reborn and reborn and reborn, without end.'

SAM B. GIRGUS

The Jew as Underground Man

A̲nzia Yezierska fought with "blut-und-eisen" to find her identity and freedom as a woman and Jew in America, and Philip Roth, in our own time, has struggled to establish his identity as a Jewish writer and man. Perhaps no other modern American writer has done so much to challenge old stereotypes and concepts about masculinity. Roth has written almost compulsively about achieving inde-pendence, authority, and maturity as an artist and man in America. The fact that his heroes are multiple guises of a single mythic consciousness of the modern urban Jew both complicates and enriches his fiction and vision of American culture. Like Yezierska's Sara, Roth's hero finds himself encaptured in a ghetto of the mind. This theme of finding one's self unable to escape the past and unable to overcome a perennial perspective from a psychic ghetto pervades most of Roth's fiction. However, another important part of his perspective as a writer is Roth's definite sense of himself as an American writer. From the beginning of his career, Roth has expressed concern about the need to understand the meaning of the American experience, and, in this sense, Roth is a major contributor to the tradition of the New Covenant. In fact, along with Bellow and Mailer, Roth has written intensively about the responsibilities of the writer to explore the American idea and explain contemporary American culture. Moreover, he has also asserted the importance of Jewish writers in developing new literary styles and tastes as both a response to their situation as Jews in America and as a way of fulfilling their artistic and literary promise. Roth, in effect, claims for Jewish writers the kind of

From *The New Covenant: Jewish Writers and the American Idea.* Copyright © 1984 by University of North Carolina Press.

linguistic initiative and leadership that characterizes the writers of the New Covenant. In Roth, one finds justification for the argument that the Jewish writer and thinker is a linguistic innovator who develops the rhetorical and narrative structures of the myth and ideology of America while maintaining the role of the modern Jewish hero of thought. After reading what Roth says about fiction and literature, it becomes easier to understand that he wants his own fiction to lead the literary and intellectual effort to help liberate people from the bonds and shackles that they put on themselves. Roth's sentiments on such matters indicate a depth of concern that many miss in the creator of Alexander Portnoy.

In his famous essay of 1960 on "Writing American Fiction," Roth argues that "the American writer in the middle of the twentieth century has his hands full in trying to understand, describe, and then make *credible* much of American reality. It stupefies, it sickens, it infuriates, and finally it is even a kind of embarrassment to one's own meager imagination. The actuality is continually outdoing our talents, and the culture tosses up figures almost daily that are the envy of any novelist." However, in spite of Roth's complaint about the intractability of American reality, his greater complaint goes against those who avoid the challenge. Thus, he expresses concern in 1960 because Norman Mailer "seems for the time being to have given up on making an imaginative assault upon the American experience." He also attacks both the beat writers who deal in cynicism and the best sellers who peddle platitudes for ultimately committing the same crime of not taking either America or their own roles as writers seriously. He writes, "The attitude of the Beats (if such a phrase has meaning) is not entirely without appeal. The whole thing is a joke, America, ha-ha. But that doesn't put very much distance between Beatdom and its sworn enemy, best-sellerdom—not much more than what it takes to get from one side of a nickel to the other: for is America, ha-ha, really any more than America, hoo-ray, stood upon its head?"

Roth's dismay at trying to reflect reality in America eventually develops into an affirmation of the writer's role. He carves out a special territory based not merely on his view of contemporary literature and culture but also on his understanding of the American literary tradition. A student of both American and European literature who received a master's degree from the University of Chicago, Roth realizes that he is not the first writer to confront the difficulty of rendering American reality. In a self-interview on *The Great American Novel*, he says:

> Later I also became a disciple of certain literature professors and their favorite texts. For instance, reading *The Wings of the Dove* all afternoon long in the graduate-school library at the University of Chicago, I would

find myself as transfixed by James's linguistic tact and moral scrupulosity as I had ever been by the coarseness, recklessness, and vulgar, aggressive clowning with which I was so taken during those afternoons and evenings in "my" booth at the corner candy store. As I now see it, one of my continuing problems as a writer has been to find the means to be true to these seemingly inimical realms of experience that I am strongly attached to by temperament and training—the aggressive, the crude, and the obscene, at one extreme, and something a good deal more subtle and, in every sense, refined, at the other. But that problem is not unique to any single American writer, certainly not in this day and age.

Roth sees himself as trying to bridge what he goes on to describe in Philip Rahv's terms as the worlds of the serious "paleface" writer and the spontaneous and more vernacular "redskin."

For Roth, this contrast between the styles and sensibilities of the "paleface" as opposed to the more aggressive "redskin" is complicated by being Jewish, which automatically enlists one in the ranks of the "redskin." The contrast between genteel sensibilities and the "redskin" reality of Jewish ethnicity and class origins creates acute tensions for the Jewish writer and intellectual. The Jewish writer has to face "being *fundamentally ill at ease in, and at odds with, both worlds.*" Roth continues, "In short: neither the redskin one was in the days of innocence, nor the paleface one could never be in a million (or, to be precise, 5,733) years, but rather, at least in my own case, what I would describe as a 'redface'." To the Jewish writer, however, such tension can encourage discomfort with ordinary stylistic conventions and make one "alert to the inexhaustible number of intriguing postures that the awkward may assume in public, and the strange means that the uneasy come upon to express themselves." In "Writing American Fiction," Roth more specifically identifies the characteristics of this innovative Jewish style and the forces that help to shape it. He writes:

> When writers who do not feel much of a connection to Lord Chesterfield begin to realize that they are under no real obligation to try and write like that distinguished old stylist, they are likely enough to go out and be bouncy. Also, there is the matter of the spoken language which these writers have heard, as our statesmen might put it, in the schools, the homes, the churches and the synagogues of the nation. I would even say that when the bouncy style is not an attempt to dazzle the reader, or one's self, but to incorporate into American literary prose the rhythms, nuances, and emphases of urban and immigrant speech, the result can sometimes be a language of new and rich emotional subtleties, with a kind of back-handed charm and irony all its own, as in Grace Paley's book of stories *The Little Disturbances of Man*. But whether the practitioner is Gold, Bellow, or Paley, there is a further point to make about the bounciness: it is an expression of pleasure.

For Roth, therefore, his Jewish background provides an important source for creative literary and linguistic invention.

In contrast to Henry Roth, Philip Roth's sense of participation in a literary movement of modern Jewish writers is consistent with his acknowledged sense of himself as inexorably Jewish in terms of experience and thought. In an interview with George Plimpton about *Portnoy's Complaint*, Roth said, "I have always been far more pleased by my good fortune in being born a Jew than my critics may begin to imagine. It's a complicated, interesting, morally demanding, and very singular experience, and I like that. I find myself in the historic predicament of being Jewish, with all its implications. Who could ask for more?" Although he has written fiction about non-Jews, such as *When She Was Good*, he clearly feels that his own experience as a Jew largely dictates his perception and understanding of the moral and psychological themes that dominate his work. Thus, in a discussion about one of his earlier and most controversial stories called "Defender of the Faith," which is about two Jewish soldiers, Roth, in "Writing about Jews," says, "Yet, though the moral complexities are not exclusively a Jew's, I never for a moment considered that the characters in the story should be anything other than Jews. Someone else might have written a story embodying the same themes, and similar events perhaps, and had at its center Negroes or Irishmen; for me there was no choice."

In terms of cultural geography, the Jewish environment that nurtured Roth was not so far removed from the experiences of Henry Roth and Anzia Yezierska a generation earlier. Moreover, in psychological terms, Roth's Newark also seems close to the earlier ghetto of the Lower East Side. Roth describes a community of his youth that considers itself under perennial siege. In trying "to transform into fiction something of the small world in which I had spent the first eighteen years of my life," Roth says that his early stories drew upon "the ethos of my highly self-conscious Jewish neighborhood, which had been squeezed like some embattled little nation in among ethnic rivals and antagonists, peoples equally proud, ambitious, and xenophobic, and equally baffled and exhilarated by the experience of being fused into a melting pot." "It was," he says in "The Story of Three Stories," "to this nation-neighborhood—this demi-Israel in a Newark that was our volatile Middle East—that I instinctively turned for material at the beginning of my writing career, and to which I returned, ten years later, when I tried to distill from that Newark Jewish community the fictional, or folkloric, family that I called the Portnoys." Ironically, Portnoy's mental state, as a reflection of this kind of environment, in some ways typifies the thinking of many of Roth's Jewish critics, who resent his uses of Jewish materials. In "Writing about Jews," Roth characterizes one of these critics as an individual who prefers "to remain a victim in a country where he does not have to live like one if he chooses" and says others prefer to hear "the oratory of self-congratulation and self-pity" as opposed to more serious and honest expressions of the life of the Jews in America.

The presence in Roth's work of this ghetto mentality is obvious. However, Roth's fiction since *Portnoy* shows the growing importance of another force—literary modernism. In fact, his essays and fiction in this period sound almost like a reader of the modernist movement in literature. Although the strongest influences are Kafka and Chekhov, there are also continual references to Flaubert, Joyce, Dostoyevsky, Tolstoy. The importance of modernism to Roth is clear in his early description of fiction as "something like a religious calling, and literature a kind of sacrament." "I might turn out," he says in "On *The Great American Novel*," "to be a bad artist, or no artist at all, but having declared myself *for* art—the art of Tolstoy, James, Flaubert, and Mann, whose appeal was as much in their heroic literary integrity as in their work—I imagined I had sealed myself off from being a morally unacceptable person, in others' eyes as well as my own." In style, subject matter, and sensibility, Roth's My *Life as a Man*, *The Professor of Desire*, and *The Ghost Writer*, as well as his own critical writings, all reflect the intensity of this modernist impulse. In addition, his editorship of Penguin's series of books entitled "Writers from the Other Europe" further demonstrates the importance to Roth today of European themes and thought. In responding to the triad of modernism, American culture, and Jewish life in America, Roth juxtaposes the American drive for individual freedom with the psychology of the ghetto and what Sanford Pinsker calls the "reflexive mode" of modernism.

Roth's special style as a writer—what we have come to think of as his unique contribution to the linguistic achievement of Jewish writers in general—derives from his insights into the styles associated with the different cultural perspectives of literary modernism, Americanism, and Judaism. The tensions, conflicts, and incongruities involved in bringing these perspectives together often account for the devastating but humorous social and cultural criticism of his prose. The different styles reflect different modes of thought and ways of life. As such they operate as checks and critical perspectives on one another—Jew vs. American, middle-class conformist vs. modernistic rebel. Brought together by Roth into one consistent style, they become the ironic consciousness and multiperspective of the modern urban Jew. A character named Nathan Zuckerman and the epithets that are used to describe him best epitomize

Roth's effort. Zuckerman, who is from Newark, would like to be a Jewish James Joyce. However, when Roth refers to him as Nathan Dedalus in *The Ghost Writer* and as "Zuckerman Unbound" in a later novel, Zuckerman's hopes are properly deflated by the dramatic tension between his middle-class Jewish background and the combination of creativity and nihilism implied in his ambitions to be a writer who can revolutionize the consciousness of his times. Earlier in his career Roth referred in an interview to the social and cultural roots of this dilemma for the Jewish writer who wants to rebel against parents who will not only protect him but will adore him to the point of expressing pride even in his rebelliousness. As a youth, he used "millions of words" as the way to fight his parents. The knowledge of his parents' undiminished love, however, effectively countered the vehemence of his rebellion. It was fear of the "broken heart" rather than of physical punishment that kept him at bay so that "even in post-adolescence, when I began to find reasons to oppose them, it never occurred to me that as a consequence I might lose their love." The difficulty that Zuckerman encounters in breaking away from such loving parents by establishing true independence from them signifies the schlemiel's prolonged adolescence that undermines any authority to his rebellion.

Like Alexander Portnoy, Nathan Zuckerman learns that even while trying to make his escape from his parents he will find them waiting for him somewhere, usually in a corner of his own psyche. The problem, he discovers, is that not only does guilt keep him close to home but being Jewish in America creates the kinds of anxieties and doubts that naturally send one back to one's roots. Thus, in his desire for independence as both a man and a writer, Zuckerman in *The Ghost Writer* psychologically disowns his father and sees an older, famous writer named E. I. Lonoff as an adopted literary father figure. However, in Lonoff's writings Zuckerman discovers his own background. Thus, Zuckerman notes that "Lonoff's canon . . . had done more to make me realize how much I was still my family's Jewish offspring than anything I had carried forward to the University of Chicago from childhood Hebrew lessons, or mother's kitchen, or the discussions I used to hear among my parents and our relatives about the perils of intermarriage, the problem of Santa Claus, and the injustice of medical-school quotas." Through Lonoff's fiction, Zuckerman finds himself able to identify with "the same burden of exclusion and confinement that still weighed upon the lives of those who had raised me." Zuckerman's condescension toward his real father and his desperate search for a new father figure dramatize how completely the insecurities of his past carry forward into his adult life.

The image of the Jew that emerges in Roth reflects modern literary sensibility, Jewish insecurity, and American ambivalence. Through these tensions Roth continues the pattern of the Jewish hero of thought. However, in Roth the Jewish hero of thought becomes a kind of underground man, a symbol of perennial Jewish isolation advanced to represent, in a manner more like Kafka than Dostoyevsky, the alienated condition of modern man. Roth relates this hero to Ralph Ellison's *Invisible Man*. In discussing Ellison's novel, he compares "the image of his hero" with Bellow's Henderson and finds the former more relevant to his own vision of the world. In "Writing American Fiction," Roth says, "For here too the hero is left with the simple stark fact of himself. He is as alone as a man can be. Not that he hasn't gone out into the world; he has gone into it, and out into it, and out into it—but at the end he chooses to go underground, to live there and wait. And it does not seem to him a cause for celebration either." The heroes of Roth's fiction are often these men from the underground even though they frequently function on the surface as seemingly successful and bright young Jewish men. They—David Kepesh, Nathan Zuckerman, Peter Tarnopol—dramatize the situation of being Jewish, modern, and American all at once.

As an underground man, Roth's modern Jewish hero is engaged in a perennial search for identity and masculinity. Roth's development of his fiction as a continuous search for a center or a "real" author conforms with the desperate search of his characters for a sense of self. An example of Roth's experiment to combine this technique of fiction and his theme of the lost or uncertain self can be found in *My Life as a Man*. In this novel, two stories, "Salad Days" and "Courting Disaster," are entitled together "Useful Fictions" and concern the character of Zuckerman. Both stories and Zuckerman himself are deemed the creation of Peter Tarnopol, the hero of the "autobiographical" third part of the novel which is called "My True Story." Thus, the fictional process of creating a "real" self is sustained by the attempt in the novel to find the real author. Roth further explains this method of searching through the self to find a real self by having Zuckerman quote to a bored class from Joseph Conrad's introduction to the *Nigger of the Narcissus*. The opening words of the quote indicate an important part of Roth's artistic creed and method: " 'the artist descends within himself, and in that lonely region of stress and strife, if he be deserving and fortunate, he finds the terms of his appeal.' " Roth's heroes not only want new identities and fathers, but they also exhibit what Tarnopol's (and Portnoy's) psychiatrist, Dr. Otto Spielvogel, terms the narcissism of the artist, thus adding to the significance of Zuckerman's reading from Conrad. The same problems also face David Kepesh, the young Jewish professor of literature who appears first in *The*

Breast and then again in *The Professor of Desire,* the later novel that anticipates the physical transformation in the first book.

Dr. Spielvogel's perceptions are important because for Roth art and psychology collaborate to mitigate the authority of an omniscient, all-powerful "authorial" presence. The multiplication of selves challenges the existence of a superior self resting in security somewhere in control of the story. Thus, Zuckerman as the creation of Tarnopol in *My Life as a Man* suggests Tarnopol's strength—until we get the true story of Tarnopol. The movement toward a true and superior writer or poet reflects the wish for a realm of objective authority and security where none exists, Roth seems to say, in either art or life. In "Salad Days" Zuckerman refers to the "amused, Olympian point of view" of the author—presumably meaning Tarnopol—and in "Courting Disaster" he discusses "the decorousness, the orderliness, the underlying sobriety, that 'responsible' manner that I continue to affect" as perhaps "the funniest thing of all, or perhaps the strangest" part of the story. While dramatizing the wish to create such a detached and final authorial presence, Roth simultaneously demonstrates how such a self demolishes itself through the ironic and inevitable process of reflection that undermines the claims of autonomy and authority through the creation of another level of critical consciousness. There is, therefore, no omniscient self either in literature or life that offers an ultimate assurance of security.

Without a final source of truth or an ultimate moral authority, fiction and reality for Roth's heroes become interchangeable. Zuckerman says that "my life was coming to resemble one of those texts upon which certain literary critics . . . used to enjoy venting their ingenuity." Similarly, Peter Tarnopol, as he tells his own story in *My Life as a Man,* justifies his decision to marry the woman he believes has ruined him by seeing himself in terms of the meaning and ethics of literary modernism. "It seemed then," he says, "that I was making one of those moral decisions that I had heard so much about in college literature courses. But how different it all had been up in the Ivy League when it was happening to Lord Jim and Kate Croy and Ivan Karamazov instead of to me. Oh, what an authority on dilemmas I had been in the senior honors seminar!" He says that he wanted his "intractable existence [to] take place at an appropriately lofty moral attitude, an elevation somewhere, say, between *The Brothers Karamazov* and *The Wings of the Dove.*" Tarnopol becomes a victim of his ambition for ultimate experience and of his literary philosophy, neither of which distinguishes between what he is and what he reads. He says, "Stuffed to the gills with great fiction—entranced not by cheap romances, like Madame Bovary, but by *Madame Bovary*—I now expected to find in everyday experience that same sense of the difficult and the deadly earnest that informed the novels I admired most. My model of reality, deduced from reading the masters, had at its heart *intractability*. And here it was, a reality as obdurate and recalcitrant and (in addition) as awful as any I could have wished for in my most bookish dreams." Tarnopol's prose often parodies and reflects a particular style of literary criticism. His vocabulary indicates that his model for such writing comes from the essays of Lionel Trilling while the subject matter suggests a particular Trilling essay entitled "On the Teaching of Modern Literature." In the essay Trilling discusses the implications of teaching literary modernism from the perspective of the academic and cultural establishment. While Roth's mimicry of Trilling's vocabulary (obdurate, recalcitrant, intractability) contributes to the humor of the piece and makes Tarnopol seem even more artificial, the clever connection to Trilling lends credibility to Roth's subject. Tarnopol illustrates the moral, educational, and intellectual issues in Trilling's essay, including the question of how the violence, nihilism, and alienation of modern literature operate upon students from conventional and stable backgrounds.

Tarnopol's confusion between his own life and the lives of various characters in great literature enables Roth to mix up the worlds of fiction and reality in a way that turns his works into studies of the issue of fiction and the fiction-making process. His recent novels dramatize some of the questions concerning fiction and reality that have been raised by such critical theorists as Gerald Graff. The title of *The Ghost Writer* symbolizes his concern for the subject through its suggestion that behind each fiction is another story writer or another fiction. Roth's penchant for including a great deal of his public self and autobiography in his novels further blurs the distinctions between fiction and reality. Thus, when Nathan Zuckerman complains in *Zuckerman Unbound* that people keep confusing him, the successful author, with the creations of his novels, we can assume that Roth is joking. In the novel Zuckerman must contend with a public who will not let him forget that he wrote a sensational book that sounds very much like *Portnoy's Complaint. Zuckerman Unbound* therefore confirms Roth's intention to diminish the barrier between fiction and reality. In *Zuckerman Unbound* a stranger says to Zuckerman about his book that " 'they arrest people for that.' " Zuckerman in turn thinks of people like the offensive stranger: "They had mistaken impersonation for confession and were calling out to a character who lived in a book."

As we have seen, however, it is precisely the line between impersonation and confession that Roth so humorously exploits in his works. He develops the tension between fiction and the real self in a way that elevates his fictional hero to the level of cultural myth. The identity of this hero emerges from Roth's public self and literary self. By writing into his recent fiction so many brilliant, internal variations of a single fictive self that so closely resembles himself, he creates a hero that lives in both literature and public life. In effect, Roth achieves a modern-day bridge in the tradition of Whitman that connects the public Roth with the literary self that searches in his novels for a solid center. As both a Jew and a modernist, Roth projects a mythic self onto American culture that seems nothing less than revolutionary in its departure from the historic model of the hero in American literature and culture. At the same time, the receptivity to such a heroic figure by the general public conveys something of the revolution in values, tastes, and style that the culture as a whole has undergone in the past several decades.

The most lasting and pervasive model for Roth of that mythic self that represents the new version of the modern American male as the underground man comes not from native grounds but from Europe in the figure of Franz Kafka. Kafka epitomizes for Roth both modern consciousness and the archetypal modern Jewish sensibility. Roth also sees in Kafka an important ability to understand the humor in the absurdity of modern man's alienated and self-destructive condition. In an interview, Roth told George Plimpton that he was "strongly influenced by a sit-down comic named Franz Kafka and a very funny bit he does called "The Metamorphosis.' " What Roth seeks to give us is an Americanized version of Kafka. In 1973, Roth wrote a story called "Looking at Kafka" in which he imagines Kafka's immigration to America to escape the Holocaust. In order to survive in America, Kafka in Roth's imagination becomes a Hebrew-school teacher, and, of course, the results for Kafka's life and work are disastrous. For example, among other things he is called "Dr. Kishka" by his students. Roth returns to Kafka as a subject in his fiction by making his memory the object of Professor David Kepesh's devotion in *The Professor of Desire.* Kepesh's reverence for Kafka is part of his overall commitment to literary modernism, on which subject he shares many attitudes and ideas with Zuckerman and Tarnopol in *My Life as a Man.* Thus, in remarks Kepesh prepares for the opening of his college class he tells his students of his " 'insistence upon the connections between the novels you read for this class, even the most eccentric and off-putting of novels, and what you know so far of life. You will discover (and not all will approve) that I do not hold with certain of my colleagues who tell us that literature, in its most valuable and intriguing moments, is "fundamentally non-referential." ' " To Kepesh, literature and the individual's experience of life are so related that he confidently says to his students,

" 'I present myself to you young strangers in the guise not of your teacher but as the first of this semester's texts.' " Roth takes Kepesh's belief in the interaction of fiction and reality to its most ludicrous extreme in *The Breast*, a story modeled after Kafka's "The Metamorphosis." In *The Breast* Kepesh asks himself how it came to be that he turned into a breast. "*Did fiction do this to me?*" he asks.

The Professor of Desire, as already noted, was published five years after *The Breast*, but its action takes place before Kepesh's change. In the later novel Kepesh only goes so far as to visit Kafka's grave in Prague. The visit occurs with the same reverence pilgrims demonstrate on journeys to Mecca and Jerusalem. Roth prepares us for the importance of this moment through a conversation between Kepesh and Professor Soska, his Czech guide who was fired from an academic position for political reasons. For Soska, understanding and loving Kafka help him tolerate the humiliation of life under Communist totalitarianism. Kepesh, on the other hand, appreciates Kafka for helping him to understand another kind of oppression. He says to Soska, " 'Of course you are the one on intimate terms with totalitarianism—but if you'll permit me, I can only compare the body's utter singlemindedness, its cold indifference and absolute contempt for the well-being of the spirit, to some unyielding, authoritarian regime. And you can petition it all you like, offer up the most heartfelt and dignified and logical sort of appeal—and get no response at all. If anything, a kind of laugh is what you get'." Both men realize that great literature can have such highly personal uses. " 'To each obstructed citizen his own Kafka,' " says Soska to Kepesh. At Soska's suggestion, Kepesh goes on to Kafka's gravesite where Kepesh sees a monument to his own anguish and suffering. Roth writes, "Of all things, marking Kafka's remains—and unlike anything else in sight—a stout, elongated, whitish rock, tapering upward to its pointed glans, a tombstone phallus." The stone for Kepesh symbolizes his own problem, while the actual grave goes deeper, so to speak, and indicates the unconscious forces that propel it. Examining the grave, Kepesh evidences surprise that "the family-haunted son is buried forever—still!—between the mother and the father who outlived him." Even in death Kafka seems caught between his mother and father, realizing in his tomb a permanence to the pain he suffered in life. Kepesh's sense of Kafka's affliction and his understanding of Kafka's role as a Jewish artist make him feel closer to Kafka than to his own father. Showing Kafka a level of respect he denies his real family, Kepesh affects a Kafkaesque sensibility and style of alienation. At the same time, Kepesh stands in awe at this gravesite of all the Jewish dead around him, many of whom died in the Holocaust. He feels an inevitable link with these Jewish dead. As he looks at the names on the monuments, he realizes that they sound as familiar as the names in his "own address book." However, even during a touching moment of realizing a bond with these dead, he finally cannot maintain his sense of relationship with this aspect of his past and identity.

As a modern sensibility and consciousness in the tradition of Kafka, Kepesh finds it impossible to achieve the solidity of a single well-centered self of the middle class. He cannot be like his father in this book or like other fathers in Roth who function with basic beliefs and have loyalties to their Jewish families and friends who see them through life. Life cannot be dealt with simply for Kepesh in commonsensical terms designed to assure security and success. Roth sympathetically portrays Kepesh's father as an example of sensitive and responsible masculinity and as a model of middle-class authority. He describes the father during a moment when he confronts both the imminent death of his wife and the weakness of his son. "He puts a hand over his eyes and quietly begins to cry. With his other hand he makes a fist which he waves at me. 'This is what I have had to be all my life! *Without* psychiatrists, *without* happy pills! I am a man who has never said die!' " In contrast to his father, Kepesh seems unable to live. He verges on a perennial death condition that makes basic functions and actions impossible to achieve. In this sense, Roth's vision relates to an earlier Jewish writer in America, Nathanael West, whose characters such as "Miss Lonelyhearts" and Tod Hackett and Homer Simpson seem to be dying men in a dying land.

Kepesh's condition of immaturity can be compared with Tarnopol's hysteria in My Life as a Man. Both men resist the manhood they claim to seek. In one fight scene Tarnopol puts on his wife's clothes to show her that he wears the " 'panties in this family' " out of a need to take what Roth called, in an interview with Joyce Carol Oates, "a sex *break*." Later Tarnopol asks, "How do I ever get to be what is described in the literature as *a man*? I had so wanted to be one, too—why then is it always beyond me?" At the end of My Life as a Man Tarnopol learns of his wife's death and wants to believe that he is "free." However, Dr. Spielvogel quickly corrects him. " 'Released is the word you are looking for,' " says Spielvogel. " 'You have been released'." Freedom is another issue beyond Tarnopol. His wife's death has released him from one imprisoning situation, but clearly he will not find any kind of freedom until he stops inventing new prisons for himself.

In his discussion with Oates about My Life as a Man, Roth seems to confirm a pessimistic view of the book's conclusion. "If there is an ironic acceptance of anything at the conclusion of My Life as a Man (or even along the way), it is of *the determined self*. And angry frustration, a deeply vexing sense of characterological enslavement, is strongly infused in that ironic acceptance." In elaborating upon this idea, Roth refers once again to Kafka—this time to the scene in *The Trial* when K looks up in hope at a priest in the cathedral. For Roth, the great irony comes through the discovery that "the man in the pulpit turns out to be oneself." The chains we put on ourselves are our greatest obstacles to freedom. He writes, "If only one *could* quit one's pulpit, one might well obtain decisive and acceptable counsel. How to devise a mode of living completely outside the jurisdiction of the Court when the Court is of one's own devising?" Roth's pessimism about man's potential for achieving freedom and his use of Jews as examples of self-bondage unite many critics in their objections to his work. Writers as different politically as Irving Howe and Norman Podhoretz tend to be more sanguine than Roth in their views of human nature and freedom. Moreover, both men also chafe under Roth's depiction of Jewish life and mores. Roth has survived such attacks and refuses to modify his views in spite of the feelings and sensitivities of others. He has continued to emphasize the perennial frustration of the individual's drive for freedom.

Roth, according to Bernard F. Rodgers, Jr., also continues an important American literary tradition. "American writers," says Rodgers, "are dedicated to the effort to liberate consciousness—an effort with which Roth allied himself early in his career." Roth has at times spoken of himself and his work in such heroic terms. For example, in an interview he once said: "I sometimes think of my generation of men as the first wave of determined D-Day invaders, over whose bloody, wounded carcasses the flower children subsequently stepped ashore to advance triumphantly toward that libidinous Paris we had dreamed of liberating as we inched inland on our bellies, firing into the dark. 'Daddy,' the youngsters ask, 'what did you do in the war?' I humbly submit they could do worse than read *Portnoy's Complaint* to find out." However, Roth is usually more pessimistic about man's capacity for freedom than this quote would indicate. Often in Roth's fiction when imprisoning walls around men collapse, others rise soon after to replace them. Almost always such new walls are constructed by the prisoners themselves. However, as a writer in the tradition of the New Covenant, Roth contributes significantly to our understanding of the nature and psychology of freedom in America.

Chronology

1933	Born March 19 to Herman Roth and Bess Finkel Roth in Newark, N.J.
1951–54	After one year at Rutgers University, Newark, attends Bucknell University, from which he receives a B.A. in English, *magna cum laude*, and is elected to Phi Beta Kappa.
1955–57	Does graduate work at the University of Chicago, from which he receives an M.A. in 1955. While there, publishes a short story, "The Contest for Aaron Gold," which is selected to appear in *The Best American Short Stories of 1956*. Also during this time, enlists in the army, but is discharged because of a back injury.
1959	*Goodbye, Columbus*, for which he receives a National Book Award, and the Jewish Book Council's Daroff Award. Continues to publish short stories, which are well-received. Marries Margaret Martinson Williams on February 22.
1962	*Letting Go*. Receives a Ford Foundation grant to write plays, and is writer-in-residence at Princeton University.
1963	Legal separation from Margaret Roth.
1965	Teaching position at the University of Pennsylvania.
1967	*When She Was Good*.
1968	Death of Margaret Roth in an automobile accident.
1969	*Portnoy's Complaint*.
1970	Election to National Institute of Arts and Letters.
1971	*Our Gang*.
1972	*The Breast*.
1973	*The Great American Novel*.
1974	*My Life as a Man*.
1975	*Reading Myself and Others*.
1977	*The Professor of Desire*.
1979	*The Ghost Writer*.
1980	*A Philip Roth Reader*.
1981	*Zuckerman Unbound*.
1984	*The Anatomy Lesson*.
1985	*Zuckerman Bound: A Trilogy and Epilogue*. Compilation of *The Ghost Writer*, *Zuckerman Unbound* and *The Anatomy Lesson* with epilogue, *The Prague Orgy*.

Contributors

HAROLD BLOOM, Sterling Professor of the Humanities at Yale University, is the author of *The Anxiety of Influence, Poetry and Repression* and many other volumes of literary criticism. His forthcoming study, *Freud: Transference and Authority*, attempts a full-scale reading of all of Freud's major writings. A MacArthur Prize Fellow, he is the general editor of *The Chelsea House Library of Literary Criticism*.

STANLEY EDGAR HYMAN was Professor of Literature at Bennington College. His books include *The Tangled Bank* and *The Armed Vision*.

STANLEY TRACHTENBERG is Professor of English at Texas Christian University and has published a book on Saul Bellow.

JONATHAN RABAN is the author of several books, among them *Technique of Modern Fiction: Essays in Practical Criticism* and an edition of poems of Robert Lowell.

BRUNO BETTELHEIM is Director Emeritus of the Orthogenic Institute at the University of Chicago. Among his books are *The Uses of Enchantment* and *The Empty Fortress*.

THEODORE SOLOTAROFF, an editor and free-lance critic, is the author of *The Red-Hot Vacuum*.

ALLEN GUTTMANN is Professor of English at Amherst College and the author of *The Jewish Writer in America*.

TONY TANNER is Reader in English at Cambridge University. His books include *City of Words* and a study of Thomas Pynchon.

IRVING HOWE is Distinguished Professor of English at the City University of New York Graduate School. His many books include *World of Our Fathers* and studies of Faulkner, Hardy and Sherwood Anderson.

JOHN N. McDANIEL teaches English at Middle Tennessee State University and has translated the work of Giuseppe Cocchiara.

SANFORD PINSKER is Associate Professor of English at Franklin and Marshall

College in Lancaster, Pa. His books include studies of Roth, Conrad, and contemporary American fiction, as well as a volume of poems, *Still Life and Other Poems*.

MARY ALLEN is Lecturer in English at George Mason University in Fairfax, Va. Her books include *The Necessary Blankness: Women in Major American Fiction of the Sixties*, a work on portrait photography, and a study of animals in American literature.

HERMIONE LEE is Lecturer in English at the University of York. Her books include studies on Virginia Woolf and Elizabeth Bowen.

SAM B. GIRGUS is Professor of American Studies at the University of New Mexico. His books include *The Law of the Heart: Individualism and the Modern Self in American Literature*.

Bibliography

Alter, Robert. "The Education of David Kepesh." *Partisan Review* 46 (1979): 478–81.

Bier, Jesse. "In Defense of Roth." *Etudes Anglaises*. XXVIe Année, no. 1 (1973): 49–53.

Charney, Maurice. "Sexuality and Self-Fulfilment: *Portnoy's Complaint* and *Fear of Flying*." In *Sexual Fiction*. London: Methuen & Co., Ltd., 1981.

Cohen, Sarah. "Philip Roth's Would-Be Patriarchs and their *Shikses* and Shrews." *Studies in American Jewish Literature* 1, vol. 1 (1975): 16–22.

Cooperman, Stanley. "Philip Roth: 'Old Jacob's Eye' with a Squint." *Twentieth Century Literature* 3, vol. 19 (1973): 203–16.

Deer, Irving and Harriet. "Philip Roth and the Crisis in American Fiction." *Minnesota Review* 4, vol. 6 (1966): 353–60.

Detweiler, Robert. "Philip Roth and the Test of the Dialogic Life." In *Four Spiritual Crises in Mid-Century American Fiction*. Gainesville: University of Florida Monographs, No. 14, 1963.

Fiedler, Leslie A. *Waiting For the End*. New York: Stein & Day, 1964.

Jones, J. P., and Nance, G. A. *Philip Roth*. New York: Frederick Ungar Publishing Co., 1981.

Kazin, Alfred. "The Earthly City of the Jews." In *Bright Book of Life*. London: Secker & Warburg, 1974.

Lee, Hermione. *Philip Roth*. London and New York: Methuen & Co., Ltd., 1982.

Lyons, Bonnie. "Bellowmalamudroth and the American Jewish Genre—Alive and Well." *Studies in American Jewish Literature* 2, vol. 5 (1979): 8–10.

Malin, Irving. "Looking at Roth's Kafka; Or Some Hints About Comedy." *Studies in Short Fiction* 3, vol. 14 (1977): 273–75.

McDaniel, John N. *The Fiction of Philip Roth*. Haddonfield, N.J.: Haddonfield House, 1974.

Meeter, Glenn. *Philip Roth and Bernard Malamud: A Critical Essay*. Grand Rapids, Mich.: William B. Eerdmans, 1968.

Pinsker, Sanford. *The Comedy that "Hoits": An Essay on the Fiction of Philip Roth*. Columbia, Mo.: University of Missouri Press, 1975.

Plimpton, George. "On *Portnoy's Complaint*." In *Reading Myself and Others*. Edited by Philip Roth. New York: Farrar, Straus & Giroux, 1975.

Podhoretz, Norman. "The Gloom of Philip Roth." In *Doings and Undoings*. London: Hart-Davis, 1965.

Raban, Jonathan. "The New Philip Roth." *Novel* 2, vol. 2 (1969): 153–63.

Rodgers, Bernard F., Jr. *Philip Roth*. Boston: Twayne Publishers, 1978.

———. *Philip Roth: A Bibliography*. Metuchen, N.J.: Scarecrow Press, 1974.

Sabiston, Elizabeth. "A New Fable for Critics: Philip Roth's *The Breast*." *International Fiction Review* 2 (1975): 27–34.

Schechner, Mark. "Philip Roth." *Partisan Review* (Fall 1974): 410–27.

Siegel, Ben. "The Myths of Summer: Philip Roth's *The Great American Novel*." *Contemporary Literature* 17 (Spring 1976): 171–90.

Solotaroff, Theodore. "Philip Roth and the Jewish Moralists." *Chicago Review* 4, vol. 13 (1959): 87–99.

Weinberg, Helen. *The New Novel in America: The Kafkan Mode in Contemporary Fiction*. Minneapolis: University of Minnesota Press, 1966.

White, Robert L. "The English Instructor as Hero: Two Novels by Roth and Malamud." *Forum* 4 (Winter 1963): 16–22.

Wisse, Ruth R. *The Schlemiel as Modern Hero*. Chicago: The University of Chicago Press, 1971.

Acknowledgments

"A Novelist of Great Promise" by Stanley Edgar Hyman from *On Contemporary Literature: An Anthology of Critical Essays on the Major Movements and Writers of Contemporary Literature* edited by Richard Kostelanetz, copyright © 1964 by Avon Book Division, The Hearst Corporation. Reprinted by permission.

"The Hero in Stasis" by Stanley Trachtenberg from *Critique* 2, vol. 7 (Winter 1964–65), copyright © 1965 by the Bolingbroke Society, Inc. Reprinted by permission.

"Two Meal Scenes from *Goodbye, Columbus*" by Jonathan Raban from *The Technique of Modern Fiction* by Jonathan Raban, copyright © 1968 by Jonathan Raban. Reprinted by permission.

"Portnoy Psychoanalyzed" by Bruno Bettelheim from *Midstream: A Monthly Jewish Review* 6, vol. 15 (June–July 1969), copyright © 1969 by the Theodor Herzl Foundation. Reprinted by permission.

"Philip Roth: A Personal View" by Theodore Solotaroff from *The Red-Hot Vacuum* by Theodore Solotaroff, copyright © 1969 by Theodore Solotaroff. Reprinted by permission.

"Philip Roth and the Rabbis" by Allen Guttmann from *The Jewish Writer in America* by Allen Guttman, copyright © 1971 by Oxford University Press, Inc. Reprinted by permission.

"*Portnoy's Complaint*: 'The Settling of Scores! The Pursuit of Dreams!' " by Tony Tanner from *City of Words: American Fiction 1950–1970* by Tony Tanner, copyright © 1971 by Tony Tanner. Reprinted by permission.

"Philip Roth Reconsidered" by Irving Howe from *Commentary* 6, vol. 54 (December 1972), copyright © 1972 by the American Jewish Committee. Reprinted by permission.

" 'I Always Wanted You to Admire My Fasting'; or, Looking at Kafka" by Philip Roth from *American Review* 17 (May 1973), copyright © 1973 by Philip Roth. Reprinted by permission.

"Distinctive Features of Roth's Artistic Vision" by John N. McDaniel from *The Fiction of Philip Roth* by John N. McDaniel, copyright © 1974 by John N. McDaniel. Reprinted by permission.

"The Comedy that 'Hoits': *The Breast*" by Sanford Pinsker from *The Comedy that "Hoits": An Essay on the Fiction of Philip Roth* by Sanford Pinsker, copyright © 1975 by the Curators of the University of Missouri. Reprinted by permission.

"When She Was Good She Was Horrid" by Mary Allen from *The Necessary Blankness: Women in Major American Fiction of the Sixties* by Mary Allen, copyright © 1976 by the Board of Trustees of the University of Illinois. Reprinted by permission.

" 'You Must Change Your Life': Mentors, Doubles and Literary Influences in the Search for Self" by Hermione Lee from *Philip Roth* by Hermione Lee, copyright © 1982 by Hermione Lee. Reprinted by permission.

"The Jew as Underground Man" by Sam B. Girgus from *The New Covenant: Jewish Writers and The American Idea* by Sam B. Girgus, copyright © 1984 by University of North Carolina Press. Reprinted by permission.

Index